September 2006

Cindy Linda Cindy
What a great time I've had
at CR with you and Jim (part time)
We will stay in touch to keep
everyone on track. Remember
on the golf course or off —

Breaking the Mold

"Take Dead Aim". If you
get past chapter 2 without falling
asleep you will be stuck
with the whole thing.

The journey of the only woman president of the United States Golf Association

By Judy Bell *with* Rhonda Glenn

Love to you and Jim,
Judy

Sleeping Bear Press

Sleeping Bear Press
310 North Main Street
P.O. Box 20
Chelsea, MI 48118
www.sleepingbearpress.com

Printed and bound in Canada.

10 9 8 7 6 5 4 3 2 1

Library of Congress Cataloging-in-Publication Data

Bell, Judy.

Breaking the mold : the journey of the only woman president of the United States Golf Association / by Judy Bell and Rhonda Glenn.

        p. cm.
ISBN 1-58536-074-0
1. Bell, Judy. 2. United States Golf
Association–Presidents–Biography. 3. Women executives–United States–
Biography. I. Glenn, Rhonda. II. Title.
GV964.B45 A3 2002

796.352'092--dc21

    2002006704

For Carl and Fred

[Foreword]

If you were an ordinary kid, you, like most of your classmates, began reading biographies in the third or fourth grade and probably wondered whether or not anyone would ever write a book about you. For most of us, the passage of time leads us to the inexorable conclusion that our life story is not as spellbinding as we would like everyone to think it is. Thus, the likelihood of seeing our biography displayed on the shelf at the local bookstore steadily diminishes as the years march on, unless, of course, we ultimately do something—either famous or infamous—that solidly fixes us in the eyes of the public. Political figures, entertainers, sports heroes and notorious criminals are only a few elements of our society that have had their lives catalogued in biographical form.

This book, I suppose, could be described as a niche biography to the extent that, outside of the golfing world, the name Judy Bell is not as widely recognized as Winston Churchill, Ronald Reagan or Albert Schweitzer. And, even in the golfing world, there is some degree of confusion. I wish that I had a nickel for each time that I was present when Judy would be introduced to someone, the two would talk for a few minutes, and the person, as he or she departed, would express their sincere desire to return to Pine Needles to play her wonderful golf course yet another time. Only one other person finds these episodes more amusing than I do—Peggy Kirk Bell herself, the real owner of Pine Needles.

So, why is Judy Bell's life story available in printed form while the rest of us previously ordinary kids grow older anonymously?

In response to that question, most non-golfers would shrug their shoulders and offer no additional response. On the other hand, many golfers would jump immediately to the fact that she is the first and only woman to have served as president of the United States Golf Association, an organization which has traditionally elected only males to its more influential leadership positions since its founding in 1894. While her election to the USGA presidency is indeed a special accomplishment, it, alone, probably doesn't warrant the writing of a biography. But those who know Judy are keenly aware of the fact that her tenure with the USGA is just one of the many noteworthy things that she has done both on and off the golf course. Among other things, she is a lifelong amateur golfer of national prominence, a victorious international team member and captain, an administrator and a highly regarded businesswoman. Therefore, my answer to the previously posed question is that this book represents both an entertaining narrative of her many accomplishments and, even more importantly, an opportunity to examine some of the personality traits that have allowed her to successfully undertake a wide variety of endeavors, only a portion of which relate to her long and storied career as a volunteer with the USGA.

There are many aspects of her personality that have helped insure her success. Most notably, they include her unwavering respect for the game and her sense of humor. But one trait consistently dominates all others. Simply put, it is "passion." And it is the basis for everything that she does—everything from determining the most effective and efficient way of incorporating disadvantaged kids into the game of golf, to finalizing both the agenda for the USGA's annual meeting and the seating arrangement for the more than four hundred people who attend the dinner that follows.

As further proof, I need only remember a telephone conversation with her that occurred last September. At one point during the call, she was so worked up about the state of affairs at a future U.S. Women's Open site that she was literally yelling into the telephone. The remarkable part of this is that it occurred only one day after she had undergone a major abdominal surgical procedure—a time when almost anyone else would have been content to lay quietly in bed and wait for their next dose of pain medicine. But not Judy Bell. If that's not passion, I don't know what is.

On November 11, 2001, I had the distinct honor of presenting Judy at her induction into the World Golf Hall of Fame. During the course of my remarks, I referenced Sigmund Freud having once said that the two most important things for a successful life are hard work and love. As you read the pages that follow, I believe that you will see that no one has worked harder for and loved the challenges that they have undertaken more than Judy Bell. And, I hope that you will come to know Judy in the way that so many of her friends do. For me, it has been one of the most instructive and rewarding friendships of my life.

—Trey Holland
USGA President, 2000-2002
Judy Bell fan, forever

[Introduction]

In 1994, when Judy Bell was vice president of the USGA, I suggested that she run for the United States Senate and write a book.

She refused to do either. She wasn't interested in running for the Senate and, she said, writing a book about her life would be presumptuous.

By 1997, I had given up the idea of Judy running for political office. She wouldn't, after all, accomplish much as a Senator—she'd spend too much time caring for every person in America and trying to solve their problems. Besides, she'd be late for every vote.

I still thought the book was a good idea.

In early 2001, four years after she left the presidency of the USGA, Judy was approached by Sleeping Bear Press to write her autobiography. She was finally open to the idea if, and only if, part of the proceeds went to charity.

Judy had one underlying principal in writing this book. A book about her life was contrary to her innate modesty and she ordered that we use the word "I" as little as possible. Her achievements, however, were sometimes so singular that the word "I" couldn't be avoided.

In recent months, we worked on the manuscript while she underwent chemotherapy. If you think she coughed up the story of her life in the whispered voice of an invalid, don't be fooled. The points expressed here were hammered out with the hurricane-like force of her incredible memory, energy, deep thought, laughter, and the gusto of her loud voice. We usually worked more than 12 hours a day. When I was exhausted, she pressed on, but then Judy has more courage than most of us.

Judy once told me that all she ever wanted was to get married and have six children. Her life went in another direction. I have always believed, however, that her genuine love for all people prompted her to raise literally thousands of "children" who benefited from her concern, guidance and caring. I'm lucky to be one of them.

Jean Marie Boylan, at that time a member of the USGA Women's Committee, once gave a speech about Judy in which she talked of Judy's ability to inspire people to their greatest efforts. Jean Marie paraphrased a poem from *Jonathan Livingston Seagull*:

"Come to the edge," she said.
"We are afraid," we said.
"Come to the edge," she said.
We came. She pushed us.
And we flew.

—*Rhonda Glenn*

Chapter 1

[The Deed Is Done]

It was January 27, 1996, at the Disney Resort in Orlando, Florida. The United States Golf Association, the governing body of the game in America, was conducting its annual meeting and, for one of the few times I could remember, the room was packed. There were no empty chairs and people were standing along the walls. I'd been affiliated with the USGA for more than 30 years and, in my recollection, we'd never had a larger gathering for the meeting.

Since the USGA was chartered in 1894, the association had elected 53 previous presidents. As the bylaws require, some had represented state and regional golf associations and I, for instance, represented the Women's Western Golf Association. Most had been members of the country's finest private golf clubs. All of them had been men. While that in itself isn't surprising, given the fact that nearly all of the major sports organizations have always been run by men, the USGA offers a slightly different arena. It isn't geared to professional athletes but serves *all* golfers, men and women, the great majority of which are amateurs.

The USGA is a nonprofit organization run strictly to protect and preserve the integrity of the game. While the association has tremendous power—writing the Rules of Golf, codifying the Rules of Amateur Status & Conduct, conducting 13 national championships, and determining which clubs and balls are legal—it has only about 300 paid staff members, including the Executive Director who is, in principle, the Chief Operating Officer.

Volunteers, some 1,300 men and women from all over the United

States, are a big part of the association. They're headed by an Executive Committee of 15 people who make a number of small and large policy decisions that determine the course of golf for millions of players in this country and throughout much of the world. The President of the USGA is, in essence, the Chief Executive Officer.

The association's traditional ruling body had changed in 1987 when I became the first female to break the mold of this all-male enclave and was elected to the Executive Committee. I was part of the USGA volunteer team. I would do whatever I was asked to do. The future was going to involve a lot of committee work. Back then, I didn't even think about becoming an officer, much less President.

I took a very active part on the Executive Committee, had some good pals on the committee, and believe me, I wasn't intimidated by my role. Having grown up being bossed around by three older brothers, when I wanted to be heard, I was *heard*.

Ever since I'd been elected vice president in 1994, the press had speculated about whether the USGA would elect a woman president. Now, two years later, I was the only nominee.

A number of men with impressive resumes had preceded me. Two relatives of United States President George H.W. Bush—his father Prescott Bush and grandfather George H. Walker—had been USGA Presidents. Richard Tufts and Ike Grainger, great authorities on the Rules of Golf, and in recent decades Sandy Tatum, Will Nicholson, Bill Battle, Bill Williams, Grant Spaeth, all lawyers; Jim Hand, a banker; Harry Easterly and Stu Bloch, stockbrokers; and Reg Murphy, publisher and CEO of *National Geographic*, had all been president.

Now it was my turn—Judy Bell, retailer, of Wichita, Kansas, and Colorado Springs, Colorado.

I really don't know that I ever thought about becoming president—I never got caught up in the whirlwind of it all and in how unusual it really was for the USGA to have a woman at the helm—but now it was happening.

All of the hoopla surrounding the event made it clear to me that it wasn't business as usual at our annual election.

Obviously, my role was in transition. Two nights before, I had arrived at the resort to find my hotel room filled with flowers. More bouquets arrived until the atmosphere had become almost funeral and I had dispatched a lot of the flowers to the conference rooms, the registration table, and the rooms of several guests. Bellmen had delivered congratulatory telegrams from Jack and Barbara Nicklaus, Arnold Palmer, Tom Kite, and Dave Marr.

On Saturday, the day I was to be elected, I lost my composure just before the annual meeting began. I had just finished an interview with CNN and was talking with Reg in a hallway.

"Reg," I said, "I'm going to miss you. You've done a tremendous job as president and it's been fun working with you."

Then I saw my two older brothers and their families. When I looked at Allen Bell, my eldest nephew, I started to get very teary. My emotions just went over the top and I excused myself to have a good cry. I lectured myself in a mirror in the rest room, giving myself the talk my late parents would have given me had they been there. "You shape up! What are you doing! You've got to grab hold of yourself."

When I came out, my family saw that I was trying to hold it together and helped me by silently taking their seats.

The annual meeting would begin at five o'clock and, as vice president, I took my place on the dais next to Reg.

A few minutes later I gave my report as Championship Committee Chairman. I was well prepared but I botched it, saying that Corey Pavin had hit a 3-wood to the final green to win the 1995 United States Open at Shinnecock Hills. I knew better, I had just read it wrong. Of course, the whole room wanted to correct me. That's the way we all are in the USGA. We know our golf.

A few people in the audience had muttered, "He hit a 4-wood," and I had been stuttery-stammery after that. I remember thinking, *My Lord, you're not going to go through the next two years like this, I hope.*

I looked out into the audience and saw that the members of the Women's Committee, a committee on which I had served for 17 years, as well as past Women's Committee chairmen, looked as if they were sitting on pins and needles. I saw that they were anxious and that they just wanted me to do so well. My family and a few close friends were sitting right behind the chairmen and every time I looked in their direction they gave me big nervous smiles.

Just across the aisle sat the other members of the Executive Committee, the past presidents, and their spouses. I knew this group was pulling hard for me to do well and when we made eye contact, they all looked very supportive. Trying to keep my composure for what was coming up, I thought: *You know somebody in almost every aisle here. In every row, you know some-*

body. You just get your thoughts together, be yourself, be the best you can be, and that's it.

Other chairmen gave their reports, then Reg and I left the dais to sit on the first row with the rest of the Executive Committee.

Bill Campbell, chairman of the Nominating Committee, was at the microphone. He read my name as the nominee for president and asked, "Are there any nominations from the floor?"

This isn't normally a tense moment, just routine adherence to the bylaws and no one is ever nominated from the floor. But you never know. My friends and family seemed to hold their collective breath. One friend later said that, at that moment, she felt as nervous as when she attended a wedding and the minister said, "If anyone knows why these two should not be joined in holy matrimony, let them speak now or forever hold their peace." Her hands, she said, were wringing wet.

But the moment passed, the obligatory voice-vote was taken, I was elected to a one-year term, and Bill said to the crowd, "The deed is done."

He looked me right in the eye and simply said, "It's yours, Judy. You have it."

Bill and I were good friends and I was very touched.

The audience stood and applauded. Some people even cheered, and some of my close friends shed a few tears. Reg turned to me and kissed me on the cheek. Sandy Tatum and Will Nicholson, past presidents and good friends of mine, each took one of my arms and, following tradition, escorted me to the stage.

I was as keyed up as I had ever been and trying to stay calm. I was just as excited as the day in 1960 when I was introduced on the first tee to play in my first Curtis Cup match and now, as then, I wanted to get going. It was time to go to the next step and there was so much that I wanted to do on behalf of the USGA.

My emotions, however, were close to the surface because in that sea of faces were so many who had been with me all the way in my life in golf.

Sandy and Will each kissed me on the cheek. I stood at the podium, looked out, and saw all of those people. I waited for everyone to quiet down.

I don't know what possessed me then, but I opened my speech by saying, "That's the first time an outgoing president has kissed an incoming president. At least, I hope so."

My wisecrack evoked a roar of laughter, broke the tension and, at long last, we were ready to go. We were away.

I started my speech by saying that when Sandy Tatum was elected president in 1986 he had been referred to as "The Pope of Golf" by Alistair Cooke, the writer and television commentator. Bill Williams, in his presidential acceptance speech at the Disney Resort in 1986, facetiously said that he rather liked being thought of as "The Emperor," adding that his election in the land of Dopey and Mickey Mouse was appropriate. Grant Spaeth was dubbed "The Pied Piper" because of his friendliness and strong affinity for state and regional golf associations, while Reg was definitely "The Birthday Boy," having been president during the USGA Centennial.

"No question about it, I'm Dorothy in the Land of Oz," I said. "Toto, we aren't in Kansas any more."

More seriously, I spoke about the United States Golf Association, what it is, and what we needed to do. The USGA is definitely hard and fast on certain core programs and principles, I said, and we'd always uphold those standards, but I tried very hard to stress that we now needed to reach out and communicate with golfers everywhere. "It's important," I said, "not to take ourselves too seriously. And remember, we didn't invent this game, we're just here to look after it."

I closed by reading a postscript from a Christmas card I had received from my 80-year-old Aunt Jo, my dad's younger sister who was in an assisted living center in Hutchinson, Kansas. Aunt Jo had written, "Be a good one." I pledged to Aunt Jo and the audience to do my level best.

After the ceremony, all of my family and most of my friends came up to congratulate me. We then filed into a big dining room for cocktails and dinner, and the evening really kicked off. People were now relaxed, and it was fun. Betsy Rawls, four-time winner of the United States Women's Open and a wonderful Rules administrator, got the Bob Jones Award for distinguished sportsmanship, the highest award the USGA gives. I had arranged for Mickey Wright, a friend of Betsy's but best known as the greatest woman golfer in history, to present the award to her as a surprise. We managed to pull that off, because Betsy thought Mickey was there to see me become president. But the whole thing was for Betsy.

Both of these great players gave outstanding remarks about the game and how it should be played, along with their strong feelings about the USGA's role in the game.

As we walked out, Jerry Pate, our 1976 U.S. Open champion, came up to me and, with that great smile of his, said, "Well, it's a great night for the ladies."

I just smiled back and said, "No, Jerry, it's a great night for golf."

It was a fun night but I now felt I could begin to work on the things that mattered.

The USGA Communications Staff had me do a press conference early the next morning, the first they had held for a USGA president. About a dozen reporters attended and they really focused on how I felt—as a woman and as president of the USGA.

"I don't know yet how it feels to be president because I've only been one for a few hours," I said. "But I know how it feels to be a woman because I've been one for 59 years."

After we settled that, we moved on to what I thought was much more important—what I wanted to *do* as president. I answered by referring to what I'd said in my speech about finding new ways to fulfill our traditional role and reaching out to golfers everywhere. The reporters asked me what I thought about liberating women in the game through open starting times, equal access at private clubs, and equal prize money at comparable United States championships.

I told them that I didn't believe it was the USGA's role to dictate course and club policy to private clubs. While I probably wouldn't join a club that wouldn't allow me to play on weekends, I said, I still thought it was the members' prerogative to set policy. And while I was for increasing prize money at the U.S. Women's Open, realistically, the market didn't believe at that time that the championship had the charisma of the U.S. Open.

I was ready for all of the hype to go away so that I could get down to business.

The follow-up articles to the press conference were as they always are when the USGA elects a new president, a small mention in the *New York Times*, and longer articles in local newspapers in Orlando, Wichita, and Colorado Springs. The only difference was the insertion of that one key line, "Judy Bell became *the first woman* in history elected as president of the United States Golf Association." Golf magazines had already run articles when I was nominated, and most included photographs. I was a guest on *Golf Talk Live* on the Golf Channel two nights after my election.

Had they been living, Mother and Dad would have enjoyed the weekend immensely. They would have been very anxious, too, because they would have wanted me to do well. But with the natural prejudice of parents, they would have been very proud. After all, they had witnessed the very first shot I played in the game and most of the others along the way.

Was I the best person for the job? I don't think it hurt that I was a woman, let's put it that way. Among men, I think that the competition for the job is keener because there are simply more men on the Executive Committee. I'm not saying that I wasn't qualified, because I was as well prepared as most people are. Certainly at that time the idea of having a woman president was attractive to people, and I was there, and those that decide thought I could do the job.

Women were very supportive. They were, I think, cheering me on and wanting me to do well. After my election I was invited to speak to a number of organizations around the country. Of course I spoke to traditionally male groups, such as golf associations, green superintendents, and Professional Golfers' Association (PGA) gatherings, and the men in those audiences seemed to take my election in stride. But many groups I spoke to were run by women. Most of those women believed the Executive Committee had a sort of male mystique as a bunch of men from private Eastern clubs deciding golf issues in a smoke-filled room and that we women were just lucky to get on a golf course on weekdays. The Executive Committee was perceived in that way.

In my experience the members of the XC, as I call it, came from various walks of life. They aren't all blue bloods or fearsome business titans. They're well-educated, however, and some of them are self-made men. Rarely do we enlist a chairman of a Fortune 500 company, but these men are successful enough—through hard work—to enjoy prosperity and spend personal amounts of up to $25,000 a year on volunteer travel, while working to keep golf the same wonderful game it has always been.

In recent years, many committee members have been business people. One is a doctor, and several are lawyers. What they have in common is that they're all passionate about golf. Perhaps they played the game as boys and, as men, found golf to be their game of choice. A few have played at the higher levels of competition.

The truth is that those guys in that room, the members of the XC, treated me just like everybody else. I'm not saying that I didn't feel certain acts of discrimination along the way, but I think that's to be expected because it's what we, as women, deal with. As women participate more and more in roles that are traditionally filled by men, they have to be at the top of their game and they've got to work at it because maybe the magnifying glass is just a little closer to women than it is to men.

Having a woman finally become president of the USGA was, I think, a great boost for women in the game. The USGA had always conducted women's national championships and the United States Women's Amateur Championship had been played since the beginning of the association in 1895. But it was good for everyone to see that women were now thought of as policy makers.

After I became president, some women were installed as board members of previously all-male golf associations and some became presidents of their golf clubs. Maybe it was just a sign of the times, but it happened and I'm sure that the USGA set the example.

One of the most monumental jumps for women in the USGA had occurred when I was elected to the Executive Committee. It happened in 1987, when Harton "Bud" Semple, a past USGA president and a good friend, evidently worked hard to have me nominated as the first woman on the committee. Bud enlisted the late Howard Clark, who was past chairman of American Express, and Bernard Ridder Jr., a past XC member who was with the Knight-Ridder newspaper chain, to quietly help lobby to get me in.

Bernie was once quoted as saying, "I'm not going to say there weren't those who questioned whether a woman could handle the job, but after many phone calls and conversations, we proceeded because we felt we had the support to do it."

After an intense but successful meeting with the people in power in the USGA, Bud told his wife Phyllis, "Well, we got it done, but she'll never be president."

Phyllis, one of my favorite people, told the story to a friend of mine not long ago. "I guess she showed 'em," she said, and winked.

And so began one of the greatest adventures of my life. I would be under the magnifying glass, but golfers had entrusted me with the opportunity to look after the game.

Last year, a friend asked me to recount my trail to the presidency. I've never thought of it as a particularly moving story—I simply lived it. But when I told her, my friend welled up in tears.

"What are you crying for?" I said. "It only took 102 years."

It was, however, an extraordinary journey.

Chapter 2

[Heritage]

Throughout life, the more that you understand yourself—this piece of work that you're dealing with every day—the better off you are. You need to know yourself and how your mind works so that when you learn about what made you who you are, the people you came from, it's very helpful. My ancestors are a source of fascination and inspiration. Those who lived in the 1600s seem so far removed and their struggles to establish towns and cities in a wild and dangerous land must have seemed insurmountable. Today, for example, it's nothing to fly from Rhode Island to Minnesota in a couple of hours. But nearly four centuries ago, how did my ancestors ever get to Minnesota when all they had were horses and mules? I'm lucky to come from some pretty strong stock.

The family members who made the strongest impression on my life, of course, were my father and mother.

Mother and Dad met in Wichita in the early 1920s on a blind date. In her early twenties, Mariam Remington Champlin was a tall, attractive woman with wonderful carriage and imposing dignity. She had lovely thick hair, strong features, impressive eyes, and the strongest pair of hands I've ever seen. At the time, she was the head nurse on the obstetrical floor at Wichita Hospital and worked for Dr. J. D. Clark, one of the town's leading doctors, so she was obviously intelligent. She was also a straightforward person —you always knew where you stood with Mother.

All of that appealed to my father, who was quite a different mix. Dad was Carl Allen Bell. He was so likeable, very warm and outgoing, with a real feel for people and a great head for business.

Dad's side of the family descends from William Bell and Hannah Dunn, my third great-grandparents. Both were born in Scotland, William in 1794 and Hannah in 1796. They immigrated to America and lived with their seven children in Berkley County, West Virginia.

William Bell's grandson, Joseph McMorris Bell, was my great-grandfather. Joseph married Emma Louise Ogle in Coshocton, Ohio, and they settled there to raise 11 children. Their eldest son was my grandfather, Fred Lee Bell, who was born in Coshocton in 1870.

I was fortunate to spend some time with my great-grandmother, Emma Bell, when I was a child. I recall one evening when her daughter, my Aunt Katherine, had a gentleman friend over for dinner. After dinner the discussion turned to politics and the guest, evidently, was a Democrat.

There were three things to know about Great-Grandmother Bell. She was small, wiry, and spirited. She was a steadfast Republican, and a staunch Methodist.

When she heard the man's decidedly Democratic political spiel, she stomped out of the living room and up the stairs to her bedroom. Apparently, she was so mad that she didn't watch where she was going and fell and broke her hip. The next thing she knew she was lying in a bed in a private room at St. Francis Hospital, which was run by a Catholic monsignor and Catholic nuns. When she awoke, she looked up to see a crucifix hanging on the wall.

"Where *am* I," she said to her son. "Get me out of here!"

They couldn't figure out what upset her the most—Aunt Katherine inviting a Democrat to Grandma Bell's home, or waking up in a Catholic hospital.

While my grandfather, Fred Bell, and his brothers and sisters were growing up, the family moved to Wichita sometime before 1893, the year in which Fred married my grandmother, Julia Henrietta Lucas.

Their second son was my father, Carl, who was born on May 8, 1896. Dad was born in Newton, Kansas, but he and his brothers and sisters— Guy, Gail, Sarah, Ruth, George, and Josephine—were raised in Wichita. Another brother, Theodore, died at birth.

Grandfather Bell was in county politics and a member of the Wichita School Board at the time that East High School was built. When he ran his political campaigns, he passed out little bells (I still have one) that had "I Ring for Fred Bell" printed on them. Naturally, Grandfather was active in the Republican Party. He was Sedgwick County Treasurer and he ran the first vault for Wichita's old Fourth National Bank. I never met him, but my three older brothers did and they thought he was the "cat's meow."

My grandfather was probably a pretty good politician, but when his party was out of office, which was quite often, he didn't have a job. So Dad left school after the eighth grade and went to work to help support the family. When Dad quit school, I think he had already figured out what the world needed him to do. My eldest brother says that he has met a lot of people who were quite educated who talked about how Carl Bell was the smartest man in the area.

By the time he met Mother, Dad had served as an Army mess sergeant in World War I and was working in the meat business. He was an entrepreneur from the word "go." I know for darn sure that he had more common sense than anyone I've ever known. Dad eventually completed his education when he earned a degree at Wichita Business College.

I'm pretty sure he just overwhelmed Mother with his personality, and there was a definite attraction between them that lasted throughout their lives.

Looking back at family history, the blood of my ancestors was pretty watered down by the time it got to me. But I'm still fascinated by my family's efforts to help build a new country.

My mother's father, Grandfather Champlin, was born in Minnesota, where a lot of Champlins had settled. In fact, the town of Champlin, Minnesota, was named for a distant cousin.

When my grandfather was 19, there was a land opportunity in the Oklahoma Territory called the Cherokee Run. It appealed to my great-grandfather Oscar and to Granddaddy, who was known as "E.R." It was 1893 and the United States was being rocked by a great depression. Few people could afford to buy land on which to live and raise crops, so a vast territory in Oklahoma known as the Cherokee Outlet was going to be opened for homesteading.

With his father and brothers, E.R. shipped horses from Minnesota to the border between Kansas and the Oklahoma Territory. On September 16, 1893, along with some 100,000 potential settlers, they lined up for the last great land rush: the Cherokee Strip Land Run. At the signal of gunshots from cavalry soldiers, a thundering herd of horses, oxen, wagons, and dusty, yelling settlers made a mad dash for claims in what was called "the greatest horse race ever."

Granddaddy used to tell the story of the fellow next to him who waited in line with his oxen and wagon. When the guns went off, everybody else took off in a wild race, but this fellow jumped out of his wagon and started to plow because that was the spot where he wanted to be.

Granddaddy got the land he wanted, then met and married my grandmother, Bessie Merrick.

My mother, Mariam, was born in Guthrie, in the Oklahoma Territory, on November 22, 1899. She was followed by Wayne Ralph Champlin, Ellen Louise Champlin, and Merrick Roland Champlin. The family moved to Wichita when she was 14. After high school, she trained as a nurse and graduated from the nursing school at the old Wichita Hospital.

As a youngster, my mother had a hard life and my grandparents were always strapped for money. While Granddaddy could give his wife and children only a meager existence in the early part of the century, he offered an interesting family heritage.

Jeffrey Champlin, my seventh great-grandfather, was the first of the line to come to America. He was born near Bideford, England, in 1621 and immigrated to the United States as a boy. By 1638 he had settled in the Pocasset Colony, which later became Portsmouth, Rhode Island.

Jeffrey was part of a group that established the colony that became Newport. He bought and sold land and was a cordwainer, a leatherworker who designed and made custom shoes, a position of some esteem in those days. His property in Newport sprawled along the south side of Mary Street, from Spring Street west to Water Street and south to the waterfront.

Jeffrey helped found the town of Westerly and was elected to the Westerly Town Council in 1680. He was Moderator of the Town Meetings from 1680-1684, Deputy in the Rhode Island General Assembly from 1681-1686, and in 1685 was assigned to survey roads.

We're descended from Christopher Champlin, the youngest son of Jeffrey and his wife Ulailia Garde. Christopher owned a 150-acre farm. He was elected to the Westerly Town Council in 1679, and served two terms in the Rhode Island General Assembly.

Christopher's great-grandson William, who was born in 1746, served in the Revolutionary War and died at Valley Forge with so many of Washington's soldiers in the bitter winter of 1778.

Oscar Ruel Champlin, my great-grandfather, was a farmer. Born in New York State, Oscar settled in Maple Grove, Minnesota, in 1854. During the Civil War, he left the farm to serve in the 2nd Minnesota Cavalry Regiment.

Oscar's son, Edward Remington Champlin, was my grandfather.

It's rare to have much record of the women in the early part of our country's history, but one of my relatives, Anne Marbury Hutchinson, had quite a life. She was my fifth great-aunt on the Champlin side. Her great-great granddaughter, Susannah Cole Eldred, married Jeffrey's grandson, Jeffrey Champlin III.

Born in Alford, Lincolnshire, England, in 1591, Anne was from a family known for Puritan leanings. With her husband and family, she immigrated to Massachusetts in 1633.

Anne advocated the preaching of a "covenant of grace," a religion based on the individual's direct intuition of God's grace and love, as opposed to the Puritan "covenant of works," which was based on obedience to the laws of church and state. She held small meetings of women in her house, where she expounded her own religious beliefs. Her criticism of the clergy rocked the colony to its foundations and in 1637 she was found guilty of making a mockery of the ministers and was banished.

Pressured by church leaders to deny her beliefs in public, she refused and was accused of lying and then excommunicated.

In 1638 she moved with her family to the wilds of Rhode Island where she and her small band of religious libertarians founded the first white colony on Aquidneck Island. The group drew up a compact as "a Bodie Politick" in order to follow their own religious convictions.

In 1642 Anne's husband died and she moved to the mainland on the shore of Pelham Bay. In 1643 she and all but one of her household were murdered by a group of Monhegan Indians. Her youngest daughter, Susannah Hutchinson, survived but was kidnapped by the Indians and later ransomed by Dutch settlers.

Frankly, I think she observed religion in the right way. But she certainly paid a price for her convictions.

Knowing my family's history and how tough those times were makes me appreciate all that they went through. I was blessed to have certain advantages that didn't exist for my relatives.

Chapter 3

[A Firm Foundation]

I was born during the Great Depression, in the summer of the greatest heat wave, the longest drought, and some of the worst dust storms in Kansas's history.

It had also been another bad summer for polio, the disease that crippled and killed children before the advent of the Salk vaccine. Since the 1920s, Dad had rented a cottage in Manitou Springs, Colorado, to keep the family away from crowds and heat, which were thought to cause the spread of polio.

While Mother was expecting me, the family was at the cottage. When it was time for school to start, Dad took my brothers Jack and Fred back to Wichita, but ordered my brother, Carl, and Mother to stay in Colorado to keep out of the heat, which on August 12th had reached a record 114°.

Mother and Carl eventually took the train back to Wichita and I was born a few days later. September 23, 1936. Judith May Bell. St. Francis Hospital, Wichita, Kansas.

The family home at 1339 North Emporia Avenue was a big house with 13 rooms. My parents weren't wealthy. But Dad, in one of his great deals, had bought that house from one of his customers for $1,000 in cash, with the balance of $4,000 to be taken out in groceries and meats.

Sixty-five years later, it looks much the same—a four-story, white Victorian house with bridal wreath spirea bushes in the front yard on a wide, shady street lined with other big houses. There's a large front porch, a porch off the kitchen, and another area off the second story that we called "the sleeping porch" because we slept out there during the hottest part of the summer. I grew up in that house on North Emporia with Mother, Dad, and three big, loud, loveable brothers.

Most of my world was contained in a one-square-mile area of brick streets. St. Paul's United Methodist Church, where I was christened and where we went to church, was two blocks from home. My first school, Irving Elementary, was just five blocks away on Market Street, and Dad's meats and grocery market was within walking distance.

We all went to Horace Mann Intermediate School at Market and 12th Street, which was actually a very progressive school at that time since the seventh- and eighth-grade classes were integrated. Carl went to school with Riley Banks, an African-American youngster who eventually worked for the railroad and later worked for us. Riley was quite a guy. He became a member of what were called the Negro Troops in World War II and was a great friend of my whole family. Later, on almost every weekend, Riley went to our farm to help my dad with farm work.

As the youngest child and the only girl, I was given a lot of special treatment. I had wonderful toys, including a miniature stove that really worked, and dolls that cried and wet and needed their hair washed.

I endured a lot of teasing, too. A friend of my brothers, Jack Newman, who lived across the street from us, convinced me that I could make firecrackers in my little stove. All I had to do, he said, was roll up talcum powder in wet paper and bake it for 15 minutes. For several hours, I worked away, rolling powder in the paper and baking it. With each fresh batch, I'd run out the door and across the street to light my firecrackers. I never could understand why they wouldn't explode.

While I took my afternoon naps, Mother polished my white shoes and when I woke up, they were sitting by my bed—spick and span—with a new pair of laces and clean socks.

The boys claim they had to walk or ride their bicycles to school, rain or snow, but that's a crock because I know they got rides. I will admit that I usually persuaded Dad or Mother to drive me to grade school.

Even then, I had the added security of never having anyone in my family say to me, "You can't do that because you're a girl." They just didn't believe in that sort of discrimination.

Mother and Dad were the strongest influences on my life. My father had a way of getting along with people, a trait that I've hopefully inherited and that I've found valuable in my own life. They both had a great appreciation for education, which I also share.

Mother was the matriarch of the family and my values certainly came from her. I'm as straightforward and up-front as Mother was. She believed that a person must never quit. She also believed that we were just as good as anyone else and capable of doing anything we wanted to do. If we made up our minds to do something, we could do it. Those principles I absolutely followed because my mother led by example.

Mother was tenacious. When she started something, she finished it. Whether it was a crossword puzzle, working in the garden, or making candy at Christmastime, she'd just stay with it.

I was about 14 when Mother and I had an unforgettable experience that showed me her fortitude. We were in Colorado for the summer and had played golf in Colorado Springs. We were coming back to the cabin in Manitou, driving up Ute Pass along a two-lane road that was very curvy and mountainous for about four miles. Early on, a man on a motorcycle speeded past us. A few minutes later, we found him in the wreckage of his motorcycle where he had crashed in front of the Red Cloud Inn, in Cascade.

Mother pulled off the road and ran over to help him until an ambulance came from Colorado Springs, which would take at least 30 minutes. She held his head in her lap, in the proper way she had learned as a nurse, talking to him and doing everything possible to keep the man alert. Unfortunately, he became unconscious. For an hour she knelt on her bare knees in the gravel, never moving, until the ambulance arrived. When the man was taken away, Mother's knees were bleeding and I remember that when we got to the cabin she had to dig out the small pebbles that had become imbedded in her skin.

Seeing Mother holding that man who was sprawled on the ground left a lasting impression on me. She was terribly brave and I don't think I could have ever done what she did.

The man died the next day.

Mother was a great source of strength for all of us. She had an upbeat outlook on life. It's important to be optimistic, to use a positive system of thinking. To visualize how you can succeed is the ultimate optimism, and this was a part of Mother's character.

I believe that my father, who was more pessimistic, gained confidence from her as he ran his business. When I think of where he started, with few resources other than a good mind and the willingness to work hard, and then built two successful businesses, I know she helped generate his success by just instilling him with her strength and optimism.

Mother gave us every opportunity to broaden our horizons. As she was growing up she never had the chance to learn to play the piano, which she had yearned to do. In her forties, Mother was finally able to take piano lessons, along with Carl, from Reno B. Meyers. She saw that each of her other children played a musical instrument, too. Carl played the piano by ear, Fred played the accordion, and Jack played the drums. I played the piano, the accordion (because we had one), and in junior and senior high school I played the clarinet. My efforts to play the piano didn't always measure up and when I said, "I can't play. I'm just no good at it," she'd hit the ceiling. She'd say the reason I wasn't any good was because I didn't work at it.

She was right, but playing the piano just never got my attention. I'd practice like a concert pianist just before a recital, but not in a steady, consistent manner throughout the year.

She honestly believed that if you wanted to be a mathematician, you opened up the math book. You were as good as anybody else and it didn't matter whether you had the background or the financial wherewithal, you could achieve anything you wanted if you worked hard enough. Everyone, obviously, can't be a great mathematician, but dedication and practice will take you a long way in whatever you do.

She also had a real fit about telling the truth. As a child, I had quite an imagination and would convince myself that whatever came out of my mouth was really true. But Mother saw through me and questioned me until I told the truth. I'd dream up little fibs, telling her that someone was walking into the house, or someone was calling on the phone or taking her car, but it wasn't often that I could fool her.

Mother and Dad's friends were easier to convince. My parents had a large group of friends and I felt close to most of them. When I was with them, I'd tell my yarns and some of those friends believed me.

Mother was very much a supporter of human beings. Forget male versus female—it didn't matter, it was how you did the job. She was very much my father's equal in making decisions and running the house. She didn't think her role was to stay in the kitchen instead of going hunting or fishing.

She was, by the way, the best fisherman in the family. While my father was a good fisherman, she was passionate about it. I hated fishing. They'd take me with them and the worst part was that I had to be quiet, which was almost impossible for me. But that was Mother's rule.

I'm also sure that Mother tried to beat Dad when they played golf

together because she was intensely competitive. My folks had an understanding that Dad would not give Mother advice on the course. However,
she didn't want advice from *any* source. Jack once caddied for Mother in
the club championship and, on the 4th hole, her opponent hit her ball into
the water in front of the green.

Mother asked Jack for a certain club.

"Why are you going to try to go over?" he asked. "You'll just hit it in the
water like she did."

"If I do," Mother said, "I will throw you and the golf bag in the water
after the ball!"

Mother managed the household money. Dad gave her an allowance,
out of which she bought my clothes, her clothes, and paid all of the household bills. If she ran out of money, she would never ask him for a dime. I can
still hear her saying, "If I have to ask him for money, I'll just go without."

Of course, Dad was very generous but sometimes didn't realize it was
taking more money to run things. When he did, he would step right up to
the plate.

When Mother worked at our market, my parents hired a live-in woman
to take care of the boys, which eased Mother's job a bit. But she still ran the
house, the hired woman, and the boys. Years later, after my grandfather
died, she also took care of my Grandmother Champlin. She was the one
person that her parents, brothers, and sister most looked up to.

Outside of my immediate family, the most important people in my life
were my Grandfather Champlin and my Aunt Gail.

Granddaddy ran Dad's produce department. He seemed stern as heck
but he did everything with me and, underneath, he was really very soft. I
remember hanging out with him in the produce section while he washed
the lettuce.

As a child I always had some hairbrained scheme, such as tearing down
wooden orange crates to build a racer, so I'd tell him about my plans and
he'd help me do whatever I wanted. He was wonderful because he always
had time for me, and he was my best pal as I was growing up.

I was with our grandparents a lot. Granddaddy Champlin and my
grandmother, "Mamuz," lived above the store and I often spent the night
with them.

Most of my elementary school friends went home for lunch, but I
walked to Bell's Market. The butcher sliced some turkey or other meat, and
Aunt Gail would fix a sandwich for me. I can see it now: a glass of milk,

potato chips, and my sandwich waiting for me in one of Dad's meat trays, fresh as could be.

My mother and father worked hard for most of their lives, but Mother was 36 and Dad was 40 when I was born. Their business success meant they were now in a financial position to be able to do things that they enjoyed, such as taking trips with their friends or going hunting. While I was too small to go with them, I was never left with a sitter. I always stayed with relatives, and I loved being with my grandparents or my aunts and uncles.

I spent an enormous amount of time with Aunt Gail, my father's sister, and often stayed with her when my folks were out of town.

Aunt Gail lived with and cared for Grandma Bell. I adored my aunt, but Grandma Bell was standoffish, a bit of a whiner, and I never liked the way she talked to Aunt Gail. I liked Grandma Bell, but she wasn't much fun. She always expected certain behavior from her children and grandchildren. Grandma Bell had no spontaneity at all. To me as a child, she was too serious and had no sense of humor. I don't know how she went through life without a sense of humor. It's the trait that keeps you from taking yourself too seriously.

Aunt Gail's care of Grandma gave her very little opportunity to have friends of her own, although she was close to her relatives. Her entire life was wrapped up in Dad's store, where she kept track of the money and took care of the charge accounts. Dad used to call her "the keeper of the dough." I can remember him saying to Aunt Gail, "I don't care how you do it. You can get a tub, put it between your legs, and throw the money in there. I don't care how you do it."

Aunt Gail was very fat and short and I was fascinated by the way she drove the pickup truck Dad bought for her. She could barely reach the gas pedal or the brake, and she drove with her foot extended way out to reach the pedals with her toe. It just amazed me. We'd go to the picture show and out to dinner in her truck, which was a stick shift that she couldn't drive very well, and that truck would jerk and buck all the way to town.

Aunt Gail stored a huge collection of china and silverware in a big room beneath the stairs to the second floor in the house at 204 South Osage, where she lived. When you think about it, she probably got all of the china and silver in anticipation of getting married and the room was sort of her hope chest. She never married but, just as I did later, found a rich and productive life as a single woman.

Each summer she visited us for a week in Cascade, Colorado and that was her vacation. We had a log cabin with a kitchen, living room, bath, and two bedrooms, but the best part was a huge room over the two-car garage where I spent time with my friends when we weren't hiking or swimming in Green Mountain Falls. I enjoyed my friends, the Sanborn twins, Nick and Frank, John Patrick Stavinak, and Ronnie Sears, one of my first boyfriends.

On occasion, Mother and Dad took me to Colorado Springs to play golf at the Patty Jewett Golf Course where I met Marian Shaw, a girl about my age. Marian and I played a lot of golf together.

My big adventure with Aunt Gail was going into Colorado Springs, where we went to the Village Inn or the Indian Grill on Pikes Peak Avenue, then to the picture show. In Wichita, she often took me to the symphony.

Aunt Gail was a remarkable, beautiful person, so kind and considerate, and her manners were impeccable. She was a good disciplinarian, too, but I found it easy to behave. I wasn't a child who caused trouble, because I always wanted to please these adults who were such an important part of my life. Aunt Gail and I just palled around, which is, I think, one of the reasons I was very comfortable with older people. I was probably another dimension in her life, just as she added a dimension to mine.

I was also very close to my aunts Jo and Ellen. Aunt Jo was Dad's youngest sister and, even when they were both a lot older, he would introduce her as, "my baby sister, Josephine." She was a lot of fun, a lot more frivolous than Aunt Gail, and a lot more laughy. She had a wonderful smile. All of her nieces and nephews just loved her because she was very much like a child herself.

Mother's sister, Aunt Ellen, was very sporting and had a great sense of humor. She played baseball and I used to watch her play big-time amateur basketball when I was a little girl. She was quite good, and played on an Amateur Athletic Union (AAU) basketball team in Wichita called "Thurston's." Her team often played against a Denver AAU team that included Babe Zaharias. Babe was a great athlete but Aunt Ellen always said that one of her own teammates, Corinne Jacks, was actually a better basketball player than Babe. Whenever the two teams played, Corinne, a guard, could contain Babe's scoring, in one game holding Babe to only two points, and Corinne led Thurston's to the final of the AAU championship.

Aunt Ellen was a good role model. She was very positive and a lot of laughs. You just wanted to be with Aunt Jo and Aunt Ellen because they were lots of fun. My three aunts were also close to each other, even though one was maternal and two were paternal aunts.

Uncle Merrick, my mother's brother, worked in the store but I don't think it was the best of relationships.

Uncle George, on the other hand, worked with my dad all his life. When he was a little boy, he stood on a box to wait on customers at Dunne's meat counter, which was managed by Dad. He was so loyal to my dad—just idolized him—and was great to me.

His second wife was as mean as anybody I ever met, but Uncle George was a prince of a guy. He was the greatest supporter, a champion of mine, and throughout his life he never forgot my birthday.

I was also very fond of Uncle Guy, my dad's eldest brother, who always had a twinkle in his eye. All the kids went to him. He'd let you do anything. Heck, even if you were six or seven years old, he'd let you smoke. Uncle Guy wasn't nearly as successful as my father, but he was a great guy. Except for weddings and funerals, I never saw him wear anything but bib overalls.

I had a lot of close, strong relationships with relatives outside of my immediate family, not just because they were family, because there were certain people that I liked and certain people that I disliked.

I'd see them at the Bell family reunion, and I'd see many more of them at the Bell-Lucas family reunions, which reached out to more people. For the Bell-Lucas reunions, we'd go to Riverside Park for a Sunday picnic. Each family brought its own food, Mother brought food for us, and Dad brought ice cream bars for everyone. It was a huge, yearly gathering of at least 150 people.

Grandma Bell's relatives, the Lucases, were all sort of short, pudgy little people, and it seemed to me that they all wore bib overalls.

Uncle Guy would always be there. Although he and my father were very close, he was no businessman. In fact, Dad tried to help with Guy's business affairs and give him advice. Uncle Guy owned some property that he farmed, but he lived on a farm that he rented and paid rent for years.

That used to drive my father absolutely berserk. "Why wouldn't you live on your own property?" he'd tell him. "You'd have it paid for by now, Guy. I just don't get it."

Uncle Guy had seven children, so just having the Guy Bell family come to the reunions guaranteed that we'd have a slew of people.

My family members were so crucial to me that I always sought their approval, even in my personal life. Whenever I brought a new beau home, some fellow that I was enamored with, I would insist that he go to one of our family reunions. That was important to me because I needed to know how he fit in and how my family liked him.

One fellow, who was just a good friend, didn't fare so well. At our family reunions, we had a tradition in which we all piled onto a fire truck that belonged to John Strube, who lived on a farm we owned in Kingman County. John would rev up the fire truck and we'd ride through the towns of Adams and Belmont, waving at everybody. On this day, when John made a turn, my friend fell off the truck.

Uncle Guy said, "You know, I didn't like him anyway. The son of a bitch, why couldn't he hold on with both hands?"

There is absolutely no way that I would have turned out as I did without these relatives. Because of all of their influence on me, my life went in a certain direction.

Chapter 4

[Bell's Market]

"Bell's Market, this is Judy Bell. Good morning, Mrs. Wilson. I can take your order for our morning or afternoon delivery. We have some very nice lettuce today."

I was 10 years old.

I knew I had arrived when I was allowed to take orders over the telephone. Until then, I had stocked shelves and worked with Granddaddy in the produce department. By the age of 11 I was running one of the cash registers, which I'd known how to do since I was about four years old. In those days, at least in our part of the country, no one seemed to know or care about any child labor laws!

Retailing is in my blood.

When Mother and Dad got married in 1921, Dad ran a butcher shop for Frank Dunne, who owned Dunne's Mercantile Company. The store was near the railroad tracks, not far from a building where fresh meat was unloaded from the trains. He then owned a store in a building he rented on the south side of 13th Street.

My folks soon had three children. My brother, Carl Allen Bell Jr., was born in 1922. Fred Lee Bell, named for my grandfather, came along in 1923, and Jack Duane Bell was born in 1926.

In 1933 or 1934, Dad wanted to buy the Dunne building, but the Depression was on and he didn't have the money to make it happen. I wasn't born yet, but my brothers told me that he took the streetcar to the Riverside section of Wichita to visit his aunt, Katherine Bell. Aunt Katherine had never married and lived in the house with Great-Grandma Bell, so she didn't have to pay rent or a mortgage payment. She also had a fine job with Wallingford Grain Company where she was Sam Wallingford's "Girl Friday." By the 1930s, Aunt Katherine had accumulated a nice savings account.

"What's the matter?" Aunt Katherine asked Dad.

"I've got an opportunity to buy this building and I don't have the money," Dad said. "Is there any chance you could give me a loan?"

"How much do you need?" she asked.

When he told her that he needed $20,000, she agreed. It was an incredible amount of money at that time.

Dad bought the building, got new fixtures, and had it refurbished. He bought inventory and equipment and still had a little cushion to help operate the business in the beginning. It was a big gamble for Dad, as he had no one to look to for repayment of the loan except himself. Now, he finally owned his own business and his decision turned out to be a great one.

Dad convinced most of the restaurants and schools in Wichita to buy their meat from him and he had a lot of good accounts, but he really had to work hard in the early days to make a go of it. His friend Pat McCoy owned a grocery store and told Dad he should expand by selling groceries and produce, not just meat.

"Mariam," Pat said, "can run the grocery side."

According to my brothers, Mother was so mad that she was ready to kill Pat McCoy, but she took over setting up the groceries and produce, kept adding items, and soon Bell's Market was a full-blown grocery store.

Some food wasn't packaged in those days and the store had big platform scales where they would measure out the sugar, beans, potatoes, and other bulk food, weigh them, sack them, and tie the bags before giving them to customers.

When my brothers were old enough, Carl worked in the office, took telephone orders, and published "The Bell Ringer," a monthly newsletter that was sent to existing and potential customers. Jack and Fred learned to cut meat, and in the early years Mother was always at the checkout counter. Everyone waited on customers.

After school, I worked at the store, too. When I was 10, Johnny Allgear, a salesman who carried the Monarch and H.D. Lee food lines, came in a lot. Johnny made a business deal with me. If I would set up a little table next to the cash register, I could demonstrate peanut butter and jelly, hand out samples, and encourage our customers to buy the products on a nice commission basis. When Fred Cochran's son, Bill, came in, I still needed to sell five cases to make my quota.

Bill, who was 23, said he would buy all five cases if I gave him a kiss.

I've always wondered what he did with all of that peanut butter.

All of us worked at our store—Dad and Mother, my older brothers Carl, Jack, and Fred, Granddaddy, my aunts Gail, Josephine, and Ellen, my uncles George and Merrick—and it was a huge part of my early life.

Our store bustled with life and noise and was a popular gathering place for Dad's friends. One of his pals was Fred Cochran, who owned Cochran's Mortuary. Every morning Dad read the obituaries in the newspaper. It wasn't because he wanted to see who had died, but to see how many of the funerals were going to Cochran's.

Dad, in his later years, enjoyed driving around Wichita to see how things were going. He'd cruise past Larcher's, our competitor, every morning on his way to the North store. Although Frank Larcher was a great friend of his, Dad would count the cars in Larcher's parking lot. When he arrived at his North store, he'd call my brother, Fred, at Bell's East.

"Skip," he'd say to Fred, "how many cars do we have in the parking lot?"

Fred would go count the cars, and come back to the telephone. "28," he'd say.

"Larcher's only has 18," Dad chortled. It was a game for him, a sort of competition, all healthy and in good fun.

Dad was an inspiring leader with a lot of great ideas. He believed in good training for his employees and also frequently asked them what they thought, which helped him develop a mutual trust. In a very real sense, Dad considered his employees to be part of his extended family. As a result, Dad's employees were very loyal to him and the business.

He also had a big hand in raising us and insisted that all of his children speak to everyone they passed, whether in the store or on the street. He had great faith in people, believing that they were essentially good, so he stuck with you and he'd never let go of a friend. Dad's great way with people won many friends and kept loyal workers with him for years.

He had a keen appreciation for making everything work together for the good of the business. When he added a produce section to the store, for instance, he saved the produce bags then sold them back to the produce companies. That money paid for the repairs to his fleet of six or seven delivery trucks.

My father always hosted a Christmas Eve party at the store. The store operated basically as a delivery business and his trucks ran morning and afternoon deliveries to Wichita neighborhoods. For that reason, we had tons of customers who'd been with us for 25 or 30 years but ordered everything by telephone and never came into the store. Dad started the Christmas Eve party so that customers could visit his place of business.

On the party menu was his "savage steak"—steak tartare that he made himself and was the best you'd ever want to eat. And he'd take specialty items, such as cocktail oysters, sardines in a variety of sauces, salmon, olives, artichoke hearts, and an assortment of cheeses and put them in flat-bottomed meat trays. For the party, Dad and my brothers scattered fresh sawdust on the floor of the suet room and lay shelving across the suet barrels, where they set up the hors d'oeuvres.

He only invited a few customers at first, but the Christmas Eve party eventually became so popular that you could hardly get in the room.

Dad's party began at noon and people came in waves, a lot of them arriving late in the afternoon. I had to make sure that the hors d'oeuvres were set out and that the trays were always filled. My brothers tended bar. Uncle Bill Friesen, who was married to Aunt Ellen, was in the police quartet and would bring his group to sing. We always had them sing "Margie," my father's favorite. The story was that Mother and Dad had heard the song on the radio when they were driving to Newton, Kansas, to get married. Even years later, when I would walk into Bell's Deli, our restaurant in Colorado Springs, Tom O'Boyle, the pianist, always played "Margie."

Dad didn't have a drink until the very end of the party. Then we'd go to Grandma Bell's house for a family gift exchange. We were a huge family, so there might be 60 or 70 people.

Grandma Bell didn't approve of smoking or drinking, but by that time Dad had a little liquor on his breath. He always gave money to his mother for Christmas, which was his favorite gift to give. Grandma Bell always took the money from him, but would then turn her head away when he tried to kiss her.

I can imagine how that hurt his feelings and it still bothers me when I think about it today.

Chapter 5

[The Land]

During World War II, my brothers were in the army overseas and in the summer, Granddaddy, Mamuz, Mother, Dad, and I lived in a cabin on our farm near Furley, Kansas, some 25 miles northeast of Wichita. Dad had always wanted a farm and bought it when he finally had the money.

My grandparents and Mother raised a lot of vegetables in a big Victory Garden. During the war, nearly every family raised fruit and vegetables for its own consumption in such gardens. At the age of five and six, I was always looking for ways to help and be involved. I made sandwiches for Mother and my grandparents and took water to them while they worked in the garden. I would then join in to hoe, weed, and help plant vegetables.

Wheat and alfalfa were the farm's primary crops. During the wheat harvest, the workers dreamed up ways to keep me busy because I had tremendous curiosity and was always underfoot. Each day the workers told me that it was my responsibility to bring water from the house. I'd load up wide-mouthed mason jars with water and ice that I chipped from a big block. I put the jars in saddlebags with a bunch of cups, and galloped my Shetland pony, "Patsy," out to the field. After about the twelfth trip, Patsy wouldn't go any more. Mother humored me by driving me out into the field for one more trip because I couldn't walk and carry my water jars, too.

When my brothers were home, they had another scheme to keep me busy. They'd say, "Go get us some ice cream." I'd jump on Patsy and ride the two miles into Furley, buy the ice cream, put it in the saddlebags, and gallop back. No matter how fast Patsy ran, the ice cream always melted. When I got to the cabin, it looked like soup.

Then my brothers would tell me, "Go back for more."

I'd usually make one more trip, taking insulated bags Mother had brought from our store, but the results were just about the same.

Dad and his friends took target practice at the farm by shooting clay pigeons. I made my extra money firing out those pigeons. I'd sit in a little hut and they'd yell, "Pull!" I'd pull, and the clay pigeons would go up.

When they drank adult beverages, I got some big tips and made what seemed to me to be a fortune out there. In reality, it was only a dollar or two. If I had a really hot day, I might make five dollars, but that could double my weekly allowance, which had to cover lunches and maybe a picture show.

There was a lot to do on the farm. I had a pet goat that I played with and my Shetland pony. In the evening, I'd go to the barn to try my hand at stripping one of the cows of milk after the pumps were used to milk her. I liked taking my goat with me when I went to the separator house to see the milk and cream come out of the separator. Our cream was so thick you had to spoon it from the jar.

Patsy was my constant companion and I rode her from morning to dusk.

There was mischief to get into as well; the farm was where I first tried to smoke. A couple of my friends and I packed my dad's pipes with ground coffee. We used hundreds of kitchen matches trying to light the pipes and left the matches lying around the outhouse. Mother found the burnt matches, of course. She didn't spank me, but pulled me into her bedroom to have a talk about the evils of smoking.

She was *not* happy about my efforts. She told me that she never wanted to catch me smoking again, certainly not until I was old enough to make my own decisions. Although Mother and Dad both smoked, she said that if she had to do it over, she never would have started.

Mother was very fair, but when you messed up, you paid the price. I was told that I wouldn't be able to invite my friends to the farm for a month.

I felt guilty about having done something wrong. Besides, my throat hurt. Each of us had worked hard to get the pipes lit, but never got anything going. I never smoked again until I was in college. Luckily, I didn't smoke much and considered it a smoking fit if I had five cigarettes on any one day. In fact, I'd go days without smoking and finally gave it up cold turkey in 1993 at the request of my cardiologist.

I loved our cabin and the farm, but when I was 13 Dad sold it and bought the 320-acre Miller Farm about 45 miles southeast of Wichita in Kingman County. It had several magnificent spring-fed lakes that he stocked with bass, crappie, catfish, and bluegill.

At the time, there was a little oil boom in the area and it became a joke that all of the local families had lived on their land for generations and the primary well was discovered on Carl Bell's newly acquired farm. Dad was always a little lucky and that oil well helped support his role as a gentleman farmer. Dad retained an owner's eighth share of the oil and the drilling company got the rest. While the wells didn't produce many barrels per day, they produced for a very long time. In fact, I'll bet they're still pumping today.

He grew wheat and alfalfa crops and we raised cattle, chickens, and lambs, which assured a daily supply of fresh milk and fresh eggs.

Dad purchased lots of farm equipment over the years. I remember when he decided to get out of the farming business and had an auction to sell the livestock and farm equipment. When he didn't think an item was going for enough money, he bid on it and bought the item back. In the end, he remained in the farm business because he'd bought back so much of his own stuff.

We sold the farm in 1998 but I look back on it as a special place. Those times at the farm with my family are among my most precious memories.

Chapter 6

[The Busiest Kid in Kansas]

I don't think I'd be the same sort of person if I hadn't been raised with three older brothers.

My childhood was quite regimented. Not only were my parents older when I came along, but my brothers were a *lot* older than I was. Even Jack, the youngest, was born a decade before I was. With all of those older people in my immediate family always telling me what to do, it was like having five parents, which is why I loved my grandparents indulging me.

In a lot of ways, my brothers and I were alike. We all loved sports, appreciated music, and had pretty good rhythm. We all knew the difference between right and wrong and if we gave you our word, we were going to deliver. Carl and I shared an appreciation for education, and we were both very verbal. Jack, Fred, and I shared a competitive spirit and love of sports. Jack and I were alike in our sense of humor, and Fred and I were alike in that we were very straightforward and had loud voices.

We were an extremely active family. Jack was a great football player in high school and also played baseball. Fred played baseball and was a basketball star. Carl was captain of the school debate team and sang in the glee club. All of them played golf.

I had my own adventures with music. When I was a senior, I was president of the North High School band. When it came time for my last audition, I stood up and raised my clarinet. Bob Hollowell, the band director, said, "Let's just talk about your golf game. I know where I'm going to seat you anyway."

He was sick of hearing me blow that thing. And he eventually seated me in the third clarinet section, almost at the end, which attested to my lack of talent. As bad as I was, he couldn't seat me in the end seat because I was president of the band.

When we were marching, I was the left guide and responsible for an entire row of musicians. But I was probably the only band member who graduated from North High School, got "A's" in music, and couldn't play the school fight song. I couldn't march and play at the same time.

Basketball for girls wasn't offered in the schools in those days. I considered myself to be a good player and badly wanted to play in an organized league. My friend, Diane Klepper (who went to another junior high school) and I went to the Wichita Department of Parks and Recreation and met with the director on two or three occasions to urge him to start a league for girls. He finally told us if we could put together three teams, he'd get the league going. Diane and I got our fathers to sponsor two teams, "Klepper's Clippers," and "Bell's Bullets". I also enlisted Janis Simmons, another friend, to get her father, who owned a plumbing business, to sponsor the third team. So we got our own league going and by the time we got to high school, it had grown into two separate leagues with 16 teams.

My brother Fred, who was big, good-looking, and athletic, was the coach of our team and the girls just loved him. He'd really get us stirred up to play hard and win. After a few years, when we girls got older, he told me he had decided that he probably should stop sending us out on the floor with a slap on our rear ends.

We could never beat Klepper's Clippers in a regular season game, but one night we played against them in an exhibition game in the Mulvane (Kansas) High School gymnasium. Fred was on a hunting trip and my brother, Jack, stepped in as the coach. One of Klepper's best players, Sally Alyward, fouled out in the first quarter and we finally ended our losing streak against their team. For the rest of the year, Jack ribbed Fred about how easy it was to beat Klepper's Clippers.

At Horace Mann Intermediate School, I had a lot of African-American friends. We'd walk home from school together and sit out on the curb to talk for long periods of time, which was frankly a source of irritation to my mother.

There was a lot of tension between the races at that time and it filtered into my school. When new African-American students were bussed to our school, they didn't know what to expect. They didn't trust us when we said we wanted everyone to get along at Horace Mann, regardless of race or color.

I was Student Council president and felt a responsibility to help work out the conflicts.

Luckily, I had friends like Thessoline Banks, Riley's younger sister. I talked to Thessoline and other students, both African-American and Caucasian, with the hope of promoting harmony. Before school started in the morning, I talked to the other children in the foyer while we waited for the doors to open. I talked to the school's athletes about having a sense of fair play when dealing with people of another race. I met with children who were leaders of their individual groups and tried to convince them to get involved in the Student Council, which they sometimes did.

I also talked to students during gym class, where the situation had become so tense that I was the only white girl who wasn't afraid to take showers with the African-American students.

"Look," I told them, "we've just got to get along. We don't have a choice."

But these conflicts were all nonsense and we got them worked out. I don't know that my efforts had any great impact, but I felt very strongly that all people had to get along. Still do.

My own childhood, I believe, was nearly perfect.

I couldn't get into much trouble because I was kept so busy, which suited me just fine. Mother signed me up for a lot of activities that I thought were stupid and enrolled me in classes with a lot of regimentation, which I couldn't stand. We all played sports, like touch football, and we played basketball all the time in our own half-court in the backyard.

At the farm in the summertime, I had to take care of my pony and my goat and had chores to do. I took all kinds of lessons, including expression, tap dancing, accordion, piano, and clarinet. Not only did I take the lessons, I had recitals for each class and Mother was always on my case about practicing.

In my piano recitals, I always played "O Sole Mio." Whenever I missed a note, I started over. Mother would force a bunch of my relatives to attend and they'd all sit there, just praying that I wouldn't miss a note and begin again.

I was also a member of a Girl Scout troop, worked at our store, swam in club and interclub swimming meets, and played golf. If Mother had ever seen any spare moment where I might possibly have been getting into any sort of trouble, she'd have signed me up for something else, I guarantee it.

My mother was not an ogre. She never pushed me to excel. She just made sure that her children had opportunities that she'd never had. The only difference was that some of it wasn't by choice. I enjoyed all of it and am very grateful, but it was a lot for a kid to *do*. I simply don't know how any child could have become a troubled youngster if they had M.R.B. for a mother.

Like every child, I had insecurities and disappointments. Some children thrive on Halloween, for example, but it was never a celebration I liked. Crestview Country Club always had a Halloween horror chamber. The club's employees, who could call all the children by name, were the ghosts and goblins. It scared me, as did any number of things when I was small. I was very impressionable and had a vivid imagination. Ghosts and goblins made me feel spooky because I could imagine that they were real.

We had hot water heat, and the water gurgling through the pipes at night sounded like someone was coming up the stairs. It scared me so much that I would leap out of my bed and run to get into bed with Mother and Dad.

No doubt some of those fears came about because I grew up in the days of radio and listened to *The Inner Sanctum* and *The Shadow*, both of which were pretty scary programs. Unlike television, radio really captured your imagination. You had to visualize, and I was awfully good at that.

Even my dolls seemed real to me. This was at a time when we could first get dolls with faces that felt like skin, and hair that was as soft and curly as real hair. I changed their diapers, cooked for them, fed them, and it all seemed very real. In fact, they seemed to like my cooking.

One night I was visiting Aunt Ellen and Uncle Bill. Bill was a detective on the Wichita police force and his assignment that night was to work at the wrestling matches at the Forum. Aunt Ellen asked if I had ever been to a wrestling match. I thought of watching Jack wrestle for his high school team and said, "Sure."

These wrestling matches were very different from Jack's matches. The small-time professional wrestlers who came to the Forum looked like big, vicious, hairy grizzly bears to me, and they threw each other all over the ring. I was so spooked that I couldn't sleep that night. Aunt Ellen came in later to check on me. "I can see you've never been to a real wrestling match, now have you?" she said.

Brownies and Girl Scouts were other groups I joined, at Mother's recommendation. Scouting today offers more interesting activities, such as sports, but in those days we moved at a snail's pace, which drove me crazy.

One troop activity took us to Sims Park, where each scout was to find several leaves and identify them. I could find the leaves in 15 minutes. Well, then what do you do? I would think about how badly I wanted to be playing on the Sims Park Golf Course, run by the city of Wichita.

One year, I went to the Girl Scout's Camp Bide-A-Wee. Mother and Dad drove me to the camp, which was just outside of Wichita but seemed to me like a week's drive away. I was to see my parents that weekend when they came to visit, but I never made it to the weekend.

I just hated camp. The mosquitoes were big enough to ride and I had to sleep in a cabin with the other little girls. They laughed and talked all night, and I couldn't sleep.

On the third day, I called home and said, "You've got to come get me, or I'm going to run away."

When they picked me up, Mother was disgusted. She disapproved of quitters. There was certainly no quit in her. None. But I just didn't like group sleeping, no matter what anybody thought.

I must have gone to a hundred slumber parties, but never lasted the night. Sleeping on the floor, with everyone talking and laughing most of the night, wasn't my idea of a good time, so I'd sneak to the telephone and call home.

"Could you come get me?" I'd whisper into the phone.

"*Why* are you whispering," Mother would say.

"I don't want them to hear me," I said. "I'll sneak out, meet you on the corner, and they'll never know I'm gone."

"This is ridiculous," Mother said. But she always picked me up, often as late as 2 A.M.

A few weeks would pass, and I'd ask if I could go to another slumber party. "Absolutely not," she'd say.

I'd wheedle and wheedle until I got her permission to go, then the process would start all over again. At first, the other girls teased me about not staying but it didn't make as strong an impression as finding a way to go home. I was never much influenced by peer pressure anyway. After four years of seeing me leave slumber parties in the middle of the night, my friends stopped saying anything.

I just always wanted to be at home. I felt safe and secure there, and I liked being around my family.

Chapter 7

[The Enchanting Game]

My parents had become avid golfers by the time I was born and were members of Crestview Country Club in Wichita.

Mother was very determined to become a good player, and worked on her game until she could shoot in the low 80s. She was also active in the administrative side of golf as president of the Wichita Ladies Golf Association. In 1950, she became president of the Kansas Women's Golf Association. Dad was active in the club and became quite a good player, shooting in the high 70s and low 80s.

By the time I was seven, I swam like a fish and loved to spend all day in the club pool. But that was also the summer that I was introduced to golf. Dave Truffelli, one of my father's closest friends and the professional at Crestview, invited me to play a few holes and took me right out on the course. If I lasted for only one hole, that was enough. There was never any pressure about staying out there, which I heartily advocate for new players.

Dave was my first instructor, a good friend, and a tremendous influence on me as I grew up. As a youngster he had worked as a caddie in Oakland, California, where he learned to play golf from John Black. Like his friends Tom LoPresti and Mike Murra, professionals who had once been caddies, he swung the club beautifully. Dave spent time with me on the golf course and had a good golf swing, so I was able to mimic him, which was a good way to begin. He kept things very simple and only showed me things that I could actually do.

I became more and more fascinated with golf. I always wanted to stay and play one more hole, eventually playing five or six holes at a time.

We had a huge putting clock, a practice putting area, at the club and in the summer it was lighted at night, which had been Dad's idea when he was chairman of the Green Committee. Families went to the club for supper, then organized a putting contest. Children were welcome, so at least I'd been putting for some time and understood at an early age that the object of the game was to get the ball into the hole.

I used Aunt Gail's old wooden-shafted clubs that had been cut down for me. As further inspiration, there was a set of shiny, red nylon head covers for sale in the golf shop and I wanted those head covers. Dave said, "When you break 35 for five holes, they're yours."

I finally broke 35 for the five holes and the head covers were mine.

I was getting the bug all along and, as it is in most cases, it was just a matter of how badly I got bitten. I enjoyed hitting the ball and liked the challenge of trying to do better every time I played. I felt that golf was something that I could do on my own, but it was also something I could do with my family.

Within a few years, my brothers and I were playing once a week during the summer. It was a battle. I was hitting the ball further and further. One day, I had already hit my tee shot over the water that fronted the 14th tee at Crestview. When Fred teed off, he hit his tee shot into the water and I laughed, not only because he had hit his ball into the water but because I was beating him at the time.

Fred quit playing golf shortly after that round and took up tennis. I still claim it was because I beat him, although he later went back to playing the game again. I was getting better, and eventually I would beat all three of my brothers. I loved it.

While we played at a private club in Wichita, during our summers in Colorado we'd play at the Patty Jewett Golf Course, a wonderful public course in Colorado Springs.

Later, my parents joined as summer members at The Broadmoor Golf Club. The membership, as at many clubs, was held in the man's name. My mother had trouble understanding the reasoning behind that policy. She thought it was stupid. Nevertheless, Mother always played in The Broadmoor Ladies Invitation, which for many, many years was a great women's tournament attracting the finest amateurs in the country.

When I was 11, I was putting on The Broadmoor putting clock while

Mother played her practice round for the tournament. Dad came over with Lynn Smith, a fellow-Kansan and the father of Marilynn Smith, who was playing in the tournament. They asked if I wanted to play in the tournament, which would start in two days. I'd never even played an 18-hole round, but of course I said, "Sure."

Dad paid my entry fee and I was a contestant.

Mother went bonkers when she found out. She was absolutely furious with him. Of course, the more excited she got, the more I wanted to play. Dad became sort of sheepish, but eventually we prevailed.

The next day, Mother and our dear friend Niente Borchert took me out for a practice round. It had nothing to do with "aim here" or "hit the ball there." It was all about manners.

They said, "You cannot walk ahead of anyone when they're hitting, you stay back." I was also told that when it wasn't my turn to putt, I should leave the green so that I wouldn't bother the other players.

Anyone who knew my mother and Niente knew you'd better do what they said, or you wouldn't be allowed to play.

I was used to rules. As a subject of adult authority I had other rules to follow and I never, ever questioned doing what I was told. I wanted to play and be accepted and if those were the rules, then that was what I was going to do.

"If I hear that you do anything wrong on this golf course, you will not be allowed to finish," Mother said. "It's that simple."

I was the only youngster in the field. I played the qualifying round with two women, Betty McDonald and Marie Roseborough, and I often think of them because they were such great sports to put up with a kid.

As I thought I'd been instructed, I'd putt then scurry off the green. I ended that first round with a score of 113, qualified for the third flight, and Betty drew me as her first-round opponent. She beat me on the 20th hole.

I then went through the consolation flight and in the final played against Marie. I won at the 18th hole. A lake fronted the 18th green, but I hit my second shot with a wood over the lake to dry land while Marie hit her ball into the water. So, that was my sort of accidental entrée into tournament golf. I just loved to play and felt really comfortable with adults, so playing in the tournament was a lot of fun.

Since the early 1940s, Ed Dudley had been the pro at The Broadmoor in the summer and had the job at Augusta National Golf Club for the rest of the year. Beginning that summer, I had a complimentary lesson with Ed every morning during our three months in Colorado. He took me under his wing and I stayed with him until he died in 1963.

Ed was a perfect gentleman with wonderful manners. He'd been president of the PGA of America. He was really a fine player, had played on the PGA Tour as a young man, and had one of the most wonderful golf swings with the best tempo I've ever seen.

Ed thought I spent too much time on the practice tee, so he played a lot of golf with me in order to teach me how to get around a golf course. It was so special to be with him because he was such a nice, nice man. His example inspired me to try to be a nice person. In that way, he was a great influence.

Ed was also a great dresser and had a lot of style. After Ed died, his good friend Jack Puffer gave one of Ed's khaki windbreakers to me. It's monogrammed with Ed's initials and I treasure it.

When I was about 13, Dave Truffelli and I went to Wichita Country Club to play with Mike Murra and his student Marilynn Smith, who was in her twenties and could outhit me by nearly 30 yards. I was pretty short off the tee and just not quite as polished as she was. I believe that Marilynn's dad probably talked to my dad about having Mike give me lessons and Dad set up my first lesson with him.

I was really torn because of my loyalty to Dave, who would always be one of my closest pals, but I wanted to be a better player and I loved learning new things from Mike. Dad also thought Mike could take my game to a new level.

Dave seemed untroubled when I switched to Mike, but his wife Esther clearly resented it. Esther worked in the golf shop and wouldn't speak to me after I began taking lessons from Mike, which always made me feel awkward whenever I went into the shop.

Mike was an exceptional teacher. Professional players such as Lawson Little, Mary Lena Faulk, Marilynn Smith, and Fay Crocker took lessons from him. Jimmy Vickers, a good local amateur, and Loma Smith, who eventually won the USGA Senior Women's Amateur Championship, were also Mike's students. He had an unbelievable quest for learning and was a great student of the game, always trying new ways to communicate with his pupils.

Mike worked on my game around the greens. He also helped me achieve a more compact golf swing, not as handsy as it once had been, and I developed more length. After working with Mike, I had a better swing and began to understand how to help myself when I had trouble. I was just fortunate to be able to hang around Mike and I took lessons from him until he died in 1966.

The close proximity of the deaths of Ed and Mike, two of the people I most admired and depended upon, was very tough for me and for a while I felt lonely. But whenever I played, I wasn't as sad because it was almost as if Ed and Mike were talking to me and I could remember many of the lessons they had taught me. I miss them still.

These men were among the key people in my childhood that I really counted on. They gave me my roots, and influenced how I felt about things. All three of those guys were top-notch, the kind of people you'd want your own son or daughter to be involved with as students.

My father, as a confident, self-made man, was also full of advice and liked to tell me what to do on the golf course. Early on, I think he discovered that it probably wasn't the best decision.

I was playing in the Wichita City Championship at Crestview one time, and we were on the par-3 12th hole, where there was quite a wait on the tee. My father walked over and told me that a previous player had used her 8-iron.

I walked over to my opponent, told her that I had received advice from someone, that I was conceding the hole, and that we needed to go on to the 13th. I thought that Dad giving advice was against the Rules. But since I hadn't solicited his advice, it actually wasn't.

My dad was shocked. He left the course, and told Mother. Mother replied, "Serves you right, Carl." Dad headed for the farm. Of course, after that, Dad was almost always on hand to watch me play. One time, a lady in my gallery asked Dad if he was my pro. Dad got a big kick out of that question and replied, "No, I'm her father and she wouldn't even let me tell her what shoes to wear."

Mother's involvement was just the opposite from Dad's. She had the right perspective on the game. The key word in that sentence is "game" because she had exactly the same expression on her face when I lost as when I won, and she would either say "Condolences" or "Congratulations." Above all, she said, it's a game. Let's don't get confused. This isn't brain surgery; it's simply a game. You tried as hard as you could, and when it was over, it was over. There were no postmortems with Mother, but Dad loved to hash over every bad shot and his favorite phrase was "If only."

Mother helped me to keep golf in perspective and taught me that I couldn't *win* gracefully until I learned how to *lose* gracefully.

It helped me that my family played a lot of games, so it was neat when I got into golf. Unlike some parents of that era, who didn't encourage their daughters to be involved in games, my parents loved sports and enjoyed playing golf with me as well.

I just took to it, but golf was always an avocation and certainly not anything that I ever considered doing for a living. We never looked at a sport as anything more than a game. As a child, I wasn't sure what I wanted to do when I grew up. I had certain goals. I wanted to win the city tournament and the state tournament, The Broadmoor Invitation, and certainly the United States Women's Amateur. My long-term goal was to make the Curtis Cup team, but I was never challenged by the idea of turning professional.

When I grew older and became a good player, if there was any financial consideration about not turning professional it was that I wanted to be in the clothing business, which I believed would generate a better income. Women's professional golf, in those days, was a lean existence.

Chapter 8

[Me? A Communist?]

I was 13 when I played in the 1950 U.S. Women's Open, conducted then by the Ladies Professional Golf Association, at Rolling Hills Country Club in Wichita. Two of the contestants, Betsy Rawls and Pat Garner, stayed at our house. I had played Rolling Hills in a Kiwanis junior tournament when I was 10 and had played in the city tournament there, so I knew the golf course pretty well and felt absolutely no pressure about performing. At that time, the Women's Open was run by the Ladies Professional Golf Association. Unfortunately, none of the scoring records have survived. What I do remember is that I felt at home on the course and had a lot of fun.

I was 15 years old in 1952 when I played in my first United States Girls' Junior Championship.

At the Kansas Women's Amateur Championship, Helen Hanna, a good player from Lawrence, told Mother about the California Girls Junior Championship, which was open to girls from any state. We had planned to take the train to California so that I could play in the U.S. Girls' Junior Championship at Monterey Peninsula Country Club. We went out two weeks early to visit Uncle Leonard Bell in Los Angeles and then I played in the California junior tournament at Del Monte Golf Course in Monterey.

Helen Lengfeld ran the California Girls' Junior and worked hard to support junior girls' golf. The tournament was great and we had a lot of fun. Helen's house was in the Del Monte Forest and every night she had all of the contestants and their parents come to her house for a buffet supper.

I won the tournament, which was a great surprise to me. And since I
was a young Kansan that nobody had ever heard of, I'm sure it was a great
surprise to everyone else.

When I arrived at the U.S. Girls' Junior the following week, there
was some mix-up about my background. It began with Winnie Milar, a
USGA Women's Committee member from Los Angeles, who ran the
Championship. Winnie was one of those women who were very provincial
and she obviously had the attitude that if you weren't from Southern
California or her social background, you didn't quite make her grade.
Winnie disliked Helen Lengfeld—possibly because Helen was Jewish—and
she started a very cruel rumor that Helen was a Communist, telling several
junior contestants, including my future business partner, Barbara McIntire.

The Cold War was intense at that time, and most people in our country were paranoid about Communism, so this was a very hurtful charge.

A couple of weeks before the Girls' Junior, the Women's Western
Amateur Championship had been played in Los Angeles, Winnie's stomp-
ing grounds, and at that time she told several of the contestants that they
shouldn't play in the California Girls' Junior because Helen was a
Communist. I hadn't played in the Western, so I hadn't heard this.

The rumor persisted. When I got to Monterey Peninsula Country Club,
talk began that because I had just played in Helen's tournament, I must be
a little Communist and my parents must be Communists, too. I wasn't aware
of the talk, but I think my parents heard the rumor and obviously the older
girls did. I never knew about it until Barbara McIntire told me years later.

Some of the older junior contestants that week, including Barbara and
Mickey Wright, stared at me as I practiced and when I was announced on
the first tee. It wasn't that they were so interested in my swing because I was
only 15. But the idea that I was a Communist made me an object of some
fascination.

When we were introduced on the first tee, the starter announced our
titles, but Winnie refused to let him announce that I was the new California
Girls' Junior Champion. I never even noticed but Cam Puget, the club's
head professional, talked to my folks about the omission and was upset
about it.

To set the record straight, Helen Lengfeld was as American as apple pie.
She started a golf program for American soldiers who ended up in Veterans
Administration hospitals. In fact, she organized friends across the country
to start these programs, which were called "Swing Clubs," at hospitals in

their hometowns. My mother organized one in Wichita. Helen's organization furnished golf balls, clubs, and guidelines for getting the Swing Clubs launched.

Helen Lengfeld later did more to support junior girls' golf than perhaps anyone in this country. Not only did she start the California Girls' Junior, she ran it and paid for it.

The U.S. Girls' Junior was my first introduction to golfers in my age group who were from all over the country. That was pretty amazing, because most of us were sort of the lone riders in our home areas. To find that many girls were doing what I was doing—loving golf—was a great revelation.

I was a pretty good player by then. That trip was my first time out as a player in big junior tournaments, but I had done well locally and I was learning new things from Mike Murra, so I wasn't intimidated by any of the other players.

I reached the semifinals of the Girls' Junior and played against Mickey Wright. Since I was only 15, Mickey seemed like a big star because she was two years older. This was her last Girls' Junior Championship. I was kind of in awe of her and didn't say very much. At the time, I didn't talk all that much anyway. Mickey was shy, too. Her personality has always been that she's very much within herself, so we had a pretty quiet match.

I felt capable of beating her, but just missed too many shots. She simply played better than I did and beat me 2 and 1. In the final, the following day, Mickey beat Barbara McIntire to win the championship.

Of course, Mickey became a genius with the golf club and has perhaps the best swing in golf. At that time, she wasn't that far ahead of everybody else in the junior field, although she was certainly special enough to win that championship. Later, she clearly became the best woman golfer in the world, no question about that, and we have remained friends.

After I lost to Mickey, we took the train back to Newton, Kansas, where my brothers had organized a big homecoming party to surprise me. They rented a bus and took the entire North High School pep band to Newton. When I got off the train, the band played the Indian War Dance, our fight song.

Some 30 friends from Crestview Country Club came with my brothers to meet me and everyone had been drinking peppermint schnapps on the trip from Wichita, so they were in rare form. I'd been away from home for two weeks and it made me feel great to see all of these people who were my friends. It was a total surprise and great fun.

Carl, Jack, and Fred were my best boosters, but they rode me unmercifully as a child. Whenever I got beat, they'd say things like, "You choked."

Oh, they worked me over, but if anybody else had said that, they would have flattened them. I've always said that putting up with those three prepared me for business and for the USGA.

I began playing in more national tournaments; the Western Girls' Junior, the Women's Western Amateur, and the Trans-Mississippi Women's Amateur, which is now the Trans-National.

My parents always took me to the tournaments because children didn't travel alone in those days. I didn't, in fact, go to a tournament by myself until I was in college. Uncle George, who called me "Sis," also came to a lot of my early tournaments. As I began to travel more, I couldn't fix things about my golf swing because I couldn't see it. Uncle George was a good amateur photographer. He bought a very expensive camera that had mechanisms to photograph swing sequences and used it to take pictures of my swing so that I could analyze my technique.

I was trying to become a better player, but I was also making friends across the country. I have some friends from those early tournament days even now. In 1987 the USGA Senior Women's Amateur Championship was conducted at Manufacturers Golf Club, near Philadelphia, and Millie Meyerson, the 1953 Girls' Junior Champion, showed up. Her name is Millie Zemering now. By 1987 she had a family and was running her kids around and had put her golf clubs aside, but there she was, a friend from more than 30 years before and it was as if we'd seen each other yesterday.

I first met Millie in California, then saw her again when she won the Girls' Junior at The Country Club, in Brookline, Massachusetts, the following year. I'd never been to New England, so it was certainly a good experience, but I couldn't get over the fact that there were certain places at the club where women couldn't go, which meant that there were certainly places at the club where children couldn't go. In 1995, when The Country Club hosted our centennial United States Women's Amateur Championship, I was happy to see that all of that had changed.

While I was getting some attention as a player, life at home remained pretty much the same and it steadied me. We were all taught the sanctity of work. It was something you had to do anyway so you might as well make the most of it. When I was in high school, Dad bought the Adeline Apartments, a red brick building with 14 apartments that stood one block from our house. Dad made me the manager and I ran the building with the help of Riley Banks. Riley and I retiled the bathrooms and picked out two color schemes that the tenants could choose from when it was time to paint. This was not a popular move because the tenants had previously been allowed to choose their own colors. Dad got several complaints over the telephone, but he stuck with me.

Chapter 9

[College]

After high school, I attended the University of Arizona in Tucson. It was a good school and, except in summer, Tucson had great golf weather. By the second semester, however, I began neglecting golf and my studies when I became very involved with campus life and my sorority, Delta Gamma. I lived in the sorority house after the end of the first semester.

I was busy, but I wasn't studying or really working on my golf game.

Every single day that I was away at school, Dad wrote part of a page to me. I remember one letter in particular. I had been partying pretty heavily with sorority and fraternity friends and had written to him to describe a beer bust where we sang that old college standby, "Roll Me Over in the Clover."

In his next letter, Dad wrote:

Dear Judy,
I don't think we should be spending our time at those beer busts and singing those kinds of songs.

While Dad's consistent correspondence may seem rare, at that time I didn't know that *every* girl didn't get a letter from her father each day.

This was the first time I had ever spent any extended time away from my parents. I can still feel that homesickness. Whenever I placed a collect telephone call home and the operator would say, "Wichita, Kansas, how can I help you?" I would start to tear up. I missed home that much. Each relative was a big part of my life and I couldn't wait to go back home. It wasn't just to see Mother and Dad, but to see and be with all of these other people that I loved.

While in college I was twice runner-up in the National Women's Collegiate Championship, losing in 1957 to Mariam Bailey from Northwestern University. In 1958, after transferring to the University of Wichita, I lost in the final to Carole Pushing from Carleton College.

Today hundreds of young women tour the country playing in regional and national college championships. When I was in school, we had no teams and the only college tournament was the National Women's Collegiate Championship, the equivalent of today's NCAA Championship. My college golf program, like the golf programs at other schools, was one class. A gym class was required so I took golf, which involved hitting balls each day at a driving range. I also tried to stay as far away from the golf instructor as possible so she wouldn't tinker with my swing.

In my sophomore year at Arizona, in 1955, I became pinned to John Benson, a fellow-Kansan who was stationed at Davis Monthan Air Force Base in Tucson. John, who was a Beta at the University of Kansas, was a couple of years older than I was. He was a sweet guy, tall, good-looking, and very smart. I was in love. After we dated for almost a year, he gave me his Beta pin.

We hadn't been pinned for very long when he was transferred. I left to play tournament golf in Florida that winter because amateur golf was something I wanted to pursue and to see how the chips fell. We didn't break up, but I returned his pin because we were going to be apart.

We both pledged to see what would happen down the road. We were still great friends but decided that we should see if the separation would make our relationship stronger or weaker. We just wanted to see how things worked out.

There was a possibility that he and I would have a long-term relationship. I wouldn't have taken his pin otherwise, because I didn't need to pin that darn thing on every day.

John's mother lived in Wichita and he and I went out every time we were both in town. On one visit, I noticed that his skin color didn't look good. I didn't know that he was seriously ill. John had cancer, but he never told me. After battling the disease for some two years, he passed away. When he died, his cousin, Sissy Wise, called my sister-in-law, Sally Bell, to break the news. I was shocked when Sally told me, and felt even more terrible about his death because I hadn't even known that he was ill.

Since I'd been traveling a lot, I hadn't seen him in a while and we seemed to have drifted apart, but his was a friendship I cherished and I had hoped that it might some day work out to be more permanent.

Now John was gone and we would never have that opportunity. I attended his funeral with Sally.

I was still in college when Mother and Dad sold our house on North Emporia in 1957. I had lived in that house my entire life but Mother and I wanted to move. The house, with four stories and 13 rooms, was too big for just Mother, Dad, and me, since I was away at school most of the time. Our midtown neighborhood was also beginning to deteriorate. Before the war, all of the houses had been single-family. Only a few single-family houses now remained and the rest had been converted into apartments. Our neighborhood was becoming very transient and while the house was only two blocks from Dad's business, the neighborhood was no longer considered a good part of town.

Mother had wanted to move for a while, but Dad wanted to stay in the house. My father hated change more than anyone I know. Then the weirdest thing happened when we were in Florida for the amateur tournaments. We were visiting Barbara McIntire and her parents at their home in Lake Park. Dad and Bob McIntire were starting the charcoal grill in the backyard. Mother and Marie McIntire were watching the evening news on television.

They watched a national feature story on the deterioration of nice neighborhoods into slum areas. Lo and behold, a shot of the 1300-block of North Emporia Avenue in Wichita appeared on the screen.

"That's where *we* live!" Mother screamed. "Carl! Carl! Come see this! They're showing North Emporia Avenue on television and they say it's the slums!"

After that, the search for a new house got serious.

My parents bought a much smaller, single-story house with three bedrooms and two baths at 6210 East 12th Street. It fitted our needs much better. Unlike my father, I looked forward to change and I was excited about the move. The new house was also closer to the golf course.

Chapter 10

[The Women's Open]

In 1955, the Women's Open was scheduled to be played at Wichita Country Club, which was now my home course.

One Friday night, I was home from college and visiting friends. We were watching the evening news on television when the sports announcer said, "Entries have now closed for the Women's Open at Wichita Country Club."

I must have turned green because one of my friends asked, "What's wrong with you?"

"I didn't enter," I said.

"Of course, you entered. You're crazy," she said. "It's at your club. What do you mean you didn't enter?"

"I swear I didn't," I said, and promptly drove home. On the way I decided that I wasn't going to panic until I became absolutely sure. Even at the age of 18, I had long been responsible for choosing which tournaments I wanted to play in and sending in my entry. I kept my entry blanks in a certain drawer of the desk in my room and needed to check to see if I had truly failed to enter.

When I opened the drawer, there was the entry blank, unmailed, and I felt a sudden ache in my stomach. I spent a restless night. I kept thinking just how stupid I had been and how I was much too lax about details. I knew that the next morning, a Saturday, would be so hard because I would have to face my brothers and my dad.

Even after they married and had their own homes, my brothers always came over on Saturday mornings to have breakfast with Dad. I got up early, as usual, and came down the stairs very sheepishly. I knew I had to tell them and might as well get it over with. When I blurted it out, my announcement absolutely undid my brothers and my father.

I knew Mother would say little or nothing, but Dad hit the ceiling.

"You've got to be kidding!" he said loudly. "Now, let me get this straight. You're telling me that the Women's Open is right here at the club we belong to and you had an entry blank and you didn't send it in? Is that what you're telling me? I'm going to call Fred Dold and I want you to tell him."

Mr. Dold was on the USGA Executive Committee and a friend of Dad's. Dad called him, then passed the telephone to me. Of course, there was nothing Mr. Dold could do. He and Dad strongly suggested that I call Joseph C. Dey Jr., the USGA's Executive Director, who was in the process of running the final two rounds of the U.S. Open at the Olympic Club in San Francisco where Ben Hogan and Jack Fleck were playing their way into a tie.

I had to explain the whole thing to Mr. Dey, which was just one more step in my humiliation over the matter. Mr. Dey said there was absolutely nothing he or anybody in the world could do because the entry deadline had passed. That was the rule. Dad was putting me through the paces so I'd never forget to enter a tournament again.

With the Women's Open coming to town, I had invited my friends and fellow amateurs Barbara McIntire and Ruth Jessen to stay with us. When I went out to the course, I couldn't play because I wasn't a member of the field. I spent all of my time explaining over and over what had happened, which was even more humiliating. Before the championship began, Mother and I left for Colorado, where I could at least play some golf. There wasn't anything we could do about the Open so it was time to move on.

The next year, in 1956, the Women's Open was to be played in Duluth, Minnesota, and I kept asking Dad if I could go.

"You're crazy if you think I'm sending you to Duluth when you couldn't even enter the Women's Open when it was right here in Wichita," he said. "You're not going."

At the Women's Western Amateur in Huntington, West Virginia, I was medalist in the qualifying round and really played well. So, I decided to enter the Women's Open anyway. Then I called Dad. He agreed that I could go, but only if Barbara McIntire and Ruth Jessen would look after me. So we caravaned in two cars to Duluth.

In those days, amateurs made up a high percentage of the Women's Open field. We got to Northland Country Club, a very good Donald Ross-designed course, and hit some balls to warm up for our practice round. Along with the other amateurs, I was intimidated by the crowd around the first tee. So we just went over to the third tee to start. No one seemed to care, so we never even played the first two holes until the championship began.

After the previous year's fiasco, I was determined to play well, and with rounds of 83, 77, and 80, I was among the top 20 players when the final round began on Saturday afternoon. In those days, we played two rounds on Saturday. I was paired with Jackie Yates, an amateur and a friend of mine from Hawaii. We heard tremendous cheering as we left the 16th green. When we asked people in the gallery what was going on, they said an amateur had just tied for the lead.

I remember walking to the 17th tee and saying to Jackie, "You know, people can really get things mixed up."

We knew that Barbara McIntire was going to be low amateur because she was far ahead of the rest of us going into the last round, but it was unthinkable that she could win. I told Jackie, "Now they've got her winning the Women's Open and all she's going to do is be low amateur. It's crazy."

Jackie and I were signing our scorecards when a sorority sister of mine came into the scoring tent, which she wasn't supposed to do, and said, "Barbara McIntire is tied for the lead."

I turned to Jackie and whispered, "She doesn't know a thing about golf."

We went to the scoreboard. Sure enough, Barbara had finished birdie-par-eagle, tying for the lead. When we went upstairs to try to find her, some reporters had stationed themselves outside the locker room door.

Today, nearly 300 reporters routinely cover the Women's Open. In that era, maybe five reporters had that assignment. Fortunately, some of them were great golf reporters, such as Will Grimsley of the Associated Press.

Jackie and I found Barbara sitting on a bench, looking as if she wanted to crawl into her locker to get away from the commotion.

Barbara and professional Kathy Cornelius were scheduled to play in an 18-hole play-off the following day. The next morning, Barbara was pretty keyed up so we hung around with her, trying to keep her relaxed just by being there. It was even more important to stay close to her because her parents weren't there (her father had just undergone surgery).

Barbara lost the play-off, shooting 82 to Kathy's 75. At the age of 19, I was still very impressionable and I was disturbed by the conduct of most of the women professionals in the gallery. They were very obviously partisan, never applauded for Barbara, and came very close to cheering when she hit a bad shot. I'd never been around that sort of behavior and it bothered me, not just because Barbara was a friend, but because all of us who were amateurs at the time had been raised to be good sports.

Perhaps because of the way the pros reacted, we amateurs became more determined to make a point of applauding Kathy's good shots, as well as Barbara's.

Although Barbara lost, her runner-up finish was a great thrill and a sense of accomplishment for the amateurs in the field.

Chapter 11

[Congratulations / Condolences]

By 1960 I had won The Broadmoor Ladies Invitation three times, which really meant a lot to me. I had wanted to win so badly because The Broadmoor was like my home course. I know my father wanted me to win that tournament more than he wanted me to win the U.S. Women's Amateur.

In the early days, there was always a Calcutta auction in the clubhouse the night after the qualifying round. In a Calcutta, people bid on various players in the championship. If the player they bid on got to the quarterfinals, there was a pretty good payoff for the "owner." The further the player advanced, the bigger the payoff.

When I first qualified for the championship flight, at age 13, my dad bought me as his player in the Calcutta. He did it because he believed that if he owned me, instead of an outsider, it would take the pressure off me. He bought me for three straight years, but I didn't play well enough to advance to the quarterfinals, so he never made a dime.

One of those years, I called Bell's Market to tell my brothers I had been defeated. "Did Dad buy you in the Calcutta?" Jack asked.

When I confirmed that, Jack said, "Why don't we send you some more money so you can just keep going. Don't even come home! Go to Mexico!"

It didn't bother me. I was used to that sort of teasing from my brothers. I would have been surprised if he *hadn't* said something like that.

But when I was 16, a business executive, John Hines, kept bidding against my dad when my name was called out in the Calcutta. As the bidding got higher and higher, I persuaded Dad to give up. John Hines won out and now owned me as a player in the tournament.

That was the year I went all the way to the final and lost to Lesbia Lobo, of San Antonio, on the 36th hole. John Hines probably made a bundle.

To his credit, Dad never said a word.

Shortly after that, the USGA took a strong stand against Calcuttas and other large gambling pools and contacted all USGA member clubs about the new policy. The Broadmoor, I'm proud to say, became one of the first clubs to honor the USGA's antigambling policy and discontinued all Calcuttas.

I was 20 years old when I finally won The Broadmoor Ladies Invitation in 1957. In the final I defeated Ann Rutherford, one of my good friends from junior golf.

After that win, I had my first taste of champagne when Thayer Tutt and Niente Borchert filled the Penrose Cup with vintage bubbly, passing the cup and refilling it again and again. Winning that tournament was a goal I'd had since I was 11 years old. My brothers drove in from Wichita to watch the final, and with so many friends and family members on hand, it was a very, very special moment in my golfing life.

On the national scene, I was a better than average player. There was a time when I was probably considered to be among the 10 best amateurs in the country. I might have been better, were I not such a perfectionist, which works against anyone who plays competitive golf. If I'd ever been able to understand that it was okay to miss greens, had not beat up on myself for missing greens, and had been able to work the ball around the greens, I might have been the player that I wanted to be.

I knew I had a shot at making the 1960 Curtis Cup team, the biennial amateur competition between a team from the United States and a team from Great Britain and Ireland, but I knew something was going to have to change.

I stayed at Arizona for five semesters, then transferred to the University of Wichita for the fall semester. My plan was to play competitive golf in the winter in Florida.

My parents bought into the deal of letting me play on the spring and summer amateur circuit and the winter circuit in Florida if I would finish college.

After transferring to Wichita, I attended the fall semester each year until I graduated and tackled amateur tournaments the rest of the year.

Since I hadn't really worked at my studies at Arizona, my brother, Carl, became my tutor. We had an awful lot of fun and Carl said that once I started applying myself, it was Katie-bar-the-door. I caught up pretty quickly and made good grades. I majored in psychology, with minors in sociology, business, and economics, and got my degree in 1961. Even though I made good grades, each year it was a little harder to go back to class after having competed in golf for the previous seven months. It was kind of a screwy way to get an education and it took me six years. I was relieved when I finally got my diploma because I'd made a deal with my folks to graduate and had now kept my part of the bargain.

That first winter after I transferred to Wichita, I took off for the Florida tournaments with Mother and Dad. We started in Fort Lauderdale with the Doherty Invitational. From there, we went to the Women's International Four-Ball in Hollywood, to the Palm Beach Championship at the Breakers, and then the National Mixed-Foursomes, which was played at LaGorce, in Miami, or at Tequesta during my day. We'd go up to Ormond Beach for the South Atlantic, and to St. Augustine for the Florida East Coast Championship.

In early February of that year I played in a unique event in Palm Beach. Michael Phipps, a great sportsman, had recently built a course called the Palm Beach Par 3 Golf Club on oceanside property owned by the Phipps family. The course was a good treat, meandering along the dunes of the Atlantic Ocean on the east, and skirting the inland waterway on the west. It was a links-style course, buffeted by the wind, and several holes were more than 200 yards long. It was like a baby Seminole golf course.

To publicize his new shopping plaza, as well as the course, Michael organized the Royal Poinciana Plaza Mixed Invitational. This was one of the first tournaments to pit six male touring pros against six women touring professionals. He also invited six male club professionals and six women amateurs.

Some big names played: Sam Snead, Dow Finsterwald, Mickey Wright, Betsy Rawls, and Louise Suggs. But Michael also invited great players from the past, such as Bobby Cruickshank and Glenna Collett Vare, the six-time winner of the U.S. Women's Amateur. It was, I believe, Glenna's last public tournament appearance and it was a great thrill for all of us to see her play.

Barbara McIntire, the reigning U.S. Women's Amateur Champion was invited. I had won the Palm Beach Championship that winter and Chris Dunphy, who was "Mr. Golf" in Palm Beach, also invited me to play as part of the amateur field. Each group of four players included a male club professional, a female amateur, and a male and female touring pro.

I remember hearing Glenna, an extremely speedy player, say that she couldn't believe how slowly the professionals played, particularly on the greens.

"They look at the putt from this side, then from another side, then another," she said. "They walk up and down the green, then they miss the putt."

In the final round, I was paired with Dow Finsterwald, Bobby Cruickshank, and Louise Suggs. Dow and Louise were tied for a time, but Louise played such great golf that day. She'd feather a 4-wood to the green, and be closer to the hole than Dow, who would hit a 6-iron. In a surprising turnabout, Louise beat the field. Dub Pagan, the pro at West Palm Beach Country Club, finished one stroke behind and Snead was third by two shots.

Sam took a lot of ribbing for that loss but he had a bad day all around. A friend of his had taken Sam's boat from Boca Raton up the inland waterway to watch him play and grounded it on a bed of clamshells, knocking a hole in the side of the boat. As the sun sank into the West, so did Sam's boat, as he stood watching from the golf course.

After the Florida swing, we'd play in the Titleholders at Augusta (Georgia) Country Club. Earlier that year, we were staying at Elinor Village in Ormond Beach for the South Atlantic Championship. My father always sent a bunch of steaks down for one of the tournaments and we'd have a cookout for my pals. I was standing out by the grill, cooking and talking to Mary Ann Downey about the Titleholders.

"What's Augusta Country Club like?" I asked.

"It's hard, a tough course," said Mary Ann, "really difficult."

"What do you mean, it's hard?"

"I'll just tell you this," Mary Ann said, "I'll bet you twenty-five-to-one that you can't break 80 every round."

At that time, I'd bet on almost anything, especially with those odds, so I said, "I'll take it."

I went inside, told another player the story and the odds, and she said, "I'll give you the same odds."

Soon, 10 people were in on the wager.

When it came time to play at Augusta, I broke 80 every round. In one round I had to hole a 20-footer at the 18th green to do it, but I was so determined to win the bet that I made the putt. I won about 300 bucks and never again played that well at the Titleholders.

Mary Ann was right. It was a tough course.

I managed to win the South Atlantic and The Broadmoor in 1958, and the Palm Beach Championship and the Florida East Coast in the winter of 1960, leading up to the selection of the 1960 Curtis Cup team.

In the spring of 1960, I was runner-up to my pal Barbara McIntire in the North & South. We faced each other in a number of battles over the years. Although Barbara and I were by then good friends, friendship never got in the way of a good match-play battle. It's never who you play, it's *how* you play. You just focused on your own game, which was never hard for either of us.

In our match, Barbara bucked tradition. Normally, if your opponent has a very, very short putt, you concede the putt. Not Barbara. After I three-putted the first hole from 15 feet, she made me putt a short one, of less than 12 inches in length, on the second green. I was down in the match on the 12th hole and had another short putt, which Barbara did not concede. After I made that one, I turned to her and said, "You'll never die of enlargement of the heart!" I lost the match, 3 and 2.

The North & South has such great tradition. I remember meeting Richard Tufts, whose family owned Pinehurst. He was always around during the week and always refereed the final. He was just such a nice man, although I didn't know then that he had been president of the USGA in 1956 and '57, and was considered one of golf's foremost authorities on the Rules.

My caddie, Fletcher Gaines, was just as memorable as Mr. Tufts. Fletcher was terrific, a great caddie, but whenever I won a match, he said, "We won." If I lost, he said, "She hit a bad shot."

In his day, Fletcher had been the caddie champion of Pinehurst. He could really play and he was great around the greens, with a great knowledge of how the greens rolled. In fact, years later when Pinehurst restored the greens of the #2 Course, Fletcher was called in to assist because of his great knowledge of their breaks and undulations. Fletcher and I used to have little chipping contests, and he always beat me.

Thirty years later, I was playing in the 1991 Senior Women's International Match at Mid-Pines in Southern Pines, near Pinehurst. Fletcher agreed to caddie for me once more.

Both of us were now on the plump side. That first day, as we were walking down the first fairway I asked him, "How old are you now, Fletcher."

"Boss," Fletcher said, "there are two things we aren't going to talk about. Age and weight."

Chapter 12

[Mrs. P]

Two sisters, Margaret and Harriot Curtis of Boston, were among the strongest and most innovative women in the history of golf. Both were fine players, with Margaret winning the U.S. Women's Amateur three times and Harriot winning it once shortly after the turn of the twentieth century. In 1907, Margaret beat Harriot in the final.

In 1898 the idea of an international match had captured the imagination of Issette Pearson Miller, secretary of Britain's ruling body of women's golf, the Ladies Golf Union. By 1905, nothing had really happened to promote the plan. That's when Margaret and Harriot sailed to England and played against their English, Scottish, and Irish friends in an informal match called "America versus England." The Americans were walloped, six to one, but the concept excited the Curtis sisters so much that they began exploring ways to formalize the event.

I met Margaret Curtis in Boston in 1960. At the time of our visit, Barbara McIntire held two national titles. She was the reigning U.S. Women's Amateur Champion and had just won the British Ladies Open Amateur. Margaret invited Barbara, Mildred Prunaret, and me for a game at Myopia Hunt Club in Massachusetts. Mrs. P. and I played alternate shot against Barbara and Miss Curtis. Even in her mid-seventies, Margaret was very feisty and, boy, was she fired up for the match. On one hole, a par 3, Barbara hit her shot to the green. Margaret asked her what club she had hit and Barbara replied, "A 5-wood."

"In my day, I hit this green with a 3-iron," Margaret said.

Margaret also came up with perhaps my favorite quote in all of golf when she was presented the Bob Jones Award by the USGA in 1958.

After she was given the award, she said, "Golf is my game and I love it. I'd play it with rocks if I had to."

I'm not a bit surprised that those two sisters were able to pull off the origination of an international match that has thus far lasted 70 years.

Their idea got a boost when our finest American amateur, Glenna Collett, took a gang of Americans over in 1930 and had a successful match with the British at Sunningdale. The Curtis Cup match, which Harriot and Margaret had tried to get going so many years before, finally became official in 1932. Its origination was an important turning point for women in the game. The Cup gave women golfers a sense of accomplishment, and they weren't so much the underdogs any longer.

From everything I've read, our first United States Curtis Cup team captain, Marion Hollins, was quite a character. Marion founded the Women's National Golf Club, on Long Island, New York, an all-female club. As the director of sports for the Pebble Beach Company, she enlisted an unknown golf architect, Alister MacKenzie, to design one of the greatest courses in the world, Cypress Point Golf Club, on California's Monterey Peninsula. She had a lot of input into the design and was particularly responsible for the character of the world-famous and picturesque 16th hole, a long par 3 over water. Miss Hollins also had the vision to create Pasatiempo Golf Club, a public course, with MacKenzie as the architect, developing it as a fabulous resort in Santa Cruz, California. All the while, she remained a top-notch competitor and won the 1921 U.S. Women's Amateur.

When we play the Curtis Cup match every two years, these women all parade through my mind as I watch each meeting unfold. The match last year, the match next year, each is just another page in that tremendous history.

My selection to two Curtis Cup teams remains one of the most satisfying and meaningful accomplishments in my life.

By 1958, I had won some tournaments but my record wasn't quite good enough and I was overlooked for that year's American team. I made up my mind to work harder, win more tournaments, and really try my best to achieve a lifelong goal of making the team. I began to rack up a pretty good record.

In January 1960, Barbara McIntire and I were partners in the Women's International Four-Ball Championship in Hollywood, Florida. We won our semifinal match and I was getting dressed for dinner when the phone rang. It was a sportswriter from the Wichita newspaper telling me that I was on the Curtis Cup team.

"I haven't been notified, and I don't believe it," I said, because, in my mind, it wasn't official since I hadn't heard from the USGA.

It was a long, restless night. I tossed and turned and didn't sleep, which surely didn't help my game for the next morning's final. In that 36-hole match, pitting Barbara and me against Joanne Goodwin and Doris Phillips, we stopped in the clubhouse after nine holes.

I was given a telegram from the USGA, inviting me to be on the United States Curtis Cup team.

Barbara, Joanne, and I had all been named to the team. Doris had not been selected. It was interesting that, when they finally beat us on the 35th hole, Doris had played better than any of us.

The Curtis Cup matches were scheduled for May at Lindrick Golf Club in Worksop, Nottinghamshire, England.

In those days, perhaps because of the cost, the teams took only seven players when playing overseas. Our team included Barbara, Joanne, Judy Eller, JoAnne Gunderson, Anne Quast, Ann Casey Johnstone, and me. Mildred Prunaret was our captain.

The members of Wichita Country Club sent my teacher, Mike Murra, to the Curtis Cup matches, which meant a great deal to me. Mother, Dad, Mike and I went to New York to meet Mrs. Prunaret and the team. Because I had only been to the city once before, we arrived early and went to the theater a couple of nights. Tommy Vickers, a friend from Wichita, took Dad and Mike to a New York Yankees baseball game and they sat right behind home plate. Oh, how they loved that.

We met with the team out on Long Island at The Creek Club, where Mr. Dey—Joseph C. Dey, Executive Director of the USGA—played. We were certainly not the favorites in the upcoming match. The American team had lost the Cup in 1952 at Muirfield, won in 1954, lost it again in 1956 at Sandwich, and halved in 1958, which meant the Cup had stayed in Great Britain for four of the last six years. We were also handicapped in that our 1960 team was made up of mostly new members. In addition, although Barbara, Anne, and Gundy had played on the Curtis Cup team in 1958, none of us had ever played overseas.

Lincoln Werden of the *New York Times*, a fine golf writer, interviewed Mrs. Prunaret. Linc asked Mrs. Prunaret what she thought of our chances.

"I have every confidence we will be successful," she responded with understated assurance.

I never forgot those words. All of us on the team took her at face value. We looked at each other and thought: *Yes. She thinks we're going to win; we probably will.* We were all pretty confident players.

Every previous American team had traveled to Great Britain by ship, but we were the first team to go by air. We were met by Ladies Golf Union officials and the British captain, Maureen Garrett, who became a great pal of mine and who had played on Great Britain's Curtis Cup team in 1948. Maureen made us all feel welcome when she greeted us, then we were put on a bus to Ye Olde Bell Hotel in Worksop, where we would stay.

The president of Lindrick Golf Club was Sir Stuart Goodwin. The club had hosted the 1957 Ryder Cup match, in which Great Britain beat the United States male professionals for only the third time since the match began in 1927. All of the newspapers were calling the Curtis Cup match "Sir Stuart's Double" because they just assumed that Britain would win the Cup.

For the first time in Curtis Cup history, our two teams mingled throughout the week. Maureen and Mrs. P. had decided we would dine together every night so we sat at the table in alternate seats, an American, then a British player, then an American, and so on. None of us knew that, traditionally, we weren't supposed to mingle with the other team.

In those days, their team had uniforms but the only item given to the American players by the USGA was a white blazer, so we decided we needed a uniform. Barbara and I had just started a mail order clothing business called "A Short Story," and we had a supplier in Boston. During our practice rounds, the weather was warm and we wore shorts. The photographers went nuts, taking pictures of us from the front and the back. We bought Shetland sweaters in the golf shop, and called our supplier in Boston to order flannel Bermuda shorts, which would be paid for by the players. Half of us would wear red, half of us would wear blue. The shipment would be delivered to Mrs. Prunaret's husband Henri, and he would bring them over to us when he came to England two days before the match.

The day Mr. Prunaret arrived it rained and turned really cold. We all gathered in a sitting room and I opened the package. A mistake had been made. The supplier sent slacks, not shorts, so it worked out great and we had our uniforms, warm enough for the conditions. Mother, meanwhile, and my sister-in-law Gwen had knitted red and navy blue headcovers for each player's clubs so we had those, too.

Mrs. Prunaret is one of my favorite subjects. I just loved being overseas with her. Her demeanor in the way she handled us and the way she interacted with the British helped us to fit in. Whether Mrs. P. was having tea, touring, whatever it was, she was our leader. Her style, her manner, and her presence were something to be admired.

We were called "Snow White and the Seven Dwarfs" and I, of course, was tagged "Dopey."

I remember when we first arrived in England, I was surprised to see that one of the older women in our USGA traveling party sported an elegant mink coat, wore it everywhere we went, and stood out in an inappropriate way. Not Mrs. Prunaret. She could have bought and sold that woman several times, but with her great humility and sense of "rightness," she wore only a simple cloth coat. She blended in and, without saying anything, she made a point about being understated as a guest in a foreign country that I will always remember.

Mrs. P. tried to keep perspective and pass it on to her players. She always wanted us to take the afternoons off and to forget about our practice rounds. She'd suggest that we go to Sheffield or do some sightseeing. Of course, we all wanted to beat balls instead. So, we'd take turns and every day one of us would break the news to her that we would go to tea in the clubhouse, but we then wanted to hit balls and practice putting. We were all pretty intense about the upcoming match.

The night before the match was to begin, a fire alarm went off at Ye Olde Bell Hotel. Judy Eller and I were staying on one floor, while the rest of our team and the opposing team was in an older part of the hotel where the fire, of unknown origin, had broken out. It wasn't a very big fire and Judy and I slept through it, but I guess the other American and British players were awakened and a lot of them were pretty worked up about it.

It was so crowded at Lindrick. Some 15,000 very enthusiastic supporters came out on trains and coaches to watch the play each day. To somebody from Kansas who had never been out of the United States, it was an unbelievable turnout of spectators.

Incidentally, the team that we once referred to as "the British team" is now Great Britain and Ireland, better known as GB&I. Since 1958, the British team had always had an Irish player. That year, Ireland's fine player, Philomena Garvey, refused to play unless Ireland's flag was raised at the opening ceremony. It's been raised ever since and, in addition to the "Star-Spangled Banner" and "God Save the Queen," a band always plays

Ireland's national anthem, "The Soldier's Song."

There has always been a lot of pageantry at the Curtis Cup match. We have a flag-raising opening ceremony whenever the match is played in America, but GB&I didn't have a flag-raising ceremony until 1984, so we didn't have that drama at Lindrick in 1960. I had, however, plenty of opportunities to develop a good case of flag fever.

Because only six of our seven players could compete each day, someone had to sit out so I was on the sidelines for the first day of the match. We took a two-to-one lead. For our team, JoAnne Gunderson and Barbara McIntire lost to Angela Bonallack and Elizabeth Price, 1 up. We took the lead, however, when Judy Eller and Anne Quast beat Belle McCorkindale and Janette Robertson, 4 and 2, while Joanne Goodwin and Ann Casey Johnstone defeated Ruth Porter and Frances Smith, 3 and 2.

On the second day, when I was announced on the first tee in my singles match against Belle McCorkindale, it was unlike any other experience. I had always been introduced as "Judy Bell, Wichita Country Club, Wichita, Kansas." Suddenly, I wasn't playing for Judy Bell. I was "Judy Bell, United States of America." Hearing that for the first time and knowing I was representing my country, I was so nervous that I found it was literally hard to swallow and I had trouble even putting my tee into the ground.

As I recall, the first hole was a straightaway par 4. Somehow I hit a good drive and a strong second shot to the middle of the green. My par won the first hole, I was 1 up, and we were away.

Belle was a very highly regarded player. It surprised me to take an early lead in the match but I was playing well and enjoyed the large gallery. When I wound up winning by a large margin, 8 and 7, it was something of an upset. Gundy defeated Angela Bonallack, 2 and 1. Anne Quast beat Janette Robertson, 2 up. And Judy Eller defeated Philomena Garvey, 4 and 3, to capture singles points. Barbara McIntire and Joanne Goodwin halved their respective matches with Elizabeth Price and Ruth Porter, so we won the 1960 Curtis Cup match, 6½ to 2½, to regain the cup, which was grand. The victory was a surprise for everyone because we were expected to lose.

Sir Stuart had ordered a large marquee publicizing the match, which was erected near the clubhouse and that's where the victory reception was staged by the USGA and LGU. As "Snow White and the Seven Dwarfs," our team had written a song to the tune of "Hi Ho, Hi Ho, It's Off to Work We Go." That night, in our joy over our win, we performed our song 11 times.

That summer, I joined Babe Zaharias as the only player to have won

The Broadmoor Ladies Invitation three times. Babe had managed to win three in a row, however, in 1945, 1946, and 1947. I was just nine years old when she won the first one and I followed her every step of the way. My memories of Babe center around the fact that she had such presence and was so outspoken, which made the gallery love her.

She was, of course, a very powerful player who hit low tee shots that ran a long way. She hit the ball a lot farther than anyone else on the golf course and certainly farther than anyone I had seen play. Her swing was far from classic, because she had a fire-and-fall-back style, finishing with her weight on her right foot, but she wasn't afraid to take chances and had a wonderfully smooth putting stroke.

It was her personality that was so memorable. In that, Babe was in a class by herself. While I never competed against her, I'll never forget her.

In 1962 I was lucky enough to make the United States Curtis Cup team again. I had won the Palm Beach Championship and a second Florida East Coast Championship in 1961.

This team included several of my old teammates—Barbara McIntire, Anne Quast, JoAnne Gunderson, Anne Casey Johnstone—and we had some newcomers too: Tish Preuss, Clifford Ann Creed, and Jean Ashley, from Chanute, Kansas. The match was being played in the West for the first time and the venue was The Broadmoor Golf Club, where I had played since the age of 11, in Colorado Springs.

Thayer Tutt, a great friend of sport, ran The Broadmoor Hotel, which was connected to the Golf Club. Mr. Tutt always did things in an impeccable way. In 1962, The Broadmoor actually flew the GB&I team first class from New York to Denver. Barbara and I felt a responsibility as hostesses and were part of the entourage that picked them up at the airport.

We were concerned about the other team's ability to adapt to our high altitude in the Rockies. Colorado Springs is some 6,000 feet above sea level and the thin air can make you feel disoriented and ill when you first arrive. People who aren't used to high altitude tend to overdo it the first couple of days. We advised our opponents to ride in motorized golf carts and just play nine holes the first day of practice. They had some lead time so they had a chance to get acclimated, and they could go back to walking as the matches got closer. We also told them to be sure to wear sun lotion.

They didn't listen. They wanted to walk, so they walked. Play was very slow, which they're not used to, and it was very warm. During one of their practice rounds we got a call from the golf course to go pick them up at the

12th hole. All of them were burned and exhausted. By the time of their last practice rounds, they were all riding in carts.

Polly Riley, the great American Curtis Cup player from the 1940s and '50s, was our captain and did a fine job. Her opposite on the British side was Frances "Bunty" Stephens Smith. These two had played a lot of historic matches against each other, so that added a nice dimension.

Whether it was because we were more rested and acclimated, or because that GB&I team was not quite as cohesive as the 1960 team, the match went our way from the start. We won every foursomes match the first day and were leading overall, three to zip. Before the start of the 36-hole singles matches on the second and final day, Polly called a team meeting. She was a good speaker with an incredible sense of humor and she tried to pump us up about the idea of a sweep, 9 to 0. It sounded good to all of us at the time. She was very determined that we become the first Curtis Cup team to whitewash the other team. But I wasn't really enamored with a sweep because these players, our opponents, were our friends. Even the inscription on the Cup, which Margaret and Harriot had composed before they had the bowl created in 1927 read, "to stimulate friendly rivalry among the women golfers of many lands."

"Many lands" to the Curtis sisters meant other countries, such as France, but it never materialized and remained a match between the USA and GB&I.

I surely wanted to win my match, but I was more keyed up about playing at my home course. There's little to be said for a so-called "home course advantage," in my opinion. In fact, most players seem to do quite poorly at home because of the added pressure of playing in front of their friends and family.

In those days, our matches were 36 holes and after the first 18 holes of the match, I was 8 down to Diane Robb Frearson. I knew the greens at The Broadmoor better than anyone playing, but putted atrociously. When Diane and I finished the first 18, I walked into our team suite for lunch. Gundy asked, "How do you stand?"

"I'm 8 down," I said.

"Quit kidding," Gundy said. "How do you stand?"

After lunch, Polly walked with me to the first tee for the afternoon portion of the match. "If anyone can win back eight holes, and win the match," she said, "you can."

But I just couldn't pull it off and my putting continued to be atrocious.

Mike Murra, my instructor, was a spectator. After I lost on the 29th hole, he commiserated with me as I walked in from the match. Mike told me that I had moved the upper part of my body toward the hole on my backswing, making me inconsistent.

It was a combination of inconsistency, poor putting, and wanting to do so well on my home course that affected the outcome of the match. I lost by the same large margin, 8 and 7, that I had won by in 1960.

Fortunately, all my teammates won their matches. So, we retained the Cup by a score of eight to one, and I was the one.

I was disappointed by the way that I had played, since it was my home course but, having talked it out with Mike on the long walk from the 29th hole to the clubhouse, I was into celebrating our team's victory by the time I got in. I was far from crushed by the loss of my match and was pretty matter-of-fact. As my mother had taught me, it was just a game. You try as hard as you can and when it's over, it's over.

The Curtis Cup is rich in history and is really the epitome of the game's sportsmanship. It's just as important how the match is played as who wins it, and I believe everyone who has been touched by the spirit of the Curtis Cup would agree.

I've made a lot of friends through the Curtis Cup, and Maureen Garrett, Belle Robertson, Diane Bailey, Angela Bonallack, Judy Eller, JoAnne Gunderson, Tish Preuss, and Barbara are still my close pals.

Mrs. Prunaret remained a great and inspiring person in my life. The American golf writer Herbert Warren Wind once told me that she came close a few times to winning the Bob Jones Award, the USGA's highest award, which is presented for distinguished sportsmanship. She would have been a perfect choice.

From 1960 until she became ill with Alzheimer's disease and moved to a care facility, I spent a couple of weeks with Mr. and Mrs. Prunaret every year. When I was in New York on buying trips for our stores, I'd go up to their home in Boston for the weekend. I went to Ireland with them several times and to the British Ladies Open Amateur twice. They were like second parents to me, to be honest, and they were wonderful.

They were sporting people who loved golf and also had the oldest beagle pack in the United States. Mrs. P.'s uncle, Chetwood Smith, had brought the first beagle pack to the United States and pioneered beagling as a sport in this country when he staged the first national championships in Aldie, Virginia. The Prunaret's pack of 30 or 40 beagles was descended from that original pack. The one thing I learned about beagling, which is when hounds account for a rabbit, is that if you can't keep up with the hounds, they run in a circle so they will eventually come back your way.

I appreciated Mr. and Mrs. P.'s obvious devotion to each other and the fact that they were such great friends. They didn't have children, so it was a different sort of relationship than what I grew up with, but they were totally devoted.

She was such a lady and an outdoors sort of person. You just couldn't help but be better off if you had the opportunity to be around Mildred Prunaret. She believed that knowledge was the secret, that if you were pre-pared and knew your stuff, you could do anything you wanted.

Mrs. Prunaret had been a member of the USGA Women's Committee and was a past chairman. She and Mr. Dey were really the ones who first got me on the Women's Committee.

I had been on the USGA's Girls' Junior Championship Committee from 1961-64. When I got a telephone call in the fall of 1967 asking me to be on the Women's Committee, I was busy, still playing competitive golf, and really didn't want to do it. But I didn't know how I was going to tell Mrs. Prunaret that I didn't want to be on the Women's Committee of the United States Golf Association. I knew I would really disappoint her. So, bottom line, I did it for her.

Over the next 13 years, I actually enjoyed my stint on the committee, particularly when we started doing more officiating, setting up the courses, and reviewing championship formats.

Thirteen years later, in 1981, I was going to be named chairman of the Women's Committee at the USGA Annual Meeting in Los Angeles. Mrs. P. was still in pretty good mental health, and she and Mr. P. flew out to sur-prise me on that special day.

I was nervous. I had lost my mother in 1969, Dad had died in 1980, and my brothers were busy with their own lives, so none of my family was on hand. I was extremely relieved when the Prunarets arrived, and when I saw Mrs. P. the night before the meeting, I finally felt that I was ready to be named chairman. When I saw her face, it all became clear. I realized that I had the knowledge, which she had said was so important, since I had been on the Women's Committee and had been involved in so many USGA activities for the past 13 years. She was my inspiration when it came to the USGA.

I had been blessed with my parents, then I had the Prunarets. I'm sure that I got a lot more out of the relationship than they did.

When I left the Women's Committee after four years as chairman, at the end of 1984, I continued as a USGA volunteer, serving on the Museum Committee in 1985. I was named captain of the U.S. Curtis Cup team in 1986 and played in my first USGA Senior Women's Amateur Championship that year as well. Although, not very well.

By 1987, we were able to pay an appropriate tribute to Mrs. Prunaret when we kicked off the United States Women's Mid-Amateur Championship, the USGA's championship for women amateurs age 25 and older.

We had been trying to get the championship going since 1984, and we finally believed we had enough interest from players in that age group to conduct the Women's Mid-Am. That first year, I threw an idea to Dena Nowotny, a friend who was chairman of the Women's Mid-Am, about a championship trophy. I thought we could name it the Mildred Gardinor (she always said she was "a one-eyed Gardinor") Prunaret Cup.

By then, Mrs. Prunaret was in the extended care facility, so I talked to Mr. P. and he was all for it. Janet Seagle, curator of the museum at Golf House, FeeFee Matthews, a member of the Women's Committee, and I tried to find the right trophy.

I thought the trophy ought to be American made and American in design. I knew Mrs. Prunaret's father had been in the silver business in Marion, Connecticut. When I next went to visit Mr. Prunaret, I said, "What I'd really like to have is one of your sterling silver beagle cups made by Mr. Gardinor, then let's get all the language polished off and make it the Women's Mid-Amateur trophy."

They had a sterling Revere bowl, made by Mrs. Prunaret's father, that they had presented to the Bryn Mawr dog show for the best two-couple beagle pack and had won it themselves so many times that they retired the trophy. So that's what we selected. It's simple, American in design, and the quality is so lovely.

Janet contacted a firm in Baltimore to make the base for the cup.

We unveiled the cup at the Women's Mid-Amateur players' dinner at Southern Hills Country Club, Dena's club in Tulsa. I was to make the talk about the special bowl and I really wanted to be top-notch, but somehow I got myself caught in the part about the beagles and the packs and it came out sounding something like, "Best Bitch in Show." The more I talked, the more I dug myself into a hole and the more the audience laughed. Thank heavens, I could always laugh at myself.

Still, the trophy is a lovely tribute to Mrs. Prunaret. I call it "the Prune's

Cup," in honor of her nickname.

By then, Mr. Prunaret, who could no longer care for himself, was also in St. Patrick's Manor, a lovely, rambling nursing home in Framingham, Massachusetts, where Mrs. Prunaret lived. He, too, was simply great and contributed a big part to my education, no question about it. They knew so much about competing and fair play in sports. They took me on trips and I learned from them about food, art, and antiques. Both gave me "expert tuition".

One day, after doing business in New Jersey, I drove to Framingham to see them both.

It was autumn and the hills were beautiful and sunstruck with red, yellow, and gold that morning. Mrs. Prunaret didn't recognize me when I went to visit her in her room. She was bedridden and everyday events weren't registering with her, so I just talked to her for a while, then kissed her and left the room.

I wheeled Mr. Prunaret out on the grounds, but the day was cold, so I went back to his room to get his sweater and tucked a scarf around his neck. We sat together, Mr. Prunaret in his wheelchair, me on a bench, and I talked and talked. He looked at me with a pleasant little smile but his eyes were vacant.

I told him about the last Curtis Cup match, the last Women's Amateur Championship, and what I had been doing. I went over some old memories, too. Finally, I got a putter out of the car and made several strokes on the grass, talking to him about technique. There was a sudden light of recognition in his eyes, and he put his hands together in a golf grip.

A little while later, I wheeled him to his room and kissed him on the top of his head.

My visits with Mr. and Mrs. Prunaret were always poignant because I never knew if it would be the last time I saw them. I'm not an emotional person—I live in the moment—but I treasured this time with my old friends.

I drove back to New Jersey that night, singing old show tunes all the way.

Mr. Prunaret died in 1991 and I attended his memorial service in Boston. Mrs. P. died in 1997. Three years later, Jeanne-Marie Boylan, one of New England's best amateurs and a member of the USGA Executive committee, invited a few of Mildred Prunaret's close friends to a private service at Brae Burn Country Club in West Newton, Massachusetts, the

Prunaret's home club. Only about 10 of Mrs. P's friends were invited, and each of us reminisced about her.

I told of when I first visited the Prunarets in their home at the corner of Frost and Winter streets in Natick, Massachusetts. That's when I discovered what she believed in. "Knowledge and knowing what you're talking about," she said at that time, "are everything."

Well, not quite everything, because it was from Mrs. Prunaret that I learned what fair play is all about.

Chapter 13

[A Short Story]

I was once interviewed by a business reporter who came to our appointment with the preconceived notion that what I learned in business made me successful in golf. I never could convince this fellow that it was the other way around. To me, the most important role has always been as a player and without that experience I never would have achieved anything in business or in the USGA.

Golf, for a player, is a very hands-on game and that's my style in business and in the USGA. I either get in, or I get out. If I'm in, I jump in with both feet.

Business is a key part of my life. I love to work. In fact, I recently told a friend that I'd work until I'm 4,000 years old. I've always kept a lot of balls in the air, numerous projects going on all at once, and I've found the best way to deal with a big workload is to spend time on one project, then switch to the next, then the next, and back again. It's a good way to stay fresh and avoid being slogged down in boredom. Some people aren't multitasked and do better focusing on one project at a time. I appreciate that, but it's not my style.

I've always worked long hours and burned the midnight oil—which you have to do when you own several retail businesses—but it has always been fun.

Barbara McIntire and I started our business selling Bermuda shorts out of the trunk of a car. A lot of the women we met while we played in tournaments liked the shorts we wore, asked where we got them, and ordered their own.

One day, during a rain delay at the Women's Western Amateur at Oak Park Country Club in Chicago, we were sitting in the locker room and decided to call Gutsteintuck, better known as G.T., Inc. We spoke with Ed Kaitz, one of the principals, and asked if we could sell G.T. shorts and slacks to various shops while traveling around the country. Ed probably had more to do with us eventually going into the retail business than he realized. He told us that he had plenty of representation on the road, but if we wanted to buy shorts and slacks at wholesale and sell them at retail, he would be glad to work with us. We began to do just that.

We placed an opening order of $500. The shorts retailed for $12.95 to $18.95, except for the Dupioni silks, and I can tell you today that H-30 was the carib linen-weave in Kelly green, and H-45 was blue.

Barbara and I both like natural fabrics—cotton, wool, silk—and we both dress conservatively (although I've been known to wear a red dress in my time). But I think we were a little surprised that this new enterprise went over as well as it did.

In 1959, we started a mail-order business. We put together a high-grade mailing brochure with tiny swatches of 17 fabrics glued inside. In fact, my mother got a hematoma on her right thumb helping us cut fabric swatches with pinking shears while we all sat on the floor of her living room in Wichita. Jack Petrie, a great friend and retailer, suggested that since our brochure was a story about shorts, we should name the business "A Short Story."

We turned one of Mother's spare bedrooms into a showroom, with fixtures, a hang rod for the shorts and slacks, and cabinets for the blouses. Two or three times a year we had showings and invited interested people.

We also ran a little ¹⁄₁₆-page ad, which featured a line drawing of our shorts, in *Golf World* magazine. The mail-order business started off well, and we thought this might be a good future. At the time, Barbara was a licensed realtor in Florida and I was going to school and still helping Dad in his business, so we were both ready for a new opportunity.

My father and brothers made me go through the wringer before we started that business. Dad sent me to see his banker, Joe Hickman, at the Fourth National Bank in Wichita. I had literally spent hours and hours preparing a business plan and a five-year projection with the help of my accountant, Jack Douglas. I went to see Mr. Hickman on the third floor of the bank building. His office was in a glass cage in the middle of a room with all of the commercial loan officers sitting at desks around him.

It was imposing, to say the least.

He was all business, and so was I. This was my first bank experience and I was nervous but prepared to talk about every number that I was submitting. When I handed my business plans to him, he glanced at the papers and threw them in the wastebasket.

He stared right into my eyes and said, "I don't care about this. I want to know if you can sell shorts."

I stammered and stuttered and tried to assure him that we could. He offered us a loan but we ended up getting a bank participation loan with the Small Business Administration. I wanted to get the whole sum from the SBA because it was two percentage points lower than what we were able to get from Mr. Hickman at the bank. My father was appalled because borrowing from a bank meant you were establishing credit, and that's exactly what he wanted us to do.

I wrote to my friend Thayer Tutt, president of The Broadmoor Hotel, and asked him about available space for a shop. I had met Thayer as a child when my parents were summer members at The Broadmoor Golf Club. He was a remarkable guy. A great amateur sports enthusiast, Thayer had successfully campaigned to bring the NCAA hockey championships to the hotel's ice rink from 1948 through 1957. He was a great promoter of sports, and sat on the boards of a number of companies. He was also known as a generous employer who knew each of his many employees by name and always asked them about their families. While his friends referred to Thayer as "a man's man," he was my longtime friend.

When my parents and I arrived at the golf club that summer, Thayer met me on the front steps to say he had a potential shop location he wanted me to see. There was an empty 500-square foot space with a display window in a building that was separate from the hotel but fronted the circular drive going to The Broadmoor South building and across from the Golf Club. We rented it for $200 a month in 1962.

Location is everything and we had one of America's most beautiful sites at The Broadmoor. The hotel, which opened in 1918, had been designed by Whitney Warren and Charles Wetmore, who designed the New York Yacht Club and Grand Central Station, as well as several New York City hotels, including the Biltmore, Ritz-Carlton, Vanderbilt, Belmont, and Commodore. The Broadmoor Hotel was an imposing Mediterranean-style structure with a red tile roof, with several adjoining buildings with rooms and shops connected by covered walkways. The hotel had always been a favored stop for people who could afford it, and it over-looked two golf courses, including the original course where I grew up. The Rocky Mountains towered over the entire property. Our shop and the front of the hotel faced Lake Avenue, which was lined with tall evergreens and fine old homes.

In summer, the scenery sparkled in the mountain air and in winter, the hotel was decked with white lights and traditional Christmas decorations. Driving through the snow on a winter night and coming up to the hotel with all those lights took your breath away.

During the day, you could hear the chimes at the Will Rogers Memorial on Pikes Peak playing "America the Beautiful," a song that was written to describe this part of the country. I felt lucky to live and work in such a lovely place.

The space for our shop was just an empty rectangle, with no storage. We obviously needed some design help, so I worked up my nerve and enlisted John Hickman of Wichita. John was a very big deal because he was one of the foremost architects in that region and perhaps in the United States. He was also my brother Carl's best friend. Carl was on the Wichita City Commission when John was hired to design a new civic center. Today's visitors to downtown Wichita agree that the sweeping, circular Century Two civic center is one of the more impressive buildings in the Midwest.

I think Barbara and I paid John $500. He helped design fixtures for the space, but his most inspired contribution was a two-foot-square antique brick pillar that stood in the opening of the shop, dividing the space and giving it interest.

Having three brothers is why I think I got along so well with the men I met in business. Many of those men not only helped us to get started but also became great friends. Among them were John and the architects who helped design our shops. Bud Roberts helped design The Second Story, and Marshall Morin, the hotel's interior designer who helped expand A Short Story in 1967, also helped with all of the interiors in our shops and in my house. Other key friends were our bankers Joe Hickman, Mark Millison, Tom Moon, and Carl Donner, and our landlords Thayer Tutt and Karl Eitel.

The fact that our store had no back room probably was the one factor that helped us survive. The reason was because every piece of merchandise had to be out front. To determine how much merchandise we needed to buy, we'd simply space empty coat hangers in a 12-inch area of our racks, count the hangers, multiply them by the number of feet of hang space, and then buy just enough clothes to fill them. In those early years we had inadvertently used a purchasing method that guaranteed that we would never be overstocked.

My dad, meanwhile, had always been a great manager of money, and he watched it closely. He had helped start a co-op called Service Supreme (which became Associated Grocers) in which independent merchants would form a coalition for purchasing merchandise and supplies. His was a big role in that co-op and he knew a lot about this kind of business.

He kept a little book in which he wrote down, on a weekly basis, what he bought and what he sold at the store. Now that I was in the clothing business, he started in on me. "How much did you buy last week and how much did you sell?"

I told him that it doesn't work that way in the clothing business. You do it by seasons.

"You gotta sell more than you buy," he'd say. "It's just that simple, and I don't give a damn what you say about the clothing business."

I wouldn't listen to him because when you're a certain age you don't want your dad telling you what to do. But it's so true, about buying and selling. In the clothing business, what you don't sell you have to mark down, so you lose your margin. Basically, what you sell in the clothing business is nearly the same as what you sell in the grocery business, just not as perishable.

Our trips for private showings were an adventure. I remember renting a big panel truck that we filled with merchandise and drove to Denver where we had showings each spring. We hung all the clothes on a rolling rack in the back of the truck. I drove the truck from my parents' house in Colorado Springs to the shop, just a couple of miles away, so that we could pick up a rope to tie down the rack and keep it from rolling. Barbara rode in back to make sure that the clothes stayed in order.

I struggled to steer the truck, unaware that in back the clothes, and Barbara, were shifting and slamming all over the place. She tried to get my attention by pounding on the wall of the cab with her fist but I never heard her. When we arrived at the shop, I opened the back of the truck and Barbara just about fell out. She had a few choice words for me that I won't repeat.

We made change out of an old tackle box in our shop and every month I'd mail shoeboxes full of receipts to Jack Douglas, the son of Henry Douglas,

Dad's CPA. Jack tallied our finances and taught me all about retail account-
ing. He was one of my greatest friends and my brother Fred's best friend.

Fred, however, couldn't believe that all the cash for our livelihood was
stored in a tackle box. Dad was so mortified he offered to buy a cash register for us.

"Nothing doing," I said. "If you want to give us the money, fine, but
Nieman Marcus doesn't have a cash register and *we're* not having a cash
register."

Fred bought a big chain and chained the tackle box to the supports of
the counter in the back room.

Thayer had the hotel carpenters build another display window, so we
had two. These triggered our imaginations. I'm fairly competitive—if you
peel two potatoes, I'm going to peel three—so I was determined to ace out
Barbara by having the best window. During the Christmas season, I had a
real fireplace with "burning" gas logs in my window. She topped me with
an outdoor scene of a front door, snow, and a decorated lamppost. When
we got our first shipment of wash-and-wear clothes, I went all out. I had
a nice "wash-and-wear" sign in my window, a display of clothes, and I
added a washboard and a tub of soapsuds. I didn't know any way to keep
the suds going other than to add sudsy water every little while, so I'd drop
what I was doing, refill the tub, and give it a big stir. In an attempt to help
Barbara one time, I put Styrofoam snowflakes in her display window. It
took her six months to get all of them out and that was the last window
she ever decorated. I've always maintained that my displays were far supe-
rior to Barbara's—or at least much more original.

In 1967, we expanded A Short Story by adding fancier casual wear and
street wear to our sports clothes. We had begun stocking some of our
women's wear in the golf shop at The Broadmoor Golf Club in 1962. In
1967, at the request of Karl Eitel, general manager of The Broadmoor, we
took over the club's tennis shop and made it twice as large. When The
Broadmoor West was built in 1975, we opened our Papagallo shop. It carried high-end shoes, jewelry, gifts, and a collection of designer clothes.

We were in the resort business, so it was just a question of supply and
demand. We did plenty of research to determine if there was a demand for
a certain type of store, like a shoe store. We would look at the environment
at The Broadmoor and try to round out the presentation of what was
needed.

Before we opened a new store, we'd get an idea about something to offer people, then space would become available in the hotel, and we'd all talk about it before the decision was made. It was a tremendous challenge to me and I'd just move on it to make it happen. Barbara was the strength behind the running of our shops once they opened.

I got into the men's clothing business with a partner, Sumner Lloyd, and opened another shop in the hotel in 1970. The business didn't do very well, so after a year we parted ways. I decided to keep the shop, however, get it on its feet and eventually sell it. A good friend from Denver, Homer Reed, was my mentor in that business, which I renamed The Men's Shop at The Broadmoor. By the time I learned how to run it we were making money, so I kept the shop.

In 1978 Abercrombie and Fitch, which had occupied a large space of about 5,500 square feet since 1962, moved out of the mezzanine of The Broadmoor South building. We rented that space for The Men's Shop and it led to the only truly terrifying experience that I've had in business.

Fifty-five hundred square feet is a lot of space, actually rather frightening. We then had to completely renovate the space, an expensive investment. I was in charge of the renovation, and it scared me so much that I moved my offices into the reconstruction project and officed among the steel beams, sawhorses, and concrete dust for some six months until the project was complete. My worry was that, after this huge (to us) investment in reconstruction and new merchandise, what if nobody came?

When the space was ready we used part of it to add The Little Kitchen, and then expanded our clothing business by opening a new shop: "The Second Story." Despite my panic, business boomed from opening day. Not only did we have lots of customers, they liked what they saw and from that day on the location was a favorite stop for locals and hotel guests.

In 1990, we added another shop several blocks away called "The Red Rabbit." It was located across from our restaurant, Bell's Deli, and in it we stocked framed golf prints and other gift ideas.

Barbara and I stocked just about everything but hardware and automobiles. The Men's Shop, for example, carried not only fine men's clothing, but colognes and shaving lotions, travel accessories, framed prints, books, antique furniture, and toys. We mounted our displays on beautiful antique desks and tables that were lit with lovely and unique lamps. It was an updated traditional statement and everything, even the display tables, was for sale.

Over the years, we had as many as 70 employees at any one time. After

I opened Bell's Deli, which became Bell's Market Grill, we had cooks, wait people, handymen, salespeople, tailors, managers, and accountants on the payroll. It was a very close and loyal group. A lot of good women amateur golfers worked for us: Tish Preuss, Cindy Hill, Jean Ashley, Nancy Roth Syms, Jeannie Butler, Bonnie Lauer, Maggie Martin Giesenhagen, and Helen Kirkland. Old family friends, such as Ellie Tutt McColl, were on the staff, but we also enlisted new people. Many of them were with us for years.

When we hired an employee, we looked for enthusiasm, spark, the ability to visit with people, and a desire to take care of people.

There's always the challenge of getting people to take pride in the job they're doing. They really have to buy into the idea. We had some employees who treated the shops like they were their own, and that was always ideal. It was a matter of them taking pride and knowing that they made a difference and that they had a voice in how things were run. We always tried to give our employees that kind of autonomy.

We spent a lot of social time with our employees. Many of us would eat lunch together at the Deli and we had frequent potluck suppers at my house. Workers sometimes brought their spouses and children for a cookout or special activities, such as an Easter Egg Hunt. We once invited everyone to bring his or her dogs to my backyard for a group picture. It was a riot. More than 25 dogs and their owners showed up. We used the photo as a newspaper ad and as a mailing piece to announce that year's summer sale.

We stressed friendly customer service. Customers could place special orders and we'd mail them anywhere. Many of our nonresident customers called from out of state and we helped them choose clothes or gifts over the phone, then mailed them out. We used high-quality bags and did beautiful gift-wrapping with unique paper and ribbon. We also tried to pay attention to the little things when wrapping gifts, such as always tucking the store tag inside the clothing or, when requested, putting the gift tag inside the package. On-site clothing alterations were done quickly. Customers could pay at the point of purchase or have a charge account. We tried hard to be a full-service organization.

To promote the stores, we had a lot of special events—trunk shows, fashion shows, cooking classes at The Little Kitchen. We kept our local customers posted on our shop activities through mailings. In any given week, we might have two cooking classes, a sale preview, and a trunk show. Good customers were invited to special evenings of pre-Christmas sales and were given the first crack at sale merchandise. We usually wrote and produced our own print and radio advertising.

Sometimes we took our shops on the road. For a big event, such as the Junior League Fairs in Tyler, El Paso, and Austin, Texas, Jimmy Nuss, one of our all-purpose employees, drove a truckload of merchandise and displays to the sites and we virtually set up new shops full of gift items. Our sales people, Nancy Gilbert and Marilyn Roberts, flew in and worked a week at each location, taking orders and doing food tastings.

In the beginning, we worked out of the shops and our houses. In 1985, we bought a wood-frame house on Cheyenne Road about two miles from the hotel. A few years later, we bought the wood-frame house next door. We renovated them, painted them complementary colors, and converted them into offices. We then built a two-story, four-car garage at the back of the property for storage.

My office at one of the homes that we renovated was a large, cozy room lined with memorabilia, books, paintings, and photos of friends. There was a brick fireplace next to my desk, a glassed-in porch on the other side, and an adjoining room furnished like a parlor. Inspired by the lovely gardens I'd seen in Great Britain, we installed a series of brick walks between the two houses with an English garden of flowering perennials. An American flag always hangs by the front door. It was a nice place to work.

Both buildings felt like home. The two houses had kitchens, which was important at Thanksgiving and Christmas. I promoted the sale and delivery of large family dinners from Bell's Deli. We usually had 40 or 50 orders at Thanksgiving and Christmas for turkeys, dressing, cranberry sauce, mashed potatoes, sweet potatoes—the works.

While most of the food was prepared at the Deli, my job was to roast the turkeys. I'd have three turkeys in the office ovens and the rest in friends' ovens all over town. I'd get up at 4 A.M. and spend the rest of the morning scurrying from place to place, oven to oven, basting turkeys.

One year, we had 45 orders for turkey dinners. I thought I'd solved the cooking problem by putting 30 turkeys in two of The Broadmoor Hotel's large baking ovens and by placing the other turkeys in the ovens of friends and at our shops.

I drove around town on my basting route but when I got to the hotel and opened the oven doors, one oven of turkeys was doing fine but the turkeys in the other oven were absolutely white as a sheet. The oven wasn't working. It was a scramble to find ovens for the additional 15 birds. I

called some friends to borrow their ovens and stuck a bird in the oven at
The Little Kitchen. The chef at the Penrose Room, an exclusive restaurant
at The Broadmoor South, gave me three ovens in his kitchen to use. The
head chef offered a couple of extra empty ovens, but couldn't spare a staff
member to watch them.

While a crowd of well-dressed diners enjoyed Thanksgiving dinner in
the Penrose Room, I lounged around the kitchen, basting and watching
my birds.

We juggled schedules, called customers and offered to deliver the birds.
It all worked out but it was a logistical nightmare.

There are ten million ways to make a living, a billion ways to make a
dime, but I have always looked upon retailing as a natural way to serve. It's
infinitely satisfying to match people with what they need and want. The
meals we served at Bell's Deli were always made from the freshest meat
and vegetables, and we tasted every dish. We stocked our shops with the
housewares and gifts that we would have wanted, and did use, in our
homes. The clothes we carried were what we believed to be tasteful, versa-
tile, and long-wearing, and we wore what we sold with tremendous
pleasure.

We first and foremost believed in taking care of customers. That was
the difference in our shops, when we compared them to others. Anybody
can buy the same merchandise and open a store, but it's the people who
work there that make the difference.

We weren't perfect, but we tried hard, and I can think of only one time
when we missed the mark. We decided to design a line of shorts made by
Daks of England. We figured out every possible measurement and sent
the specs to the manufacturer. When the shorts arrived, the crotches
were almost down to the knees. I kept those shorts in the storeroom to
remind myself that we needed to *buy and sell* clothing and stay out of the
design business.

We had begun doing the United States Curtis Cup team uniforms in
1970 and it was a lot of fun. In 1974, we even did the sweaters for the GB&I
team. The matches that year were to be played in San Francisco but the
team arrived without sweaters. We had a good stock of white cashmere
crew-neck pullovers at that time so we flew some of them to San Francisco.
The GB&I players were very pleased to have cashmere sweaters from
Scotland shipped from a Colorado shop.

We were in the right business. We offered quality merchandise, and it gave us great satisfaction in bringing it to people at a fair price. We were fortunate, but we also worked very hard to be successful. We were successful for more than 35 years.

Chapter 14

[Hot for Nine Holes]

One of my finest days on the golf course is memorable not just because I played well, but because it was so wacky and weird.

The 1964 United States Women's Open was played in July at San Diego Country Club. Today's contestants find it hard to believe, but in those days Women's Open contestants played 18 holes on Friday and Saturday, then wound up the championship by playing 36 holes on Sunday.

I came down with a bad case of strep throat just before leaving for the championship and there was a question about whether or not I could make the trip. A friend of mine in Colorado Springs, Dr. Jim Brady, was actually a psychiatrist but could, of course, prescribe medicine. Jim gave me the antibiotic declomycin to fight the infection so that I could play.

Dad, Barbara, Jean Ashley, who was a good amateur friend from Chanute, Kansas, and I made the trip. Unknown to me, the declomycin made me sensitive and allergic to the sun. During the practice rounds, I was absolutely cooking myself. When we went out to dinner after practicing, I complained that I felt as if I was frying.

Dad, Barbara, and Jean would chime in, "Well, it's July. It's hot." And "Quit being a baby. It's just hot."

After dinner one night, I went to a druggist and asked about the combination of sun and declomycin. He told me a reaction was possible.

I shot 79 in the first round, but I was miserable. After the round I saw Dr. Roger Eisenhower, who wanted me to withdraw from the championship. I told him that I came to play and I was going to play, so he gave me a shot, protective sunscreen, and orders to wear protective clothing.

Because I'd brought only shorts and summer shirts, I went shopping. Of course, in July it's awfully hard to find slacks, sweaters, and long-sleeved shirts. We finally found some clothes that I could wear for the rest of the championship and, boy, was I decked out. I had on a white turtleneck, a yellow cashmere sweater, lime green slacks, brown socks to protect my ankles, two brown golf gloves, and a wide-brimmed straw hat. Not an inch of my skin was exposed, but all of the clothes were in bright colors and none of them matched.

Of course, I *would* be paired with Barbara Romack on the final day. Barbara was a friend of mine, a three-time Curtis Cup player who had turned professional and was regularly atop the best-dressed list. There I was in my weird getup when Barbara showed up on the first tee, a vision in apricot; apricot silk shorts, a gorgeous shirt, an apricot Lemmer-meyer alpaca sweater, apricot socks, and custom-made apricot golf shoes with silver snakeskin saddles and kilties.

I may have been a funny-looking sight but I began playing well right off the bat. The course was set up at 6,470 yards. On the front nine, I came out of the chute with a birdie on the par-4 first hole. I parred the second and third holes then I missed the 4th green when I hit my second shot just a little short of the putting surface. I surprised myself, more than anyone, when I chipped in for my second birdie, because I'd never been good at chipping. I guess that inspired me because I birdied the next two holes for three in a row. I parred the 7th hole. On the 515-yard par-5 8th hole, I hit my third shot through the green. Guess what? I chipped in again for my fifth birdie in eight holes.

On the 9th hole, I had a birdie putt of about 15 feet for a score of 30 on the front nine. As funny as this may sound, at breakfast that morning, Frank Hannigan, a USGA staff member, came over to a table I shared with Barbara and Jean. He had a sheaf of papers in his hand and asked if any of us wanted to turn professional. He was holding declaration sheets because, at that time, you could turn pro in the middle of the Women's Open and collect a check.

I had jokingly said to Frank, "If I shoot 30 on the front nine, I might think about it."

When I came down the fairway of the 9th hole, he was standing in back of the green. I almost made the 15-footer for birdie when my ball ran over part of the hole, but I had to settle for a par and a five-under-par front nine of 31.

"If I hadn't missed that putt, I might have signed your paper," I told Frank. Believe me, he was as surprised as I was about my performance that morning.

Suddenly, my name appeared on the leader board.

On the back nine, I birdied the 10th hole and the 14th, both par-5 holes. All the rest were pars, except for the 17th, where I missed the green to the left.

The Women's Open was being televised locally and camera platforms were behind the 17th green. I chipped to the green and needed to mark my ball, which was in Barbara's line. Suddenly, I discovered a wad of gum on the spikes of my left shoe.

I've got to get this gum off of my shoe, I thought.

I poked at the gum with my gloved right hand. Now the gum was on my glove. When Barbara saw the mess I was in, she offered to mark my ball for me. When she reached into her pocket for a coin, her pocket seam ripped out and a handful of coins and tees scattered on the green.

We were in a pickle. I was in a mess and I looked up to see that the camera was still rolling. But not for long because the producer soon switched to a more graceful group of players. That was fine with me, since I didn't care for my costume and I was paired with this vision in apricot.

I missed my putt for a par and had my only bogey of the round.

When we finally left the green, Barbara whispered, "If you hadn't been such a klutz, we would have had more air time."

I couldn't respond.

I parred the 18th hole and finished with a one-under-par 36 for a total of 67, six under par.

Barbara Romack was pulling for me and seemed awfully supportive on that back nine, saying, "You can do it, Judy," as we walked down the last few fairways.

My score that morning tied the previous low round in the Women's Open, a record that had been set by professional Marilynn Smith before the championship came under the auspices of the USGA.

As an amateur, I got a lot of attention for that record round, but after having opened with two rounds in the upper 70s, I was more shocked than anyone.

Mr. Dey met me behind the 18th green and after I signed my scorecard he walked with me to the clubhouse. News of my round had filtered throughout the course and he said that a number of reporters wanted to talk to me.

"Now, Judy, you just go into the locker room, have your lunch, rest, and get yourself ready for the afternoon round," he said.

In the afternoon round, I didn't change a thing but shot 43 on the front nine, 12 strokes more than in the morning and to the very same hole locations. I felt as if I was taking one step forward, and two steps back. Probably the best nine I played, under the circumstances, was my 40 on the back nine of that final round. The way I was going, it would have been easy to shoot 50. I remember thinking during those final, frustrating holes that *Golf is like a butterfly. You never quite catch it.*

I finished with an 83, and my score of 79-78-67-83—307 didn't even win a medal as low amateur. Barbara McIntire beat me by three strokes for that honor.

The front-nine score of 31 is still in the USGA record book, and after 38 years remains the second lowest nine-hole score in the Women's Open. I've gotten a lot of mileage out of that 67. After I became USGA President, I would consistently be introduced by someone who mentioned that round. Sometimes they quoted the score as 67, but more often it was noted as a 65, a 64, or even a 63.

One of these days they'll get me down into the 50s.

Chapter 15

[Losing Mother]

My mother died of a heart attack in 1969.

She had suffered the first of three heart attacks in 1961. When she had her first attack I was 24 years old and living at my parents' house at 6210 East 12th Street in Wichita.

It was autumn. Barbara McIntire was visiting and we'd all been at the farm fishing. Mother, Dad, Barbara, and I had driven in from the farm that day and shortly after we arrived, Mother, who had gall bladder problems, thought she was having another gall bladder attack. She walked the entire length of the house toward her bedroom, and lay down, groaning in pain. It was worse, she said, than childbirth.

We rushed to her side, called my brother, Carl, who lived a block away, then called an ambulance and Mother's doctor. They all arrived at about the same time and Mother was rushed to the hospital. Her doctor knew right away what had happened. She had suffered a heart attack.

If Mother made it through the first 24 hours, then 72 hours, we were told she might then be out of danger. The waiting was excruciating and for three days we milled around the hospital, sick with worry. I never left and slept in a chair in her room or the waiting room.

Mother pulled through and after several weeks came home.

My brothers, my father, and I had just one goal: to get her well. It wasn't easy. It's not that Mother was a bad patient but her activities were severely limited and I knew she wasn't going to be satisfied with playing just nine holes of golf or not being allowed to go fishing in her favorite spots.

We managed to keep her from overexerting, then when she was able to do a little more we increased her activities.

I was determined to take care of her and remained close to the house, paying attention to every detail of her care. Mother was an early riser, so I'd get up early and fix her breakfast. I tried to make everything just right, cooking healthy foods, and seeing that she rested and was without stress.

When one of my sisters-in-law, Gwen, Sally, or Jack's wife, Ruth, came over for a couple of hours I'd go to Wichita Country Club and play nine holes with my friend Paula Petrie. The fresh air, golf, and Paula's company were a bit of an escape, but Mother was never far from my mind.

After a month at home, Mother seemed much better and we were all able to go on with our lives but we now knew that, with heart disease, her life would never quite be the same. While she hadn't worked at Bell's Market for some time, she was still a very active woman who was involved in the community and enjoyed her friends and family. Golf and her fishing and hunting trips with Dad had been a big part of her life, but those activities were now restricted. For Mother, who had always done exactly what she wanted to do, it was an unwelcome adjustment. She was bored.

Three years later, in 1964, I was living in my parents' house in Colorado Springs. Barbara and Jean Ashley, one of our fellow amateur competitors, lived there, too. Barbara and I had opened our shop, A Short Story, in 1962. It was doing well and we were excited about our business prospects.

One winter afternoon, while Barbara was in Florida visiting her parents, I was the only one working in the shop when the telephone rang. My brothers were calling from Wichita. Mother had suffered a second heart attack. This time, she had lost consciousness.

Bill Rounds, a family friend who owned the Breckenridge (Colorado) Ski Resort, figured out a way to get me home. If I would meet Bill at the airport, he'd fly me to Wichita in his plane that night. I just locked up the shop and took off, hurrying home to throw a few things in a suitcase. I was frantic and heartsick. The first heart attack had been a warning, but I knew that this second attack was more serious and I was afraid that I'd seen Mother alive for the last time.

I would not come back to Colorado Springs for four weeks.

Mother had been unconscious for a longer period of time than was considered safe but, once again, we were lucky and she pulled through. After a couple of weeks in the hospital she was allowed to come home. Her activities were now even more severely limited and it was a constant battle to keep her from doing the things she wanted to do. She was on a low-fat, saltfree diet. I did all of the cooking and Dad and I ate what Mother ate. Neither of us complained.

She still awoke early, dressed, and joined me for breakfast. Then she was at loose ends. Staying in the house reading magazines or going for a drive around town were not going to keep her happy. She was extremely agitated at not being able to be her own person and make her own decisions, a position I could well understand.

We had to almost sit on her because she was just by-God going to do everything she'd always done. She even quit playing golf because she wasn't allowed to play a full round, saying, "I wouldn't put on my shoes to play nine holes."

I remember how guilty I felt when I later became Chairman of the USGA Handicap Committee and successfully pushed for nine-hole handicaps. It was because of what Mother had said.

One day, she surprised me by buying a sewing machine. She'd never shown any interest in sewing and didn't know how to sew, but she just took it up and began making clothes. It was typical of Mother, who liked learning new things on her own. The challenge of learning to sew eased her frustration, I think, and for a while she took great pleasure in showing us what she had made. She became interested in ceramics and had a kiln installed in a workroom at the farm, where she made ashtrays, bowls, and platters. I still have some of them. They're not especially fine examples of the craft, but they're great because she made them.

After her second heart attack, I again supervised her care and I wouldn't have traded anything for being there. She had taken care of me all my life and I felt it was a privilege to have the opportunity to now take care of her.

One little sidelight of this period was that every morning I went into town and spent a couple of hours with our accountant, Jack Douglas. Jack taught me how to enter our figures in the ledger and I literally did all of the bookkeeping for our business.

The days passed slowly but Dad, Mother and I fell into a routine and after about a month, Mother was stronger so we went to Colorado Springs to their house on Sequoia Drive. Barbara and Jean still lived there. Mother did some of the cooking but, once again, was extremely frustrated that she couldn't do everything she wanted to do. She wanted to go up to Green Mountain Falls to fish, for example, but her doctors wouldn't allow it.

Because the altitude was higher there, they knew she would be in danger of another heart attack.

The atmosphere at home seemed very different because Mother's tremendous energy had always been at the center of our family. Obviously more fragile, she moved around the kitchen more slowly now. But we all grew accustomed to it and for a few years, life seemed almost normal.

In 1969, Mother and Dad were alone at our farm in Kingman County. One winter night, they had finished eating dinner when Mother said she didn't feel well. She wanted to go to their bedroom and lie down. She died that night in her own bed. She was 69 years old.

I was in the house in Colorado when the telephone rang. One of my brothers told me Mother was dead.

I was devastated. One of the hardest things in life, I think, is to lose a parent. We were such a close family and my childhood had seemed so perfect. Throughout my life, Mother had been my strength, my pillar, and I had no better friend.

I couldn't imagine life without Mother. But we had to go on and there were things to be done. First, I called Barbara, who was in Florida, and for the second time she rushed back to run the business. I caught a plane to Wichita. My brothers picked me up at the airport and we drove to the farm.

I went in to see Dad. He looked so lonely and seemed utterly lost. They'd been married for nearly 50 years, had raised a family, and had enjoyed so many things together. They were very close. Mother had been in poor health for several years, but he had never prepared himself to lose her. He was nearly in shock.

The following day we drove into Wichita and made the funeral arrangements. Dad had given Mother her rings and a diamond necklace and he wanted her to wear them to the grave. Dad said, "I gave them to her and they're hers." But Bill Cochran, a friend of the family and owner of the mortuary, talked Dad out of it.

I said, "We're going to bury her in a dress that she made," and we did.

The arrangements, the reactions of people who loved her, all of it seemed so raw, but it was necessary to help us all deal with our grief. I can remember when my grandmother, Mamuz, came to see Mother. She said she wished it were she and not her daughter who had died. She went to the casket, leaned down, and gave Mother a kiss.

Mother's funeral was at St. Paul's Methodist Church. Fred and Sally hosted a luncheon before the service. We closed the store and the wholesale meat company that day so that everyone who worked for us could come. The church was packed. Dad had the organist play "You'll Never Walk Alone," saying that it was Mother's favorite song. In truth, I believe that it was *his* favorite song. Mother had always loved another Rodgers & Hammerstein song, "Climb Every Mountain" from *The Sound of Music,* and its message of finding your dream had been something she had taught us long before that song was written.

A couple of days after the funeral I went back to Colorado Springs. It was very hard to leave Dad. I began going back to Wichita to see him about once a month.

When we lost Mother, I was 32 years old. I still had Dad, but I felt I was without the other most important person in my life.

After Mother's death, I changed a lot.

Until she died, I'd been a sort of laid-back person. I was happy to work hard and loved a good time, but preferred to low-key it and stay in the background.

Shortly after Mother's death I had surgery to have my tonsils removed. I was at home in bed in Colorado Springs—just a quiet, laid-back person recovering from surgery—when Barbara McIntire and Ellie McColl brought a milkshake in to me. I took a sip and the coldness of the milkshake made my throat hurt so I surprised myself—along with Barbara and Ellie—when I heaved the milkshake against the wall.

I don't know why I did it, unless the anesthesia caused that reaction, because I'm somewhat allergic to anesthesia, but I was never the same person after that.

Until Mother's death, I'd always been indecisive and could count on Mother to make my decisions for me. Now that she was gone, I realized that I had to step up to the plate and that I was now the only person I had to answer to. I knew that I'd better make sure that what I did was right. From that day forward, it was Katie-bar-the-door and there was *never* any doubt about what I was thinking. I had grown up.

When Mother died, her will left everything to Dad, except for one checking account over in Kingman that had only one other name on it— mine. I could tell that Dad was surprised and a little upset, because he never knew about that money and it was as if she had had a secret.

In 1964, she had begun collecting Social Security. She never spent the money, shared it, or put it into running the household. She opened the account in Kingman and deposited her checks there. She told me she was socking her money away to remodel the kitchen in Colorado.

She put my name on the account, yes, but she had wanted to do that kitchen and knew Dad would go through the checking account records and ask her how much she was spending. She wanted to be independent.

At the time of her death the account had about six thousand bucks in it, which was quite a little nest egg at that time. It gave me great satisfaction to use that money to remodel the kitchen in the way that I thought she would have wanted.

Mariam Remington Champlin Bell was a very direct person. You always knew where you stood with her. She was tough. She was capable. She was a loving person. She took care of people. She believed in dreams. She was all of those things. She was my mother and I loved her dearly. Her imprint remains on my life forever.

Chapter 16

[Volunteering: My USGA Start]

I became a volunteer with the United States Golf Association more than 40 years ago. My first assignment was as a member of the 1961 United States Girls' Junior Championship Committee. I didn't really do anything on that committee and, to be honest, I went to only one championship. People come up to me today to say they remember me at the Girls' Junior, which amuses me because I was a lousy volunteer then.

As the years went on, I became more dedicated. Volunteering was something I'd been raised with. Mother was a member of a women's circle at St. Paul's Methodist Church, and belonged to the Eastern Star, the Wichita Club, the Wichita Red Cross, and the American Legion Auxiliary. When someone in our community needed something, she was always willing to help.

Dad was active in a number of organizations in Wichita and was a charter director on several boards. He certainly volunteered his time. In 1963, my brother, Carl, was elected Mayor of the City of Wichita and was a great leader with a very progressive agenda.

So I grew up around people who volunteered and it was something I think I felt strongly about, even as a child. We all believed that if you're asked and you have an opportunity to give back, you just step to the plate and do what you can.

In the USGA, volunteer committees run each of the 10 national amateur championships with the aid of the staff. Various subcommittees deal with Regional Affairs and Women's Regional Affairs, Communications,

Implements and Ball, Green Section, Amateur Status & Conduct, and on and on. All of these committees are made up of volunteers, without which the work of the USGA couldn't be done.

When I first went on the USGA Women's Committee in 1968, by tradition we really weren't allowed to do much. My first USGA Annual Meeting as a Women's Committee member was in New York. With the other WC members, we'd meet from 10 A.M. to noon, have lunch with the Executive Committee, meet for another hour after lunch, and that was it. By 2 P.M., I was always at Bloomingdale's looking at their merchandising displays.

That was the year Joseph C. Dey Jr. resigned from the USGA to become Commissioner of the PGA Tour. Several of us were disappointed that he was leaving the USGA and his resignation came as a huge shock to others because Mr. Dey had been the persona of the association since the 1930s. In 1968, however, the PGA was locked in a struggle between the tournament players and the club professionals. Key players, including Arnold Palmer and Jack Nicklaus, sought to draft Mr. Dey to become commissioner because they believed his impeccable reputation and vast knowledge of the game could heal the differences.

I remember sitting in the Commodore Hotel over Grand Central Station and hearing Mr. Dey give his resignation speech at the Annual Meeting. He said that he felt the USGA was in good shape, and that the PGA Tour was also part of the game. And, he said, he believed he should therefore try to help and serve the PGA tour, which was in trouble.

"When I went to the meeting to talk to the PGA about it," he said, "I wore this tie," and pointed to his USGA tie. I'll never forget it.

When I began playing in national championships and met Mr. Dey, it really meant something to me. I was 16 years old when I first met him at the 1953 U.S. Women's Amateur at Rhode Island Country Club. He became someone I loved—his looks, his stature, the way in which he spoke. He was Mr. Rules of Golf to me.

When I made the 1960 Curtis Cup team and we went out to his house on Long Island and practiced at his club for two days, I began to feel that I knew him.

Over the years, he'd always look me up, and I began to feel that I knew him pretty well.

I was still on the Women's Committee when he retired from the PGA Tour. He continued, however, to work as a Rules official at the U.S. Open every year that he was able. When I was put on the Executive Committee in 1987, I rode around with him at least one day at each U.S. Open.

Each time, he'd say, "Miss Bell, if you don't call me Joe, I'm never going to call you Judy again."

I'd think, *I just can't. I can't do it. It isn't me. I cannot do it.*

But I tried, so I'd say, "Okay, Joe."

Maybe we'd then stop and watch the play on a hole, and I'd say, "Well, Mr. Dey, what do you think about this."

Mr. Dey was definitely someone I looked up to and I much admired his honesty, integrity, and discipline. I went to a lot of Rules of Golf seminars that he conducted and gleaned from him his sense of history of the game, which I very much respected.

Joe Dey was a man for all seasons.

In the beginning of my time on the Women's Committee, there wasn't enough going on to even keep my interest and I found it hard to be on the committee. I was still playing competitively and also thought I should be working harder on our businesses.

Cynnie Alexandre, who later became Cynnie Fochet, was named chairman of the Women's Committee in 1978. Just before becoming chairman, however, she was diagnosed with cancer. I'd been thinking of resigning from the WC to attend to other things when a USGA President called me. He said the Executive Committee didn't think Cynnie could manage the job because of her health and asked if I'd be willing to step in and help set up courses for our women's championships. As I understand it, Kay Jackson, another WC member and a good friend, got a similar call and was also asked to also help out.

"Absolutely not," I said. "I won't step in. She can do it and I'm going to be there every inch of the way to support her."

Now I had committed to stay on for three more years to give support to this brave, dedicated woman who was just a wonderful person. So, my new plan was to get off the WC when Cynnie's term was over.

But in late 1980, I got a call from then-USGA President Will Nicholson, of Denver, Colorado. Will asked if I would be the next Women's Committee chairman.

"What's the deal with Cynnie?" I asked.

"She's served three years and wants to step down," Will said.

I asked him to call me back. By now, I had become serious about resigning but I talked to Barbara about taking on this new responsibility in regard to our business. She thought I should do it. Once again, I talked to Mr. and Mrs. Prunaret and they were behind me becoming chairman one hundred thousand percent. So I volunteered for the job, and remained chairman for the next four years.

As chairman from 1981 through 1984, I saw a lot of changes. We had been accepted as Rules officials at our national championships since I first went on the WC in 1968. Now, with approval of the USGA Management Committee, we began selecting members of teams representing the United States and we were taking a more active role in running all USGA women's championships.

I believed, however, that WC members didn't have enough knowledge about the USGA, which was a big challenge. We needed more education, so I enlisted Frank Hannigan, Executive Director of the USGA, to give a seminar about Amateur Status & Conduct. Frank's presentation was the first of several and other staff members spoke to us about the Rules of Golf, the equipment-testing center, the Golf House Museum, Regional Affairs, and the championships.

Executive Committee members always received a "blue book" before each meeting, which gave them background on all sorts of USGA-related topics. So, I put together a blue book for the Women's Committee with a lot of interesting background material and an agenda for each meeting.

In typical Judy Bell fashion, I didn't publish it in time. I put it together in my office at home with the help of my assistant, Susan Collazo, and handed it out at the next meeting so WC members didn't have a chance to read it ahead of time. But it was a start.

At that time, our four women's amateur championships were each run by a committee headed by a member of the Women's Committee. Those committees were beefed up by appointing more WC members to give the chairman of the championship needed support.

I made it a point to attend every USGA women's championship, where I served as a Rules official, and went to the championship committee meetings and the players dinners. In my term as chairman, I attended 16 women's championships.

In my first year, 1981, P.J. Boatwright, a great friend of mine who was the USGA's Senior Director of Rules and Competitions for many, many years, had reworked some of the exemptions to the Women's Open. Exemptions are special invitations issued by the USGA to players who would then not have to qualify to play in a championship. At the time, these exemptions were awarded to players who finished in a certain position on the LPGA money list, a number of past Women's Open champions, and to amateurs who had reached a certain level of achievement, such as the reigning U.S. Women's Amateur champion and members of the current U.S.A. Curtis Cup team. I believed in what P.J. had done, but also believed that P.J., Will Nicholson, and I needed to completely rework the exemptions.

First, I had to sell the idea to the WC. In those days, we had meetings with the contestants before each championship, so the new format had to be presented to them at the 1981 Women's Open because the new exemptions would take effect in 1982. No one would be grandfathered in.

It wasn't a popular move. Some professionals lost their exemptions, and amateurs lost theirs if they turned professional.

We also finally changed the process for special exemptions. When I first went on the WC, we always gave special exemptions to veteran players Patty Berg, Louise Suggs, and Marilynn Smith. Once a player got invited, it was like your annual Christmas party, as if she was on a guest list and would be invited every year. I wanted to put more teeth into the special exemptions and give them only to outstanding players who had won the Women's Open and were still competitive. On occasion, wonderful players such as Kathy Whitworth and Nancy Lopez, who had not won the Women's Open, received special exemptions.

Susie Maxwell Berning, a three-time Women's Open champion, wanted a special exemption and was given one, but she thought she was entitled to a lot more and was very disappointed when she didn't receive more than one. From time to time, these special exemptions have certainly been criticized and they're a popular topic among reporters as a sort of guessing game each year.

Exemptions were a big issue and yet our new way of deciding them hasn't changed, except for minor tweaking, from 1982 until this year.

At the 1981 Women's Open, my first as chairman, I was fumbling around, deciding what my role was. When I went to LaGrange Country Club, near Chicago, on the Monday before the championship, I had no idea what I was supposed to do.

Committee assignments are a key part of the chairman's responsibilities. The chairman would assign committee members to various jobs and P.J. had said he would help me with my list. On Tuesday when I got to the course, I asked for his help. He looked over my list, said, "That looks good," turned around, and walked away.

The Women's Open would start on Thursday. I knew I needed to tweak my plan and was awake all of Tuesday night. I'd make the assignment list, then discover I'd left out two people. As I got sleepier, I'd make another list and find I had booked someone in three separate places during the same shift. I finally dozed off at about 5:00. When I woke up a few hours later, wadded up sheets of paper were all over my bed.

I quickly decided to spread the job of making the assignments within the committee, because I didn't think the chairman ought to be dealing with it. So, the first thing I did was appoint an assignment chairman who made the list then gave it to me to review.

I was also striving to give committee members more authority at our championships. I urged them to make good recommendations to the Championship Committee and the Executive Committee. My goal was to be sure we were involved in the recommendations when it came to women's golf because we were closest to that side of the game. On some issues, I was fairly pushy, such as developing more detailed records on players being considered for international teams, working on a better team selection process, and review of championship formats by a subcommittee every year. Quite a few of these innovations came about because of the insistence and support of men.

That same year, P.J. instigated the tradition of the WC chairman refereeing the final match of the Women's Amateur Championship, a job he had always done in the past. He said, "I'm not going to do this, you're going to do it. There's no reason you can't do it. I'll walk around with you." So I became the referee for the match between Juli Inkster and Lindy Goggin at Waverly Country Club, in Portland. At that time, it was an 18-hole final, not the 36-hole final we have today. On the par-3 16th hole, Lindy hit a pitch shot and her ball landed on Juli's ball, knocking it further from the hole. Luckily, I was standing by the side of the green and knew the exact spot where Juli's ball had been, so she was able to replace it.

Juli won that match, 1 up, for the second of her three straight Women's Amateur championships.

At the 1983 Women's Open, Bill Campbell and Jim Hand, the president and vice president of the USGA, called me into a room the evening before the final round. "You're not going to like it, but we think you and Marty Leonard (WC vice chairman) ought to referee the last two groups and we'll serve as your observers. It isn't up for discussion."

I'd never had any disagreements with either of them, but I said, "I think you're wrong. It's an honor for a player to have the president of the USGA as her referee in the last game of the day. If I were president of the USGA (never thinking that I was going to be), I would be the referee. But I'm not, I'm chairman of the Women's Committee."

They said, "We told you, it's not up for discussion."

In the final round, I refereed the last pairing, which included Jan Stephenson, who was leading the championship. Bill Campbell was my forward observer. He would stay ahead of the players, tracking their shots. When both players' balls had been located, Bill would go to the landing area of the next hole and prepare to track their next tee shots.

On the 71st hole, Jan was still in the lead with two holes to play. Bill had gone on to the landing area for tee shots on the 72nd hole when we had a Rules dispute. Jan's caddie at that time was a former lawyer. He insisted that Jan should get a free drop. There was a small tree between her ball and the green, but it didn't interfere with her swing. After a long discussion, Jan and the caddie insisted that she was going to play back toward the front fringe, that the nearby cart path would interfere with such a shot, and that she should therefore get a drop away from the cart path. If I had given her the drop because of her announced intention, the tree would now be out of play, she could then turn around and hit right toward the hole, unobstructed.

My sense was that she was simply trying to get away from the tree and it wasn't reasonable. I looked around for Bill and saw the top of his cap way down the 18th fairway. I didn't see P.J., either, so I thought, *You've got to make up your own mind.*

I told Jan, "No. You have a shot and that's the way you play it. I'm not giving you relief."

When the caddie started arguing, I said, "I do not want to discuss this with you. It's the player's shot and I'll discuss it all day long with the player, but not with you."

They continued to argue with me but I just stayed right with it. When I stepped back a couple of paces into the front row of the crowd, I smelled smoke from a pipe, then heard a man say, "Stick to your guns." I turned around. It was P.J.

I understand that Jan gave a golf clinic some six months later and told everyone about this bad ruling that she had received from Judy Bell at the U.S. Women's Open. I know I was right, but that was the biggest incident I ever faced as a Rules official.

Today, the Women's Committee is very proactive and really determines the direction of the women's side of the game in this country. The committee members accept that responsibility and they're accountable for it. The committee makes the decision on who is selected to the U.S.A. Curtis Cup team. It selects future women's championship sites and makes recommendations on those sites to the Championship Committee. Any change of the format of a women's championship begins with the WC.

It's a hard-working committee. Not many people I know who are worth their salt want to volunteer and not get involved, not make any recommendations or decisions. That's boring and most people would get out of that.

My term as chairman of the WC rolled along for four years. I was chairman under three USGA presidents; one year with Will Nicholson, two years with Bill Campbell, and one year with Jim Hand. I got to know them very well, because we worked closely together.

Will Nicholson lived in Denver, just up the road from Colorado Springs, so I went to him about a lot of issues and he did a great deal to move the WC along. Bill Campbell kept me very informed about what was going on and would either talk to me or write to me once a week during his presidency.

Under Jim Hand, we formed our first women's nominating committee, similar to that of the Executive Committee. This was a big step because, in the past, the Executive Committee nominated members to the various women's committees. But each of these three presidents thought there should be a proper process for nominating women to the Women's Committee and they thought these women on the committee should be more involved in every facet of the game.

They were each very supportive when I wanted to make changes and, to be realistic, it wouldn't have been possible to make changes without their support.

Bell Family Portrait in 1939. My father, Carl, and mother, Mariam, flank me with my three brothers behind (*left to right*) Jack, Fred and Carl. (*Courtesy Judy Bell*)

My high school senior picture from Wichita North, 1954. *(Courtesy Judy Bell)*

Practicing during my amateur career. (*USGA*)

Winning the 1957 Ladies Broadmoor in Colorado Springs. Club President Thayer Tutt (*right*) and Mrs. Paul Borchert, tournament chairman, present the trophy. (*Broadmoor Golf Club*)

Putting during the 1964 U.S. Women's Open at San Diego Country Club.
I finished 14th and shot a then record 67 in the third round. (*USGA*)

A fashion statement—me at the '64 U.S. Women's Open! (*USGA*)

My first appearance on the Curtis Cup team at Lindrick Golf Club in England in 1960. My teammates (*front row, left to right*): Barbara McIntire, Captain Mrs. Mildred Prunaret, Joanne Goodwin. (*Back row, left to right*): Anne Quast, JoAnne Gunderson, me, Judy Eller and Ann Casey Johnstone. (*USGA*)

Bell Named Member of Curtis Team

USGA Honors Wichita Star

Meet English Foes Next May

NEW YORK (AP) — The U.S. Golf Assn. Saturday named a young team to try and regain the Curtis Cup from Great Britain next May.

It also increased the prize money for the U.S. Open championship to $50,000, and invited the amateur champions of 40 nations to play in the 1960 U.S. Amateur championship.

The actions came at the annual USGA meeting, at which John G. Clock of Long Beach, Calif., was elected president. He is the first Californian to head the body.

Named to the Curtis Cup team, which will play a British women's team for the International Trophy May 20-21 at Nottinghamshire, England, were four members of the 1958 Cup team and three newcomers. Only one is over 25 years old.

The youngest is 19-year-old Judy Eller of Old Hickory, Tenn., who won the USGA Junior Girls Championship in 1957 and 1958. She reached the quarter-finals of the U.S. Women's Amateur last year.

The other newcomers are JoAnne Goodwin, 23, of Haverhill, Mass., runner-up to Barbara McIntire in last year's Women's Amateur, and Judy Bell, 23, of Wichita, Kan. Returning from the 1958 team are Miss McIntire, 25, of Lake Park, Fla.; two former champions, JoAnne Gunderson, 20, of Seattle and Anne Quast, 22, of Marysville, Wash., and Mrs. Ann Casey Johnstone, 37, from Mason City, Iowa, who won the Trans-Mississippi and North and South tournaments last summer.

JUDY BELL
Young Golfer Honored

Left: Newspaper article announcing my selection to the 1960 Curtis Cup team. (*Wichita Eagle*)

Below: Me and my good friend and business partner Barbara McIntire at the 1961 North & South Amateur. We met in the finals but she prevailed, 3 and 1. (*Golf World*)

Judy Bell Wins Title 10-8;

Wichitan Keeps State's Crown

Mary Frazier Bows In Tourney Finale

TOPEKA, KAN., June 28.—(*P*)— Judy Bell, 16-year-old defending champion from Wichita, won her second straight Kansas Women's Amateur golf championship here today by defeating Mary Frazier of Topeka, 10 and 8.

Miss Frazier, 17, and playing in her second state tournament, held a one-up lead at the end of the first nine holes, but never won another hole as Miss Bell settled down to play the last 10 holes in 82 strokes—four over par.

Miss Bell shot a one over par 38 on the second nine to take a four-up lead at the end of the morning round.

The Wichita miss clinched the championship by winning the first three holes of the afternoon round. She sank a 35-foot putt for a par four on the first hole. In the morning round she hit a 30-foot putt for a birdie three on the first hole.

The only holes Miss Frazier won were No. 7, 8 and 9 on the morning round. Miss Bell sliced her drive into the rough on No. 8. On No. 9 Miss Frazier shot par five, while Miss Bell had a six.

The closest match Miss Bell had during the tournament, which opened Wednesday, was 5 and 4. She was tournament medalist with an 82.

There was heavy rain during the first nine holes this morning, but the sky cleared and some 400 spectators watched play on the last 19 holes at the Topeka Country club course.

WINNER AND STILL CHAMPION—Judy Bell (above), Wichita's gift to the golfing clan, repeated as champion of state's women golfers when she stroked out a lop-sided 10-8 triumph over Mary Frazier of Topeka in the tourney's final match at Topeka Sunday.—(Eagle Staff Photo.)

My largest margin of victory in three straight Kansas Women's Amateur championships. (*Wichita Eagle*)

McIntire Jinx Broken 2 and 1

Victor Gains Leg On Kenan Trophy

From The Eagle's Wire Services

ST. AUGUSTINE, Fla. — What a difference a year makes.

That's what Judy Bell of Wichita found out here Saturday as she defeated long-time friend Barbara McIntire 2 and 1 to win the 1960 Florida East Coast Women's Golf Tournament championship.

Last year, Judy, a three-time Kansas champion, went all the way to the finals in this tourney before tumbling. On Saturday, however, the story was different.

Judy, who knocked off Mrs. Ernest Smith of Ponte Vedra Beach, Fla., 3-1; Lanny Cranston of San Marino, Calif., 6-5; and medalist Phillis Preuss of Pompano Beach, Fla., 3-2 to reach the final round, went in front by one up at the turn and then held on to edge past the 1959 National Amateur champion.

After turning one up, the U. S. Curtis Cup team member went two-up on number 11.

Barbara Slices Edge

Miss McIntire cut the margin back to one when her opponent's ball went into a bunker on the 16th.

Miss Bell on the deciding 17th sent her shot to the green while Miss McIntire ran into bunker trouble. She conceded the hole after Miss Bell sank her ball for a birdie 3.

The victory was Miss Bell's first in the 32-year-old tournament over the Pence de Leon Course. It gave her a leg on the Mrs. William R. Kenan Trophy. It also marked Miss Bell's first decision over Miss McIntire in tournament competition.

"I'm real, real pleased and that puts it mildly," said Miss Bell. "Barbara is a wonderful player and it's always a thrill to beat a good player."

Judy Ends Jinx

It was the first time in four tries that she defeated Miss McIntire, 25, of Lake Park, Fla., also member of the U.S. Curtis Cup team. The two young women are close friends and roommates on the winter tour.

They are ranked as two of the nation's finest women golfers, and this spring will compete in England against Great Britain's best amateurs.

They halved the first five holes, then Miss McIntire went one-up on the 6th when she chipped from about 35 feet for a birdie three, shooting against the wind. She carded a 37, one over men's par, on the first nine holes compared to her opponent's 38.

On the 11th hole, Miss Bell fell short of the green but made a neat recovery for a par. Miss McIntire, who missed four putts of less than five feet, missed a 10-footer for a bogey on the 12th, dropping her two behind.

She staged a brief comeback on the 16th when her tee shot landed on the green and Miss Bell bunkered and conceded the hole.

On the 17th, Miss Bell placed her second shot within four feet of the cup and Miss McIntire fell short and conceded.

At long last, I finally triumphed over my friend, Barbara McIntire, at the 1960 Florida East Coast Women's Tournament. (*Wichita Eagle*)

One of my all-time favorite trips, to St. Andrews in 1979 with good friends (*left to right*): Mary Lena Faulk, Maureen Garrett, me, Joanie Birkland, Tish Preuss and Barbara McIntire. (*Courtesy Judy Bell*)

132

Me, front and center, as Captain of the 1988 Curtis Cup team. Members of the team were (*front row, left to right*): Pat Cornett-Iker, Tracy Kerdyk, me, Cindy Scholefield and Pearl Sinn. (*Back row, left to right*): Carole Semple Thompson, Caroline Keggi, Leslie Shannon and Kathleen McCarthy. (*USGA*)

171 Factory Pond Road
Locust Valley, New York 11560
516: 676-7879

October 10, 1986

Dear Judy,

How splendid that you've been nominated for membership in the USGA Executive Committee! The warmest of congratulations to you.

Of course, the USGA is to be congratulated on having the benefit of your services and your wonderful spirit, in a role never before occupied by a lady.

You'll bring a lot of knowledge to the USGA's policy-making and, after all your golfing experiences, the game will be richer for your presence on the committee.

Mrs. Dey joins me in affectionate regards and good wishes.

Sincerely,
Joe Dey

A congratulatory letter from the late Mr. Joe Dey when I became the first woman nominated and eventually elected to the United States Golf Association Executive Committee in 1987. (*Courtesy Judy Bell*)

With Tiger Woods at the 1992 U.S. Amateur players dinner at Muirfield Village in Dublin, OH. Tiger had just won his second straight U.S. Junior Championship as a 16-year-old. (*Courtesy Judy Bell*)

With Reg Murphy at the 1994 U.S. Women's Open at Crooked Stick, outside Indianapolis, IN. Reg was of immense help in preparing me for what would eventually become a highlight—the Presidency of the USGA. (*USGA*)

A typical tournament day for me—two phones and nobody listening! (*USGA*)

Trying to find papers at the 1996 U.S. Girls Junior Championship in Sioux Falls, SD. There's always much to do at a tournament. (*Courtesy Judy Bell*)

The Next Gen(d)eration: Judy Bell Nominated as USGA President

The USGA put me front and center on the cover of *Golf Journal* as I began my Presidency in 1996, the first ever woman in over 100 years, to attain the highest elected position in the Association. (*USGA*)

Presenting the U.S. Open trophy to Ernie Els in 1997 at Congressional Country Club. Support from the players always made me feel good about my role in the Association. (*USGA*)

Receiving the 1998 Donald Ross Award from the American Society of Golf Course Architects with outgoing President Alice Dye and incoming President Bob Lohmann. (*Courtesy Judy Bell*)

Accepting the Distinguished Service Award for contributions to state and regional golf associations in 1998. Presenting the award was Brett Marshall, also a Kansas native, and friend for many years. (*Courtesy Brett Marshall*)

Chapter 17

["Captain"]

I've been captain of four American teams in international competition. I always make the record book in interesting ways. I followed a Women's Open record 67 with an 83. I was the only American to lose a point in the 1962 Curtis Cup match at my home club.

It also turned out that I'm the only person in the world to captain a Women's World Amateur Team and a World Amateur Team, which is made up of men. That adventure comes up later.

I was named captain of the United States Curtis Cup team in 1986. The match was to be played at Prairie Dunes Country Club, in Hutchinson, so I knew that it would be a special thrill to be back in Kansas and at one of my favorite courses.

Perry Maxwell and Press Maxwell designed Prairie Dunes, a links-style course right in the middle of Kansas, and it had proved to be a great test during the 1964 and 1980 U.S. Women's Amateur. It will also be the site of the 2002 United States Women's Open, which will be a real treat.

In 1986, however, I had a very inexperienced Curtis Cup team. Certainly that team was good enough to win. Golf, however, had changed throughout the world by the mid-1980s. Golf scholarships to American colleges had given many foreign players the opportunity to play here, and in some areas of the country they could play year-round and develop their games. Those opportunities made the bench stronger for the 1986 GB&I team.

None of our 1986 American players had any Curtis Cup experience. The United States had previously dominated Curtis Cup play, so some of our players from the college ranks looked at the match as a sort of ho-hum team event. It's true that we led in the series at that time, 19 wins, two losses, and two ties, but I never could convince my 1986 team that we could lose. One of my players even said to me, "Well, don't we always win this thing?"

The Captain is the team's official spokesperson. She's also the planner, mapping out the day, arranging transportation and meals, and most importantly, deciding which players will play in which slots. When your team members are playing, you're out there cheering them on. It's exciting, of course, but it's a lot of responsibility, too, so you just have to keep mushing on.

My job was also to educate my players about the history and importance of the match, and I certainly tried, but we never got away to a good beginning.

Prairie Dunes, with two par 3s in the first four holes, has a neat start. But in the first 12 matches we were down or all-square through those first four holes. We just got our backs up against the wall early on and couldn't get going. We lost the 1986 Curtis Cup, 13 to 5.

The U.S team consisted of Leslie Shannon, Kathleen McCarthy, Danielle Ammaccapane, Dottie Pepper, Kandi Kessler, Cindy Schreyer, Kim Williams, and Kim Gardner. Strange things happened. In the first foursomes match, for instance, Danielle inadvertently built a stance in the bunker at the third hole. The U.S.A. team lost the hole and it was a very unsettling beginning for Danielle and her partner Dottie. They wound up losing, 2 and 1. In another foursomes match, one of the U.S.A. players played twice in a row instead of alternating shots with her partner. We just weren't as sharp as we needed to be. Lillian Behan and Jill Thornhill of GB&I defeated Kandi and Cindy, 7 and 6. And in the last foursomes match, my old friends Belle Robertson and Mary McKenna of GB&I won on the 18th hole, 1 up, when Belle holed a 40-foot putt. Belle had gained her revenge from when she lost to me in singles in 1960.

We had been blitzed in the first day's foursomes, three to zero.

GB&I edged us out in the singles that first afternoon, 3½ to 2½ and one of the matches went to the 18th hole before we lost it. The score at the end of the day was 6½ to 2½. We had our work cut out for us.

We got drilled again in the foursomes the second day, 2½ to ½. Again we lost one of our matches on the 18th hole. The score was now 9 to 3 with only six points left to play for.

At lunch on the second day, one player asked me, "How many points do we need this afternoon, Captain?"

"All of them!" I replied, a little annoyed that my players weren't all keeping up with the scoring.

In fact, winning all of the afternoon points would have merely given us a tie. But because we were the holders of the cup, we would have held on to it.

Some of our players were stunned by our loss. I wasn't, because I knew this GB&I team was capable and I had a lot of respect for their players and for Diane Bailey, the GB&I captain. Diane Bailey hadn't come over here to finish second, and I knew that because she was the one who had defeated me in a singles match in the 1962 Curtis Cup. She had also captained the 1984 GB&I team when the match was played at Muirfield, in Scotland, and with Tish Preuss as captain, the U.S.A. team had squeaked out a win by a single point.

Diane meant business. Her players were better prepared for Kansas's summer heat than we were because while back at home, they had been hitting balls while wearing rain suits, which simulated the intense Kansas heat. They'd had a trainer while practicing in GB&I and when they came to Kansas they followed the trainer's orders by drinking supplements, and weighing in before and after each round. They were not only better prepared, they played better than we did and deserved to win.

That GB&I team was the first foreign golf team—men, women, professionals, or amateurs—ever to win on American soil. Our players were very disappointed.

In 1988, the Women's Committee decided to give me another chance and I was again selected as U.S.A. Curtis Cup Captain. Diane Bailey was once again GB&I Captain and the match was played at Royal St. George's Golf Club, in Sandwich, England.

We had a very interesting team, including some players who had Curtis Cup experience, so we went over with high hopes. Unfortunately, the weather threw us off balance. During practice it was balmy and sunny with very light winds. The night before the match began, however, the heavens opened up. I awakened in our hotel in the middle of the night to hear the wind howling and rain beating on the building.

When we arrived at the course the next morning, not only was the wind so strong that it was difficult for the players to stand up, but it had shifted to the opposite direction from our practice days. Not that we shouldn't have been able to play in it, believe me, but this time we played the opening holes well but not the home holes. We lost at the 18th hole five times during the match and won only twice.

In the first day's foursomes, Leslie Shannon and Caroline Keggi halved with Jill Thornhill and Vicki Thomas. Their ½ point was our total accumulation for the morning.

In the afternoon, just as in 1986, they edged us, 3½ to 2½. But the real story was in the lead match, Lindy Bayman of GB&I playing against Tracy Kerdyk. Tracy was 1 up playing the 18th hole. It was Lindy Bayman's 40th birthday.

Lindy missed the green with her approach shot hole-high to the left. She faced a chip shot of about 25 yards, through a swale, to an elevated green. Lindy putted the darn thing and holed it! Just moments before, Tracy had hit her approach to within 15 feet of the hole and had looked as if she would have an easy win. Now, they had tied, each winning ½ point for their team.

In the second match, another cliffhanger, Julie Wade of GB&I defeated Cindy Scholefield at the 18th. Both played beautifully. Julie shot 70 and Cindy shot 72.

You can always count on Carol Semple Thompson and in the third game of the afternoon she defeated Susan Shapcott, 1 up. Shirley Lawson of GB&I defeated Pat Cornett-Iker at the 18th hole, 1 up, in the fourth match. Pearl Sinn, who later that year won the U.S. Women's Amateur, had a good win over Karen Davies, 4 and 3. In the bucket seat, Leslie Shannon lost, 3 and 2, to Vicki Thomas, of Wales.

The score at the end of the day was 6 for GB&I and 3 for us.

The second day, the wind shifted again but it was still very blowy. Golf is different in Great Britain in that you must keep the ball low in that kind of weather and we never hit the ball low enough or straight enough. Neither was our putting top-form.

In the morning foursomes we managed to eke out one point in the first game when Tracy Kerdyk and Kathleen Scrivner defeated Lindy Bayman and Julie Wade, 1 up. Our opportunity was with the second game but we couldn't get it done. Karen Davies and Susan Shapcott beat Leslie Shannon and Caroline Keggi, 2 up. Jill Thornhill and Vicki Thomas won easily over Cindy Scholefield and Carol Semple Thompson, so the midday score was GB&I – 8, USA – 4. They needed only two points in the afternoon to win the cup again.

We were once again in that awful position of having to win every point in the afternoon to win the cup back.

Tracy Kerdyk said to me, "Captain, you can count on my point." Tracy was extremely patriotic, and she could play. She kept her word and defeated the British Ladies champion Julie Wade, their lead player, 2 and 1.

In the second game, Susan Shapcott won what was, in my mind, a surprise victory over Caroline Keggi, 3 and 2. To clinch their win, GB&I now needed a single point. It happened in the third game, once again at the 18th hole when Lindy Bayman defeated Pearl Sinn, 1 up.

Although we had already lost the cup again, by tradition the last three games continue to conclusion. Kathleen Scrivner and Carol Semple Thompson each won their matches and Vicki Thomas defeated Pat Cornett-Iker.

Once again we had lost, this time 11 to 7. As in many team matches, it was closer than the score indicates. Had the ball rolled just a bit differently on the 18th hole in several matches, we could have won. It was that close.

Enid Wilson, the great English golf journalist, wrote of that match, "Now our girls have learned to putt."

There's no question that they outputted us. They just putted the eyes out of the hole. We had a good team and, as I said at the presentation, "We loved it all, except for the score."

After the match, the team stayed over to play in the British Ladies Open Amateur at Deal. I caddied in the qualifying for Cindy Scholefield but then had to leave for the U.S. Open at the Country Club in Brookline, Massachusetts.

Certainly, I have a special affection for the players from those 1986 and 1988 teams. They've since looked me up, or I've seen them at the Women's Open and many of them still call me "Captain."

In 1988, by chance, I also became captain of the United States Women's World Amateur Team. Marty Leonard, past Women's Committee Chairman from Fort Worth, Texas, had been selected but couldn't make the trip to Sweden because her mother was very ill.

I'd planned to go to the championship anyway, so I was asked by the Women's Committee to serve as captain. This was very much a last-minute deal and the team had actually been alone in Sweden, without a captain, for three days while we ironed out my transportation and I finally arrived.

We had a wonderful team of Carol Semple Thompson, Anne Sander, and Pearl Sinn, who had won the 1988 U.S. Women's Amateur and U.S.

Women's Amateur Public Links Championship.

In the Women's World Amateur Team Championship, all three players compete each day, but only the best two scores count toward the team's total. Pearl was our batter-in. On the final day, she was our only player remaining on the course when she arrived at the 71st hole, a par 3.

In this competition it's hard to know where your team stands because the scorekeepers at the leader boards have a hard time keeping current. Meanwhile, you have three players on the course for most of the day. It was only my best calculation that we were one stroke ahead of the Swedish team of Helen Alfredsson, Eva Dahllof, and Helene Andersson.

The 71st hole was cut in the front-left portion of the green. Pearl hit her tee shot into the front bunker. The Swedish player, Eva Dahllof, who was outscoring Pearl that day, hit her tee shot about 12 feet from the hole.

I'll never forget what followed. Pearl got in the bunker and waved her arm to move people from behind the green. Was she preparing to blade her shot over the green?

Oh, this *is positive*, I thought.

But Pearl played a good bunker shot, just outside of Eva's ball, and holed the 14-foot putt for a par. Eva missed her birdie putt and we went to the 72nd hole, still one stroke to the good.

Pearl had previously struggled with the par-5 18th, making a triple-bogey eight in the first round. She probably had a little trepidation about playing the hole now with everything on the line. In this championship, players are allowed to ask their captain for advice and as we walked up the steps to the tee, she asked me what club she should use for her drive.

Both sides of the drive zone were lined with bunkers, and another bunker crossed the fairway. It was either a driver or a 3-wood shot, and I told Pearl to hit the driver.

She swung and there was a nice "crack" at impact, but I didn't see where her drive went and asked her.

"I hit it left," she said.

Not only had Pearl hit it left, she had hit it left *of the bunkers*, way over in an area of the rough where none of us had ever walked before. *And* she was next to a tree. Eva had hit a good drive down the middle of the fairway.

I got over to Pearl's ball and told her not to play until I moved all of the people out of the way, because the Swedish spectators were getting pretty excited at the prospect of Eva picking up one or two strokes and tying or winning the championship. I cleared out the crowd. I wanted Pearl to have every chance.

Because of the tree, Pearl had to keep the ball low. She said, "I need my 2-iron."

"Where is it?" I asked.

"In my hotel room," she said.

"Well, what do you want me to do, go get it?" I asked.

With that she pulled out her 5-wood. I sat on my shooting stick nearby. When Pearl took her stance, she played the ball off her left toe, which in my mind would make her hit it high, and we needed a low shot.

Here goes the Women's World Amateur Team Championship, I thought.

But Pearl hit a miraculous golf shot. It started low and climbed. I had my binoculars on it, but I was so excited I didn't follow the ball all the way to its landing.

A bunker stretched across the fairway about 60 yards short of the green. "Did I reach the bunker?" Pearl asked.

"No, you hit a perfect shot," I said, although I actually had no idea whether she was in the bunker or not.

How she stayed out of that bunker, I'll never know, but Pearl had hit it down there in the fairway to right of the bunker. Now we came to her strength, her short game. She hit a nice little pitch onto the green.

Eva, meanwhile, had her problems, beating it down the left side of the hole, and finally hitting a great fifth shot to within three feet of the hole to save a bogey. Pearl two-putted for a par and we won by two strokes over the home team. It was a cliffhanger. GB&I was third, 10 strokes back.

Our team competitions are played in friendly spirit, but these are international contests—country against country—and I always wanted to win for the U.S.A. The Women's World Amateur Team title was great and I was excited by what my team had done. And while the two U.S.A. Curtis Cup losses as captain are not my favorite memory, I loved it all.

Except for the score.

Chapter 18

[Hello, Sir: Joining the Executive Committee]

I finished my term as chairman at the end of 1984 and after 17 years finally made my exit from the Women's Committee. In a way, it was a great relief. I had finished my volunteer service. Now approaching the age of 50, I was going to play competitive amateur golf as a senior.

I'm really going to play some golf and maybe finally win a national championship, I thought, which would have been extremely important to me. I had continued to compete when first named to the Women's Committee, but had never competed since becoming chairman.

So I went off the WC and served on the Advisory Committee of Past Women's Committee Chairmen. I even played in a couple of senior events, but my game had suffered from several years of inaction and I failed to play very well.

Two years later, in the autumn of 1986, I got a call from Bud Semple, chairman of the Nominating Committee and a past USGA president. Our conversation was very brief and to the point.

The committee, he said, would like to nominate me to be on the Executive Committee. They thought I would be a sound addition, and that it was time for a woman to play a role on the XC.

You could have knocked me over with a feather. There had been no preliminary conversation. Their decision was hard to fathom. Not that I held the Executive Committee in such high esteem, but a position on that committee certainly wasn't anything I'd ever thought about. I just accepted the fact that the XC was the men's committee and the WC was the women's committee and I'd been very proud to spend four years as its chairman.

I had definitely wanted us to make the recommendations on anything that had to do with the women's side of the game. I knew that nearly all of our recommendations had to go through the members of the XC, because that was the structure, but I had never thought about being one of them. Not ever.

While some women might have jumped at the chance, I hesitated. I told Bud, "I've got a business to run, and I've got this, and I've got that. I've got to think about it."

Bud told me that he thought I'd be terrific and we hung up.

I talked to my brothers, to my business partner Barbara McIntire, and to the Prunarets. They were unanimous when they said, "You've got to do it. You don't have a choice."

They thought, I believe, that being named to the XC wasn't just an opportunity for me but a big new opportunity for women.

My decision making process went as follows: If I decline it, I'm being selfish and I'll just be saying no because I want to play senior golf. I have to press on and take the job.

After a couple of days, I got back to Bud and said simply, "I'll do it. I accept your nomination."

Bud said he was really pleased and that his wife, Phyllis, was pleased. "I think you'll be a great addition to the Executive Committee," he said.

After the call from Bud, I was nominated in November 1986 and in January 1987 went to Seattle for the USGA Annual Meeting where my nomination would be confirmed by vote. I remember that Bob Ihlanfeldt and Edean Ihlanfeldt, the 1982 USGA Senior Women's Amateur Champion, had a nifty cocktail party for me that week, a really nice occasion. Barbara McIntire, who was on the Women's Committee at the time, and Ellie McColl came but I didn't even invite my family as it was such a long way to travel from Wichita.

I had no idea of what I was getting myself into.

I'd become the only woman who had ever been welcomed to the XC meetings as a member of the group. Because of the support of men, I had broken an old barrier of 93 years, during which the Executive Committee had been an all-male enclave.

In XC meetings in Seattle that week, the men on the committee didn't make any big folderol and I felt very comfortable. I was told that because I had not yet been elected, I had a voice, but no vote, at the first meetings.

I said only three words in those gatherings, which was okay with me as I considered this a learning experience. M.T. Johnson, an XC member from Amarillo, suggested that I be put in charge of looking at the USGA's merchandising effort. I said, "Thanks a lot," which brought a little laughter. In two days of meetings, that's all I said, which was *most* unusual for me and probably the first time in my life I had said so little.

The Women's Committee met with the Executive Committee for about 40 minutes on Friday afternoon. As the WC filed in, each woman said to me, "Hello, Sir. How are you, Sir?" Their levity made everyone laugh.

I love the game so, and I love all of the people involved, so I took to the Executive Committee like a duck takes to water. I was just fascinated with all of the projects that had to be worked on.

Having grown up with brothers helped me when it came to dealing with the USGA's Executive Committee. Within the XC, there could be 15 opinions, but you had to weigh it all and come up with your own. A lot of people would be intimidated by that. But the way I was raised, in a family where everyone had an opinion and everyone's ideas were respected, we eventually worked out our differences.

Some of the more difficult issues faced by the XC during my term included exemptions for the U.S. Open, whether we should have a satellite golf museum in a different part of the country, and the language about junior golfers in the Rules of Amateur Status and Conduct. We also had financial issues, such as the U.S. Open prize money and projected costs of expanding the USGA's administration building and equipment test center.

When people I dealt with in the USGA opposed my way of thinking, I never took it personally. I tried to look at their opposition with Dad's tolerance, which was, "That's just people being people."

In November the XC had a long-range planning session in New Orleans. A study of our merchandising effort was my first big assignment. Chris Johnson, the USGA Director of Merchandising, and I tackled it by analyzing what the USGA was presently doing and found one department selling Rules of Golf books, another department selling something else, and another selling gift items. In fact, the USGA was mailing out 21 different brochures selling publications or memorabilia.

My whole premise in long-range planning was to make people more aware of the USGA's identity through merchandising. I believed that we ought to offer merchandise to people other than those who bought a ticket to the U.S. Open. Anyone who wished to experience the national championships should be able to do so.

I believed we needed just one USGA catalog, which would be mailed a couple of times each year. The XC bought into the idea, but there was always a lot of dissension about it because some XC members didn't think the USGA should be in what they called "the rag or trinket business." I spent the next several years defending a position.

An XC member would say, for instance, "I don't think the USGA should be selling trinkets. What do the professionals at our member clubs think about us competing with them?"

I'd say, "I think that USGA members who want to purchase a U.S. Open ball marker or shirt or hat, ought to be able to do so."

It's not as if USGA members had a choice, because only a certain number of U.S. Open tickets are sold. If you lived in Spokane, you might not be able to go to the Open when it was played at Shinnecock on Long Island. In fact, you may *never* have the opportunity to buy a U.S. Open ticket.

Our merchandising effort was at zero, which didn't bother anyone on the committee because they never thought about it. We could only go up from there. At the time, only one clothing manufacturer was doing a brochure for the USGA. All the available products were printed on a single page and, for what they had going, it was successful. We eventually published a four-color, multipage catalog and we were very careful about our selection of products and the writing. We also offered special pricing for USGA members.

It did very well and is even more of a success today. Both the catalog operation and the merchandise licensing business have greatly expanded into sales of over seven million dollars.

Although I was now a member of the Executive Committee, I stayed in close touch with the women's side of the game. Our 1988 U.S. Women's Open, at the Five Farms course of Baltimore Country Club, went to a new level, thanks to Reg Murphy. It was Reg's home course. Using innovations like a Dixieland Jazz band near the clubhouse, free parking, and tasty food that was reasonably priced, he generated some of the largest galleries in Women's Open history. Reg later said that he called in every favor he was owed in Baltimore to help bring out the crowds and produce the sizeable corporate hospitality effort.

In the final round, there was a hair-raising battle among several key players, and a new star, Liselotte Neumann, of Sweden, emerged to win.

This was not only her first Women's Open victory but her first professional title in the United States.

All of the right ingredients—lots of spectators, a great course, and a good battle in the final round—made me think about having the USGA produce a video of the championship. That may not seem like a big project today when tournament videos flood the market, but in 1988 there were no videos of women's competition.

We'd had a U.S. Open video for many years, but we had never offered a Women's Open video to our USGA members and the public. I just said, "We have one for the U.S. Open, so we should have a video of the Women's Open, too."

John Morris, USGA Director of Communications at the time, was only mildly supportive and pictured the video as something just for the viewing of the WC, although he had always put together the U.S. Open video.

I talked to Katherine Graham, Chairman of the WC, and we decided the project could be done on our own with outside help. We enlisted Rhonda Glenn, coauthor of this book, who had a broadcasting background and a lot of USGA experience as a member of the Women's Mid-Amateur Committee. And we drafted Mary Capouch, a WC member from Mandeville, Louisiana, who served on the ad-hoc Committee for U.S. Women's Open Promotions and had been a magazine editor. I offered to help. It was strictly a volunteer project for all of us but we were determined to get it done. Until then, neither Mary nor I had any production experience. When we finally finished, we felt like experts.

The technical part was more difficult than it should have been. When a network broadcasts a golf event, a videotape of the action, called a "clean feed," is recorded in natural sound. It includes crowd noise and the sounds of the action without the announcers' voices. Clean feeds can then be used to put together a highlight video, complete with all of the natural sounds of a clubhead striking the ball and spectators cheering, with a new announcer's voice over the action.

John said he didn't have a clean feed of the Women's Open. Instead, he sent videos of the television broadcast to us, complete with commercials and the announcers' sound track. For weeks, Rhonda was bogged down in just rerecording the highlights, with no sound at all, then building an appropriate sound track by dubbing in crowd noise and golf sound effects. It was a torturous process and an obstacle that shouldn't have been in our way.

I stopped in Dallas one afternoon to see the early cut. The first five minutes looked beautiful. To avoid paying music royalties, the soundtrack was classical music that, in my mind, included an awful lot of violins. Another problem, I thought, was that Rhonda's script gave away the name of the winner right off the bat.

"There's no suspense here," I said. "You shouldn't let the audience know what happened until the end of the tape."

"But the Women's Open was decided more than two months ago," she said. "Everybody knows who won."

"Let it build," I said, "and get rid of those screeching violins."

I left town and she went back to work. When it came time for the voice and music track and the final edit, Mary and I went to Dallas. We all holed up in the studio early the first morning and, by dinnertime, had only reached the 12th hole of the final round on the video. Mary and I were supposed to leave by 8 P.M. I said I wasn't leaving until we finished this video. Mary agreed, so we stayed and worked through the night.

That's when I got some unneeded hands-on education. Mary and Rhonda drove off to a restaurant to pick up food and left me stranded with a catastrophe. We were producing the segment on the 12th hole. Colleen Walker, a player I liked, had made a big number on the hole and I was in the production hot seat, trying to help the editor put in shots that would show what happened but not go through the entire tortured scoring process. I got production experience, but fast.

We wrapped up the tape with a truly wonderful sequence of film of all past Women's Open champions, with a dramatic piano score.

Although we ran into a lot of roadblocks, we managed to produce a tape of which we could all be proud. It remains the best-selling of the 13 Women's Open videos that the USGA has since produced. The project took nearly two months to complete and although I was juggling a lot of projects and business at the time, the romance of producing the first Women's Open video was right at the front for me.

Chapter 19

[The PING Case]

In really simple terms, the mission of the United States Golf Association is "for golfers, by golfers." It's taking care of the very essence of the game that has been a part of golf since its inception.

In the beginning, golf had only 14 Rules, but you'll see that same spirit in the Rules today. If we didn't have that foundation, those roots in the Rules, the setting of equipment standards, amateur status, and all the rest —then we would have chaos.

The USGA is the governing body of golf in this country. Someone has to set and maintain standards and it is the USGA because other parties might be too self-serving. For example, should the PGA Tour make up the rules of the game its members are playing? Should the LPGA do it? No, I don't think so.

Should each regional and state golf association write the rules? We'd then have all kinds of rules. In Kansas we'd have wind rules, in California we'd have sun rules, and in Seattle we'd have rain rules.

Who, then, should govern the game in this country if not the USGA? The USGA was formed in 1894 to be the caretaker of the game. Its mission is so solid because it's about preserving and protecting this ancient and honorable game. That mission hasn't been touched in more than 100 years, but the way that the USGA accomplishes the mission has changed a lot.

Through the years, the association has had to grow and today it's a lot more complicated in the way that it fulfills the mission. The USGA, for example, is on the information highway and has more linkup with state and regional golf associations—in terms of support and communication level—than ever before.

But almost every responsibility of the USGA has remained the same for many years. The association still conducts the national championships. It still writes the rules. It still works for improved access to the game for all golfers. It remains committed to environmental research. And it continues to protect golf's integrity with the scientific testing of clubs and balls.

The USGA is the honest broker on the street and that's why it should be the governing body. In reality, there aren't a lot of conflicts with the USGA's mission and what it actually does. As I once said in a speech, those of us who are volunteers must never forget that the USGA didn't invent this game. We're just here to look after it.

One of the USGA's key issues in 1987 when I was put on the Executive Committee was the case involving sets of irons manufactured by Karsten Solheim's company, PING.

The USGA's Implements & Ball Committee deals with equipment issues. Right from the get-go, I sat in on the I&B Committee meetings. At the time of the PING issue, I'd been nominated to the XC and was invited to the first meeting, although I had not yet been elected. It was quite an interesting experience because the PING issue was one of the great controversies to face golf's governing body.

PING had manufactured new irons, and the space between the grooves on the clubface was at issue. At that time, most people thought it was the size of the groove itself, but the whole thing boiled down to the space between the grooves. The smaller space between grooves, which PING had incorporated into its new irons, allowed more grooves on the clubface and supposedly more spin on the golf ball.

That first meeting was intriguing. The president of the USGA, Bill Williams, was there, along with the members of the I&B Committee. Karsten Solheim, PING's founder and CEO; Frank Thomas, the USGA's Technical Director; and Frank Hannigan, who was the USGA's Executive Director, also attended.

Frank Hannigan and I got along great and I always thoroughly enjoyed him. He's one of the brightest people I've ever known and has great perspective. For the most part, we pretty much thought alike and, most importantly, Frank was always for the players.

When I became chairman of the Amateur Status Committee, he helped me to understand why a rule was written in a certain way, why we had it in the first place, and what the bottom line was. Frank was very, very good at cutting to the chase.

For the longest time, I talked to Frank on the telephone once a week. The USGA's sale of television rights was one of the few areas in which Frank and I totally disagreed. For many years, USGA championships had been broadcast on ABC and Frank had helped work through that contract. When he retired from the USGA, he went to work as an expert commentator for ABC, so he was very disappointed when the USGA considered another network.

Our Television Committee looked at all of the possibilities and came to the XC recommending that we sign a contract with NBC, ending our long-time relationship with ABC. I certainly asked all of the questions that I wanted to ask and supported that decision. Frank and I disagreed about that, for sure, but I always had the greatest respect for his opinion.

Frank had the unique knack of expressing very complicated subjects in laymen's terms, so he laid out the real issue about the PING irons and made it understandable. When Karsten and Frank Thomas began to draw formulas on a blackboard, however, I looked around the room and saw that nearly everyone's eyes were glazed over. That, at least, made me feel better about my own lack of comprehension of this very complicated subject.

USGA committee people and staff members occupy a position of trust. Revealing what goes on in a committee meeting is something that most of us just will not do. To repeat what people said would gag them in the future. If people fear that what they say in a closed-door meeting will be repeated, they have no true freedom of speech. I've always respected the confidentiality of meetings. And I've always been a person who, if you confide in me and tell me not to tell, I absolutely will not tell. Ever. I'm not that kind of player.

I will say that the USGA people in that meeting left the session unified in their support of the USGA's position.

Once I understood it, I totally supported that position because I believed it was the correct one. The idea of having anything in the game besides a player's skill affecting the result of a shot is disturbing to me.

Our position wasn't a personal vendetta against Karsten, his family, or his company. It was just a difference of opinion on the way that a golf club should be constructed.

The issue went to the courts and finally an agreement was worked out. It was an interesting time. I would estimate that USGA administrators in those years were spending more than 70% of their time on this controversy. This kind of Implements & Ball issue, particularly when it gets into the courts, is not only detrimental to the game itself, but detrimental to the USGA and the way it functions because it's a subject that's all-absorbing.

I&B issues are tough. On one hand there are manufacturers who are entrepreneurial in spirit. They develop products and want to have a better product than the guy next door.

USGA specifications include a tolerance factor but, in my opinion, that's a factor that needs to be reduced because the manufacturing processes and improved technology of most companies are now so good they can work right to the edge, and the tolerance level becomes a plus for them.

So, we have business people who want to build a better mousetrap than their competitors in order to sell more products. At the same time, we have the governing body of the game that wants to see technology handcuffed, to some extent, when it affects the outcome of a golf shot beyond a player's skills.

I don't see this conflict ever going away. I don't see I&B issues ever not being a difficult situation. Obviously, the question has come up as to whether the USGA should be setting equipment standards. Yes, absolutely. It's central to the USGA's mission and exactly what the association ought to be doing.

It's just as important as any rule of golf.

Chapter 20

[Jack, Tiger, and Augusta]

I first served as a rules official at the Masters in 1988. Members of the Executive Committee are traditionally asked to help out as Rules officials at Augusta. I'd been a rules official at the 1987 U.S. Open, but hadn't been able to go to Augusta that year, although I had been invited to serve. It may seem strange to pass up such an opportunity but I still had responsibilities with the business and I was forced to make an unscheduled merchandising trip when the husband of one of our buyers underwent heart surgery. Through the years, I served as a rules official at the Masters nine times.

There's no question that Augusta National is a beautiful test. Watching the tournament on television makes it obvious, but being there is even better. Where else could a spectator put a chair out on the golf course, leave for six hours to walk around, then come back to find their empty chair in the same place? There's no other place like Augusta National.

Beginning in 1934, when Bob Jones and his friend Clifford Roberts initiated their little springtime gathering of friends, this course, often called "the Cathedral in the Pines," inspired some of the most dramatic moments in the game. For 53 years, however, it was an all-male party—male players, and certainly male Rules officials. In 1988, the Masters was about to change because of my role as a rules official.

They're very good to you at Augusta. Rules officials at the Masters always work with another rules official and on my very first day of duty, I worked on the 10th hole with Dow Finsterwald, former PGA champion,

Ryder Cup player, and a buddy of mine for years as Director of Golf at The Broadmoor Golf Club.

I wore a gray skirt and a blazer, along with a "rules official" armband. Dow was stationed at the 10th green. I sat on my shooting stick over to the side of the drive zone and the spectators seemed to stare at me as they walked past. I kept looking around because I couldn't figure out what they were staring at.

After an hour or so, Dow and I switched posts and as we passed I said to him, "I just can't get over this. Everybody is staring at me when they go by. Is my slip showing?"

"No," Dow said.

"What do you think it is?"

"Well, Jude," Dow said, "I don't think they've seen too many women wearing that rules armband."

For the final round, I was assigned to a post at the ninth hole with Jake Carey of Hutchinson, Kansas, who I'd known forever.

We sat on the end of a bleacher row where we could see everything and easily get up and down to make rulings. We were right by an area that the players walked along as they came off the green.

Jake turned to me and said, "Can you believe this, a little boy and a little girl from Kansas sitting here at the Masters *and* working as rules officials?"

It was the icing on the cake.

When Hubert Green walked off the green, he glanced my way and saw my armband. He stopped, pushed his hat back on his forehead and said, "Lordy, Lordy. What *is* the world coming to? A woman referee? My heavens, I never thought I'd live to see that."

The way he said it was funny. Everybody laughed, and I laughed. I didn't think much about it except that it was funny. Anyway, by the final round I'd begun to realize that I wasn't just your everyday, standard Masters Rules Official.

During the competition, two players whom I'd known walked over to acknowledge me—Arnold Palmer and Ben Crenshaw.

After that first year, I wasn't such a standout from the norm.

A couple of years later, I finally had a rules post at the Masters all by myself. I was assigned to the first hole and, of course, everyone knew nothing ever happens on the first hole at Augusta.

The day I was there was cold and blustery. The volunteer marshals on the first hole were all doctors, including Bill and Betty Storms from Colorado Springs. Through them I met the others and with no rulings coming my way, we mostly talked, watched golf, and tried to keep warm. There were no incidents until Jack Nicklaus and Andrew Magee came along, about four groups from the final pairing of the day.

Until then, the only thing I'd had to do was get the green crew to bring a blower to rid the first green of pine needles, which you have to do at times at Augusta. I was sitting behind the green when I was suddenly called to make a ruling in the drive zone. Jack met me as I was halfway down the fairway. He said that Andrew wanted relief for an imbedded ball and that he was not entitled to it.

There's a special rules card given to the players specifying, among other rules, that the players were allowed relief for an imbedded ball through the green. I knew that and had the card out and could plainly see the rule. But I'll tell you something, you're not sure *what* you know when you see Jack's steely blue eyes while he's talking to you in a serious situation.

Jack was adamant about it but I said, "We're playing the embedded ball rule through the green."

I wanted to talk to Andrew because the Rules official's obligation is to talk to the player involved. I told Andrew what he needed to do and read the rule to him, something I'd learned from Mr. Dey, who always said, "Read the rule, if there's any question."

Andrew's caddie said, "We could have looked up the rule. All *she* did was read it." The key word in that sentence, obviously, is "she." But Andrew picked up his ball, dropped it properly, and away they went.

Jack, of course, is a terrific guy and I have tremendous respect for him as a player and as a man. In golf, you run into the same people over the years and we've since had a number of friendly encounters. In 1996, when I became USGA president, one of the first congratulatory letters I received was from Jack.

In 1998, Jack named me a member of the Captain's Club, a committee of friends that help Jack and his charming wife, Barbara, with the Memorial, the outstanding tournament he hosts at his wonderful Muirfield Village Golf Club outside of Dublin, Ohio.

In 2001, I attended a reception given by the PGA of America when I was named a "First Lady of Golf." Two years earlier, Barbara Nicklaus had become the first to receive the honor. Jack kept a low profile at the reception and avoided reporters. "I just came to support you and Barbara," he told me. Knowing Jack and Barbara has been a great pleasure and their friendships are among the many that I treasure in this game.

Another one of the great experiences of Augusta is spending time with and getting to know people from the Royal & Ancient Golf Club of St. Andrews and the members of other allied associations. The R&A works with the USGA to write and uphold the Rules of Golf and the Rules of Amateur Status & Conduct. We also work hard to cooperate on other issues.

When I was chairman of the USGA's Amateur Status & Conduct Committee, a job I loved, Miles Boddington, from England, was chairman of the R&A's Amateur Status & Conduct Committee and had held that post for several years. We were assigned to the same rules post at the Masters one year so we were able to spend a whole day together on the 11th hole. At one point, I said, "Miles, I've been thinking that the Rules of Amateur Status are written too negatively. I think we ought to reorganize them, rewrite them, and make them more about what you *can* do and not about what you're *not allowed* to do."

I had a lot of ideas.

Miles was very wise. He never discouraged me, but said during the course of the day that he'd thought about that a lot, and had attempted a rewrite several times, but it just didn't work out because it was more cumbersome than what we already had. What Miles was saying, in effect, was that maybe this wasn't the thing to be doing and in a nice way he had shed a little light on the matter for me.

It was great to sit out on that wonderful course at Augusta with people from allied associations with which the USGA had relationships. Out there all day on a rules assignment, we'd get to know each other and usually had quiet time to talk. That's the way I felt about being with Miles and, later, with Richard Cole Hamilton when I was USGA president and he was chairman of the R&A's General Committee. It's a really good opportunity for an exchange of ideas.

There's no question, however, that one of the greatest pleasures of a rules assignment is to be able to closely watch the greatest players in the world play one of the most beautiful courses on earth.

While I was USGA president in 1997, I worked as a rules official at Augusta when Tiger Woods made history as the first player of African-American heritage to win the Masters.

I had certainly known Tiger because he had captured three straight United States Junior Amateur Championships and three straight United

States Amateur Championships before turning professional. His last U.S. Amateur victory came in 1996 at Pumpkin Ridge Golf Club in North Plaines, Oregon, when he defeated Steve Scott on the 38th hole. As president, I handed Tiger the Havemeyer Trophy at the presentation ceremony.

Tiger is a pleasant young man, poised, down-to-earth, and seemingly unencumbered by his role as a very great player. He wears the mantle lightly.

I had previously spent some time with him at the 1994 World Amateur Team Championship. Tiger had played on the United States team, and we had chatted over cheeseburgers in Versailles, France, so I knew him a bit.

Before the start of the 1996 U.S. Amateur, Fred Ridley, a member of the Executive Committee, and I had separately invited Tiger to represent the United States on our team in the upcoming World Amateur Team Championship in Manila, the Philippines. Tiger had accepted.

I was therefore surprised and certainly disappointed a few days after he won the Amateur when a press conference was called and Tiger announced he was turning professional.

As his opening remark, Tiger grinned and said, "Hello, world."

Since he had committed to play, I would have been more pleased to hear him say, "Hello, World Amateur Team Championship."

I felt he could have handled the situation gracefully by telling Fred and me that he couldn't commit to a spot on our team. Or, he could have turned us down flat. But he had said he would play, and then backed out.

Tiger's victory in the 1997 Masters, however, was as dramatic as any in golf. A wonderful young talent won a great tournament that African Americans had only been allowed to compete in during the last few decades.

I was happy for him, for the members of Augusta National Golf Club, and especially for the wonderful members of the clubhouse staff who embraced Tiger's victory with such personal pride.

At the end of the final day of play, a Champions Dinner was held in the dining room of the clubhouse at Augusta National. I was already seated when Tiger and his parents entered the room. The entire clubhouse staff, including the kitchen staff, came out into the dining room and congratulated him with a rousing round of applause. Knowing the history of the game, I found it to be a special moment in time.

In golf, the Masters is truly the first rite of spring.

Chapter 21

[A Scare]

The first time I ever set up a Women's Open course alone was at Colonial Country Club in Fort Worth, Texas, in 1991. P.J. had become ill with cancer. The USGA's long-time Senior Director of Rules and Competition, P.J. Boatwright had endured shoulder surgery in the winter of 1990 and just couldn't travel to do setups, so he told me to go on—that I could do it. I told him I didn't want to do it alone. Without our banter, it just wouldn't be as much fun. We lost P.J. in April 1991. That was the first Women's Open course setup in many, many years that didn't have his fingerprints on it.

I remember going to Colonial some 12 times during the year because I was a little nervous about the setup without P.J. David Fay, by now the Executive Director of the USGA, said that with all those trips we ought to have this course right. A Colonial member, Paul Cato, general chairman of the championship and chairman of the club's Green Committee, became a great friend of mine.

My numerous trips to Colonial involved diplomacy as well as technical expertise. Paul was suffering from cancer and while he toughed it out to try to make this a great Women's Open, we kept butting heads with the green superintendent. The superintendent had his own way of doing things and neither Paul, Tim Moraghan, our manager of USGA Championship Operations, nor I could convince him to prepare the course as we directed. We would specify certain mowing patterns for the fairways and rough, I'd leave town, then get a phone call from Paul telling me that the superintendent was disregarding our instructions. Paul became very frustrated. So did I, so I returned to Colonial again and again. Finally, we managed to get through to the superintendent and got the mowing patterns we wanted.

One of the things we tried to do at Colonial continues to be used today. We redefined the mowing pattern on nearly every hole, particularly around the greens where we had the grass cut to fairway height in order to emphasize the chip-and-run as part of the players' examination. It was controversial at that time. I can remember Frank Hannigan, who had ended his term as the USGA's senior executive director two years before but was at Colonial on behalf of ABC Sports, telling me that all I was doing was putting a putter in the player's hands and making it easier. But I always thought it wasn't right to have the players using only one shot around the greens—the wedge from the high rough we used to have—in the national Open, although the wedge shot out of long grass is often more difficult than playing out of a bunker.

For me, variety is the key. The complete player must be able to work the ball. Anyway, it turned out fine. No records were broken, and we got to see a lot of interesting shots.

We lost Paul to cancer just a month after the Women's Open. His family saw to it that Paul's 1991 Women's Open Championship Chairman's badge was buried with him.

When I was chairman of the Championship Committee, and vice president of the USGA in 1995, David Eger, then USGA Director of Rules and Competitions, Tim Moraghan, Director of Championship Operations, and I extended the closely mown areas around Shinnecock Hills on 11 holes for the U.S. Open. Virgil Sherrill, a Shinnecock member, had been U.S. Open chairman in 1986 when the Open had been played at the club. Virgil had a hissy fit about two months before and right through the championship because he feared we'd made it too easy, and if it was such a good idea, why hadn't P.J. done this in 1986? He had a point. But P.J. had virtually invented the long grass around the greens as a signature of the modern U.S. Open. It was his mark.

Despite Virgil's trepidation, our test stood up, with Corey Pavin winning at even par for 72 holes. In the end, Virgil agreed that we had produced a great test.

In my mind, in certain situations, the long grass around the green traps the ball after an approach shot, leaving it closer to the hole, rather than letting the ball end up of its own accord. Today's players also carry a bundle of wedges in their bags that make the shot out of long grass much easier, so our new mowing patterns demand more versatility.

We also changed mowing patterns at Oakmont for the 1994 U.S. Open, at Oakland Hills for the 1996 Open, at The Broadmoor for the 1995 U.S. Women's Open, and at Pine Needles for the 1996 and 2001 U.S. Women's Open. In fact, I'm sure this type of mowing pattern will be used on a few holes at the 2002 U.S. Open at Bethpage State Park and at one of my favorite courses, Prairie Dunes, for the 2002 U.S. Women's Open.

All in all, it has been very successful, because it doesn't produce a cookie-cutter look. It makes the person in charge seriously consider each option on a hole and how it can be played. I have my fingers crossed that the USGA will always continue to look at this option.

In 1991, I was elected treasurer of the USGA, the first woman officer in the history of the association.

I was pleased, of course, but I knew that it absolutely did not mean I was going to move up through the chairs into the top job. I had, in fact, been told by one of the past presidents that this *wasn't* a signal that I was going on to be president. I was told that the purpose of naming me treasurer was to make my experience available for the Management Committee, and the office of treasurer was also reward for all the effort I'd given to the USGA.

Oddly, I was the first treasurer in many years that was not named chairman of the Finance Committee. Since then, I'm happy to say several people have joined me in that position. When Reed Mackenzie and Trey Holland later became treasurer, I made darn sure that neither one became chairman of the Finance Committee because I sure didn't plan to stand alone in that role.

The reluctance of the president of the USGA to make me Finance Committee chairman didn't bother me too much, I suppose. I just joked that they didn't want me to get my hands on all of that money. It certainly didn't hurt my feelings. I have a sense of self worth that comes from my mother. If, for example, you believe that you have the ability to be chairman of the Finance Committee, and you're not chosen, so what? Now, if you think that you aren't good enough, that's another deal.

Because of my business acumen and ability to run a small business, I think I was helpful on the Management Committee. That's because the USGA is more like a niche business, such as A Short Story, than a big corporation, such as General Motors. The USGA is a big business, in a way, but it's also unique in that it's like a specialty operation, just the type of businesses I'd been involved in.

I served as treasurer for one year. Then, in 1992, I began to ascend the USGA ladder when a past USGA president said, "I want you to move up to secretary. I'm asking you."

Once again, I was elected. As the only woman on the committee, secretary, of course, was the perfect role for me. They all thought of me as "the secretary," and they'd say, "She is the secretary. Judy Bell, secretary of the USGA." Their comfort with me in my new role amused me.

When I'd previously been introduced as treasurer, it had made some men uncomfortable, and it seemed to me that they'd sort of wince when they heard, "treasurer." It was as if they were thinking, *You mean we're letting that woman get her hands on all the money?*

When I became secretary, a higher office, they were all comfortable with me in that role, perhaps because it has a historically feminine connotation.

I had a lot of, shall I say, *interesting* experiences along the way. From 1988 through 1992, I was chairman of the Handicap Committee and served on the Handicap Procedure Committee. The Handicap Procedure Committee always tried to have a meeting at the U.S. Open site for the following year. Our 1989 meeting was set for Medinah Country Club in Medinah, Illinois, where we would also play golf. A few days before the meeting, I got a telephone call from P.J. who told me he wanted to move the meeting to the Chicago Golf Club.

He explained to me that only on one appointed day per year would Medinah allow women to play their Number 3 course, where the U.S. Open was to be held, and he was very adamant that we change the venue of the meeting.

"No, I'm not going to be able to come until that evening, anyway," I said, "so let's keep it at Medinah Number 3."

I didn't want our committee members to miss the opportunity to play the course where the U.S. Open was going to be conducted. As much as I love the Chicago Golf Club, this was an easier way to handle it.

The day chosen for golf turned out to be freezing cold. I'm not sure how much the committee members enjoyed the round, but I got there at five o'clock, went to the meeting, and we didn't miss a beat.

As everyone knows, discrimination does exist. Ever since the USGA was founded, the Executive Committee has traditionally hosted what is called "The Links Club" dinner during the week of the USGA Annual

Meeting. It's always held at a private club, and many of those clubs are traditionally male oriented. While I was on the XC, some clubs made an exception to their "men only" rule, or the USGA staff joggled around to find different sites that permitted women. David Fay always managed to find a place.

I didn't feel discrimination as much as I could have, because of the way the other members of the XC treated me. I didn't feel any of that.

In 1991, I was asked to go to the White House with the United States Walker Cup team to meet President George H.W. Bush. The president's grandfather, George Herbert Walker, was USGA president in 1920 and had started the Walker Cup matches. The president's father, Prescott Bush, had been USGA president in 1935, so he had some very close ties to the USGA.

Reg Murphy had made the arrangements and was also attending. I was asked at the last minute and I've always thought it was because they felt they needed to have a woman on hand, but I was thrilled to have the chance to meet the president under any circumstances.

As always, I was rushed in my packing and barely got to the Colorado Springs airport in time for the flight. I have quite a reputation of missing flights, probably because I seem to put off packing until the last minute. In my heart, I hate to leave home. Before boarding my plane, I suddenly realized I'd forgotten to bring earrings, so I called a friend who lived near Dallas-Fort Worth Airport.

"I'm on my way to the White House and I forgot to bring my earrings," I said. "I'll be changing planes in Dallas. Can you bring a pair of earrings to me at DFW?"

I knew that she had several nice pairs of gold earrings, which would have been perfect. Like nearly all of my friends, however, she knew that I often misplace jewelry, purses, briefcases, and nearly anything that's in my possession while traveling.

When I got to the gate at DFW, she was there. She handed me two pair of earrings. One pair was white plastic; the other pair was a small, conservative set, but certainly not made of gold.

"I won't wear the white pair and this other pair will make my ears turn green," I protested.

"I certainly wasn't going to give you a pair of mine and have you lose them," she said. "I bought these at the supermarket a few minutes ago. Wear the second pair. No one will know they're not real. Just remember, Barbara Bush wears fake pearls. She'll probably love to see you in these."

I tossed the earrings in my briefcase and off I flew.

When I arrived at the White House, the team had already arrived. I went to the security gate to check in. While the guard looked for my name on his list, a number of tourists approached me and asked me for directions, probably because, in my navy blue blazer and USGA blazer patch, I closely resembled a National Park Service guide.

I finally got in and hooked up with the team. President Bush led us to a small putting green on the grounds. There were some balls there and a couple of clubs, and he asked the team members to hit some chip shots. When they finished, they asked him to hit a few.

They were all hitting from a terrible place, a downhill lie in gnarly, rough grass, and I'm afraid the president didn't have much luck, shanking some of his attempts. But he was a great sport, and his friendly charm put us all at ease.

I had a wonderful visit in Washington, another highlight of which was lunch with Nancy Kassebaum, the Republican United States Senator from Kansas and a close friend of my brother Carl and my sister-in-law Gwen.

I brought back several small mementos from the White House. Today those mementos, and the earrings, are in a box in my dresser drawer.

In February 1993, I checked into the hospital for minor foot surgery. The anesthesiologist came in and asked when I'd last had a heart attack. I sat straight up on the gurney and informed him I had never had a heart attack. He said my EKG was abnormal, and he would not give me an anesthetic that morning.

It was a misread by the anesthesiologist. When my friend and doctor, John Hays, read the EKG, it was similar to others he had taken, which meant it was normal. One thing, however, led to another and my friends Ann Beard, Joanie Birkland, and Barbara McIntire kept on me about going to a cardiologist. Just to shut them up, I finally made an appointment with Dr. Buzz Sellers.

I checked out perfectly on an echocardiogram, but had problems with the stress echo test. The angiogram showed a blockage in the left ventricle, which called for surgery. Believe me, I struggled with the idea of having gone to the hospital to get my foot fixed and ending up with a heart bypass.

In March 1993, I decided to go ahead with the heart bypass. There wasn't much choice. My family had a history of heart disease. First Mother, then my brother Jack. Jack had died of a heart attack in 1991 at the age of 65.

I loved Jack. Of all three of my brothers, Jack had been the one I'd grown up with most closely. During the war, he had been at home because he couldn't get in the service. Here was this big, strapping guy who had played right tackle in high school football and again at the University of Wichita and he had flat feet, so the Army wouldn't take him.

Jack had a very dry sense of humor and loved to kid people. He was a great teaser about any sports I played, in particular when I got beat in a golf match. He was also a golf devotee and played nearly every day of his life, which isn't easy to do in Kansas.

I went to Wichita for the funeral. Now, it was just Carl, Fred, and me. I couldn't help but think that Mother and Dad would have been proud of how their children had turned out. All of us had strong work ethics and strong family ties. Carl had become a successful lawyer and was giving a lot of his time and effort to his community by serving on the Wichita City Commission and eventually serving as mayor. He helped get the Urban League of Wichita organized, on a pro bono basis. He was active in his church, after he had once considered becoming a minister as a young man.

Fred was a hero. He had served in the 104th Infantry Division, "the Timberwolves," of the VII Corps in Europe during World War II. His division was decimated by the Nazis shortly before the Battle of the Bulge. So few of his buddies remained alive that the 104th wasn't even large enough to send into the battle, but fought on the perimeter about five miles away. With his machine gun, Fred had cleared the way for American riflemen to eliminate a Nazi machine gun nest, for which he was awarded the Bronze Star. After the war, he came home and attended the University of Wichita while working at Dad's store. He was a solid member of the community and a great family man.

Carl's wife, Gwen, Fred's wife, Sally, and Jack's wife, Ruth, were like sisters to me. I had no say in choosing my sisters-in-law, but I've always thought my brothers made great picks. We'd never had any divorces.

Jack's funeral was a sad time for us and we would miss Jack. I still miss him today. We are blessed to have these people and to share our lives with them, but as it says in Ecclesiastes, "There's a time to be born and a time to die." Death is part of the plan. If I went around with my head down every time I lost someone, I'd be in mourning a lot of the time. That's no way to live. I believed we would all be together again anyway.

My heart bypass was serious stuff but I had no fear of meeting the Man Upstairs. I was older now and, at that point, had a lot more friends and family members "Up There" than I had down here.

I believed I was more likely to die from the anesthesia than from the surgery itself. I wrote an addendum to my will and checked into the hospital. My family and several friends were all there for the surgery.

It went well. In the recovery room, I opened my eyes to see Barbara McIntire, Tish Preuss, Ellie McColl, Bill Giesenhagen, Helen Kirkland, and my brothers and their families standing in a circle around my bed with big smiles on their faces. It was a nice way to wake up.

Cards, letters, funny gifts, and flower arrangements kept coming to the hospital and we finally just started having the flowers delivered to the children's ward.

Now I had to recover.

My house on El Encanto Street was next door to Barbara's house. After the workday was over, we had almost always eaten dinner there with a group of friends, Tish, Ellie, Paula Petrie, Helen, Mary Lena Faulk, Dow and Linda Finsterwald, whoever was in the neighborhood. During my recovery, Barbara and Tish pretty much moved in to look after me and friends continued to drop by.

Tish and Barbara never invited anyone to dinner, but I'd get on the telephone and invite everyone over. After a nap, I'd come out of my bedroom to have dinner, never really knowing who was going to eat with us.

During the day, my assistant, Susan Collazo, and our accountant, Dolly Wong, brought in my piles of paperwork and I'd press on, trying to keep up with business from my home.

I was fairly stoic about my health, which comes from my mother's example. Mother never, ever talked about her health unless someone asked her, then she was matter-of-fact about it. She wouldn't skirt it, nor was she one to deny that she'd had a heart attack. But she didn't dwell on it.

During my recovery, my big, sweet yellow Labrador retriever, "Bear," was the latest in a long line of dogs in my life. Barbara's yellow Lab, "Glenna," was Bear's sister, named after the great amateur Glenna Collett Vare. Bear and Glenna seemed to instinctively know that I wasn't well. They stayed by my side and were great company.

A strict diet and exercise were imperative, so I swam in a heated pool and took walks on a regular schedule. We lived near The Broadmoor Hotel and that winter I seemed to have more appreciation for the beauty of the neighborhood than ever before, with the snow and the bare, towering trees outlined against the sky.

A sequence of classes started right after I got out of the hospital and Barbara dragged me to each one. I wanted to go, so I went to a nutritionist, an exercise class, in fact the whole medley of instructive classes. My recovery called for cardiac rehab and seminars about heart disease, including a stress management class with several other heart patients.

One day the instructor told us to think of the one word we associated with the word "stress."

I was the only one to yell out, "Opportunity!"

Chapter 22

[Eight-sided Boxes]

As volunteers for the United States Golf Association, Women's Committee members probably spend $10,000-15,000 each year of their own money on USGA expenses. Executive Committee members spend perhaps $25,000 a year, simply because they take more trips and attend more meetings.

When I first went on the XC, I didn't spend that much. Some years, I spent more. When I was making so many trips as president, some of my expenses were reimbursed, just as they had been for other presidents.

My Women's Committee work, from 1968 through 1984, lasted almost 17 years. As a member of the XC for 11 years, I was certainly committed financially. Now, if I told you that you were going to spend this amount of money for 28 years as a USGA volunteer, most people wouldn't sign up for that army.

There were several times along the way when I was going to get out of the USGA. The longer I volunteered, however, the more involved I obviously became. More than that, I just love the game. I'm passionate about the game of golf, which has given me so much sheer joy and pleasure that I have always wanted to give something back to it. Without question that's really what my volunteer efforts have been about.

As I became involved in various USGA programs, I wanted to see them through, so I thought, *I'll stay on a couple of more years.* I really loved my committee work and when I was on the WC and chairman, I got tremendous enjoyment out of seeing that committee's role grow.

Working well within committees isn't much different than running a business. I believe that certain concepts lead to success in both: educate yourself and your group; invite ideas; know what's right, and wrong; listen to your head and heart; lobby to build a consensus; be open to opinions; invite feedback from people you respect; be secure about your strengths; and, don't ever worry about who receives the credit for success.

Committee people have to know the subject, what the sides are, and all of the background. They also must know that their participation and ideas are welcome. That's one of the real keys to working with volunteers.

It's much the same as running a business. In our business, I wanted our employees to be very, very knowledgeable about what they were trying to sell. Education is the key.

I've had a jillion ideas that I've never pursued because somehow a monkey wrench would get thrown into them. But it's never good to jump into something that doesn't wear well and I don't think you can do anything without studying and having as much knowledge as you can possibly have.

A number of things kept me going in business and in the USGA, even if they came about in the process of making some mistakes. Emotion, my mind, what I believe to be right and what I believe to be wrong, all of those help me to decide whether to pursue or drop a project. You've got to get inside yourself to find out what motivates you.

At times, I've reached a conclusion that, in the whole scheme of things, a project is no longer worth the effort. So, I dropped it. Just a few years ago, we found some space in a new shopping center on the northeast side of Colorado Springs. We wanted to put in a kitchen shop, incorporating all of the accessories people need for their homes, as well as stocking blooming plants. After much research, we decided that the rent was too high, particularly for a concept that had no track record.

Then, there are times when I should drop an idea, but don't. Once I commit, I simply have too much of my mother's stick-to-it trait. I'll shake the tree, I'll do everything possible to see a project succeed. For example, I probably had no business getting into the grocery and meat business in Colorado Springs in the late 1970s, but that was an emotional decision because that was the business I came from. I believe this because the food business is tough. Many of the products are perishable and, often, you wind up being on the manufacturing side of the business as well as in sales.

We finally sold the food business in 2001, but not without a great loss of money and a lot of wear and tear on me. At the time of the sale, no one could have paid me enough for that business to give me all that I'd invested in dollars and hard work. But that's okay, because I got my "education," as my dad used to say.

In the early 1990s, Lyda Hill, who owned a visitor's center at the Garden of the Gods, near Colorado Springs, invited us to upgrade the food concession and begin a catering service. We tried everything to make it work. We redesigned the food operation and restaurant and offered a totally new menu, running the operation like a bistro. We were working nearly around the clock to put the operation in service by the opening day of the visitor's center. We offered an array of homemade desserts, soups, and fresh made-to-order sandwiches.

Some days we'd have a nice crowd, other days would be a famine. We had a hard time setting a schedule of staffing for the lunch service, consequently if we guessed wrong and put too many staff members in the restaurant on a slow day, our costs didn't relate to the sales.

We served breakfast, lunch, and dinner. While the catering had potential, a lot of supplies such as tables and chairs had to be provided for each client who had us cater their private party. This ended up, again, hurting the bottom line. On the positive side, the restaurant had the greatest view in Colorado.

We had two really spectacular days. Each year, on Mother's Day and Easter, we had special brunches. Advertising helped draw large crowds and we took reservations. We'd be sold out for many of the seatings just after we announced them. We tried hard to have a big array of choices and still keep the meal price down so we offered a quality meal at an affordable price.

Bill Robb, a friend who had retired after 20 years as maître d' at The Broadmoor Hotel, volunteered to do our seating on Mother's Day. He was a pro, but I'm afraid the rest of his staff—including me—didn't know what to do with a huge crowd. We had more than 400 reservations and could seat 100 at any one time, so we had four seatings. The problem this day was that people didn't show up on time. Many, who had arrived late, hadn't finished their meal when many more would show up early for the next seating.

We finally got through the fourth seating, then had to begin to clean up and get ready for a regular visitors center day on Monday and transport the frozen food to our walk-in cooler. The first Mother's Day, I took the last load of breakfast pork chops to the cooler at 2 A.M. It was an exhausting business for all of us. And in the end, we just couldn't make it work. The landlord wanted a larger percentage of our profits and the numbers just weren't there. There just weren't enough people interested in coming out to that visitor's center to eat lunch, even with the spectacular view. I learned that I needed to be more sure of a location and more sure of traffic patterns, or there was no way to make such an enterprise work.

In other investments, I had better experiences.

Just after the clothing business became successful, my accountant told me to buy either real estate or oil interests. I decided to buy some oil interests with some good friends in Kansas. Our first well hit, the next one hit, and the next one hit.

It was only after the third oil well hit that I told Dad. Dad lived with me in Colorado in the summer and at breakfast one morning, I was just so full of myself that I blurted out, "Dad! I've invested in three different oil deals. And guess what, we've hit every one of them."

Dad never looked up from his newspaper. Nothing. He just turned a page and said, "You'll get your education."

He meant it in a general sense, and he was right. In those oil deals I actually made some money, although we had a few dry holes, but I got my education later in the food business.

Not long ago, someone asked me about my adventure in that business and whether I'd had previous experience.

"Well, yes," I said. "I worked in my dad's grocery store when I was a little kid and grew up in the business before I started my own.

"And," I said, "I have about a $200,000 education in it, too."

Besides "education," I operate within a committee by consensus. A long time ago, my father told me, "You've got to be able to count. If there are 16 people involved, you'd better have nine votes if you're trying to get something done."

It's that simple. Certainly you don't always have the votes. If you talk to a few committee members and find that your idea is dead in the water, then there's no reason to take your idea in for a vote.

It takes work to build a consensus and there's a huge difference between how men and women work to build one. Women conduct more business in the meeting room. Men conduct more business in the hallways or on the golf course.

In 1997, my last year as USGA president, we conducted meetings at the U.S. Open at Congressional Country Club. We had come to a very big discussion point. We were about to make a decision about an implement and ball matter, but this wasn't going to be a patsy deal that could be pushed through and there were obvious differences of opinion. I thought it would be a good time to take a break.

At that time, my friend Carol Semple Thompson, a great champion and the daughter of Bud and Phyllis Semple, had become the second woman elected to the Executive Committee. After a short break, Carol and I came back into the meeting room. We sat there and sat there, but the men on the Committee didn't return. So I walked down to the men's rest room, pounded on the door, and yelled, "Either you come out, or Carol and I are coming in."

The men weren't trying to exclude us. I don't believe they'd thought of that. They were all down there trying to figure out what to do. That's just the way guys do business. They work the halls or the rest room, and there's nothing wrong with it. Anyway, one by one they came back into the meeting room.

I seldom felt excluded because I'm a woman.

Although I didn't go into the men's rest room, if I was out in the halls and saw three guys talking, and if I were interested in their opinion, I'd just get involved in their conversation. I never felt as if I was intruding or needed to find out what they were saying. I just felt comfortable with the men on the XC. If I didn't understand something, I didn't hesitate to say, "I don't understand what you're talking about."

At the same time, it never bothered me to express a differing opinion, particularly one-on-one, which is the best way. If I didn't agree with someone and we were on a committee, I would never stand up and carry on in front of the entire committee. I talked it out one-on-one. I'd try to understand the opposing viewpoint and give them a shot at mine.

I've always sought a lot of input from people I respect. My mother used to say it was because I couldn't make a decision.

"If you give Judy a four-sided box, she's going to see six or eight sides," Mother said. "She's just that way. She just can't commit and get off the dime."

What I like to do is to get all of the feedback in the world, then make up my mind. If I were going to start a new business, I'd get a lot of feedback from people I respect. I may, however, open the business even if everyone I consulted said no. I believe we must reach our own conclusions.

When I ended up taking over the Men's Shop at The Broadmoor, I couldn't get anyone—including my brothers, my father, or my closest friends—to go in it with me. They all told me I was foolish.

I said to Dad, "If I don't do this, the shop owes money and I'm going to lose $30,000."

He said, "What are you going to do, wait until you lose $100,000?"

I did it anyway and, luckily, it was a success.

So, it's not necessarily that I poll people and if six out of ten give me one opinion, that's the way I'll go. Getting different viewpoints from people that I respect is just part of my thought process—in business or at the USGA.

Chapter 23

[Old Friends]

In the 1980s and '90s, I was involved in the care of the woman I had called my best friend since I was ten years old.

Ella Engle was born in Pennsylvania in 1896 and in 1916 came to Colorado Springs, where she worked at the Printers Home and lived in the YWCA.

By 1946 she was in the catering business and also working in the women's locker room at The Broadmoor Golf Club. When my parents joined the golf club, Mrs. Engle and I just hit it off.

She was a quiet, demure little person and a hard worker. She was a real lady, but also had a delightful sense of humor. Since there were so few children at the golf club, I'd practice for a while, or play a few holes with my parents, then, by choice, have lunch with Mrs. Engle in the locker room.

Although she was 40 years older than I was, we remained great pals through the years. She showed me genuine affection, and when she bought a little dog, she named it "Judy Bell."

When Barbara and I opened our shops at the hotel, we shared our plans with her. "Oh my," she said years later, "I can remember when all you could talk about were the new shops."

Mrs. Engle's husband, Frank, worked for Railway Express. After he died, she continued to live in her little house in town. Although she had a son who lived on the East Coast, he seldom visited and seemed to have very little communication with his mother.

I tried to visit her frequently but as she neared the age of 90, I could see that she was having trouble managing herself. We began bringing her pack-ages of precooked food and we always brought her to my house or Barbara's for Christmas, Thanksgiving, and Easter. I'd drop by her house every few days to see how she was getting along.

When it became clear that she was no longer strong enough to handle paying her own bills, I called her son and told him of the problem. Rather than offer to help, he drafted me to do it. So, we began paying Mrs. Engle's bills out of our business office. We hired people to tend her yard and her house and as the years went by I hired people to stay with her so that she wouldn't have to move into a retirement home. Friends such as Jane Hecox, Barbara, and Tish helped care for her when she was ill.

In the late 1980s, Mrs. Engle began to think about "passing on," and asked me to help her set her affairs in order. Together we visited a funeral home she had selected and we walked from room to room, looking at cas-kets. I tried to keep the experience light. "Why, look at this one, Mrs. Engle," I said. "It has some cute little flowers painted on the top and a nice soft satin cushion. You'll be very comfortable."

She'd just laugh and say, "Oh, Judy. Stop it."

We celebrated Mrs. Engle's 94th birthday on April 5, 1990. She died in 1994 at the age of 98. I suppose she was a grandmotherly figure in my life but she was just a lovely person to spend time with and her grace and dig-nity made a lasting impression on me.

Another dear friend was Mary Lena Faulk, the 1953 U.S. Women's Amateur Champion who was a fine professional and a truly great teacher.

When Mary Lena retired from competing on the LPGA tour, she gave golf lessons in Palm Beach during the winter, and in the summer at Allegheny Country Club in Pennsylvania and later at Westchester Country Club in New York. I took a lesson from her at Westchester when the Curtis Cup was played at nearby Apawamis in 1978. I knew The Broadmoor was looking for a woman teaching professional, so I told Dow Finsterwald, the director of golf, about Mary Lena. He offered her a job in 1979.

She rented a small house for a few years then stayed with me in the summer. We called her "M.L." and I knew she was on her way to Colorado Springs when big cardboard cartons of clothes and possessions began arriving in the mail.

M.L. was a gentle soul with a wide range of interests. Art, music and gardening fascinated her. She loved people and was always a good dinner guest because she could discuss a variety of subjects.

In midsummer, when I chaired The Broadmoor Ladies Invitation, we housed the younger contestants who couldn't always afford rooms at the hotel. M.L. became a sort of unofficial tournament instructor and would stroll up and down the practice tee at The Broadmoor, offering help to contestants who were suffering with wayward swings. She had studied under Harvey Penick and was a very fine teacher, helping Barbara McIntire, Tish Preuss, and me on any number of occasions through the years.

In September of 1979, M.L. and I took a trip with Barbara, Tish, and Joanie Birkland to Scotland. We hooked up with Maureen Garrett and other past Curtis Cup players during our travels. While there, we played Dornoch, the home course of the great golf architect Donald Ross. Ross always maintained that Dornoch influenced his designs in America. Since the course has become more famous, there's a widely held theory among dedicated golfers that "all roads lead to Dornoch."

When we played this special course, which is now Royal Dornoch, a cold wind howled around us and it rained in blustery gusts most of the day. But we pulled our trolleys and golf bags up and down the craggy slopes, marveling at the design.

When we finally finished, the golf professional said, "Sorry, Miss, that you weren't able to play the whole course."

"Are you kidding?" I said. "We played the whole course, and this was the greatest day of golf I've *ever* had."

One night at dinner with Mary Lena, Barbara, Tish, and some other golfers, we discussed sportsmanship. A question arose about whom we had each most looked up to as a great sport. One of our guests, a somewhat younger amateur, said that she had always looked up to Barbara as a gracious player. She asked Barbara who she had looked up to, and Barbara replied, "Mary Lena and Peggy Kirk Bell." When Mary Lena was asked whose sportsmanship she admired, she said, "Glenna Collett Vare."

In that moment, we had a tie from generation to generation, back to some of the earliest days of American women's golf.

Like any number of us, M.L. enjoyed having a drink, but she also smoked heavily and in the early 1980s was diagnosed with lung cancer. Her situation was more precarious because she had no health insurance. We persuaded one of the golf magazines to carry a small blurb on a fund I had started to pay her medical expenses. Before long, a number of generous people from all over the country, and several from Great Britain, had contributed enough to pay M.L.'s medical bills.

She recovered and resumed teaching at The Broadmoor two summers later, but it was always a battle trying to keep her from smoking.

In the mid-1990s her lung cancer reoccurred and, this time, there was no stopping it. Mary Lena died in Florida in 1995, shortly before the reunion of past champions at the 100th anniversary of the U.S. Women's Amateur Championship.

I had lost a gentle, gracious friend and another delightful companion.

Chapter 24

[A Big Birthday Bash]

The 50th anniversary edition of the United States Women's Open Championship was played in 1995 at my home course, The Broadmoor Golf Club. It was a dream come true.

For women, today's U.S. Women's Open is the Masters, the British Open, and the U.S. Open all rolled into one. We've made a great effort to get terrific venues and we have such an international field that it has to be the finest women's championship in the world.

The 1995 Women's Open was exciting to me personally because I'd played the course since I was 11 years old. Memories of that original course have been with me in all of the intervening years, and I often think of its subtleties and beauty when I'm seeking peace of mind.

By 1995 the original Donald Ross design, which was wonderful, had changed a bit. I knew that old course as well as the back of my hand and was asked to contribute my thoughts on how the course should be set up for the Women's Open.

Our idea was to try to restore some of the subtleties of the original holes because it was impossible to restore the original course as the hole sequence had been changed. Chuck Clark, The Broadmoor's Director of Golf Courses, and I took out all of the existing mowing patterns, widened the areas around the green, and widened the fairways. Then we brought them back, allowing new rough to outline the shapes of the greens and fairways.

We expanded the size of some greens, creating additional hole locations on a few greens which had become smaller over the years. When I was young the course had demanded a lot of running shots, so we tried to create new areas that would call for those types of shots.

We let the rough grow higher around the greens, cleaned up the green surrounds, widened the entrances, and brought the fairways in slightly to make them more narrow.

The holes had been rerouted somewhat over the years, so our major change was to use Ross's original home holes for the final three holes of the championship. Those same finishing holes have been used ever since.

Barbara McIntire and I were co-vice-chairmen and Karl Eitel was general chairman. Karl was perfect for that job. He had been director of the Colorado Springs Chamber of Commerce and had served on the board of the Colorado Golf Association. He was the person who was really responsible for bringing the Women's Open to The Broadmoor.

He was also a great personal friend of mine, and a great advisor. Karl became manager of the hotel shortly after we opened our first shop in 1962, so he was also our landlord for many years and a very good friend, both personally and business-wise. I got a sound education from Karl and played a lot of golf with him. He was one of the finest individuals I've ever known and it was a pleasure to work with him on the Women's Open.

Several months before the Women's Open was scheduled to begin, I received an invitation from Greg Jones, who headed the Association of Disabled American Golfers. Greg asked me to come to Denver to present prizes at his association's annual golf tournament.

I arrived to find an amazing group of golfers. All of them had disabilities, some of which made it difficult to move around, but they all played golf that day using specialized equipment and golf carts to help them get around the course. It's inspiring to think of how disabled golfers have to work hard to get around a golf course, a task that to us seems so simple.

I attended their reception before a dinner and it was just like any other reception before a golf awards dinner. The only difference was that these participants were all sitting down.

At their trophy presentation, I made a short speech. I told the contestants how honored I was to be in their presence, and congratulated them on behalf of the USGA. I ended by telling them of Bob Jones's return to St. Andrews, Scotland, when he was made an Honorary Burgess of the Borough, the first American so honored since Benjamin Franklin. Younger Hall, where the ceremony took place was packed. Jones made a wonderful speech. Now totally disabled, Jones had left the ceremony, riding down the center aisle in an electric golf cart as the whole hall suddenly burst into the old Scottish song, "Will Ye No' Come Back Again?"

"I know that if Bob Jones had been here," I said, "he would have been extremely proud of you and your efforts to play the game."

When I handed out the prizes, one of the winners was seated near the very back of the room. He struggled on crutches with arm braces to make his way to the front. I whispered to Greg that perhaps I should meet the man halfway down the aisle.

"No," said Greg. "Let him come."

We waited. Haltingly, the man made his way to the presentation area, smiling with pride when I gave him his trophy.

At the end of the evening, there was a drawing for door prizes. I apologized for not thinking to bring U.S. Women's Open tickets for the drawing.

"What we would really like to do is marshal a hole at the Women's Open," Greg said.

I never blinked. I said, "Okay, let's work this out."

I called USGA President Reg Murphy and told him of my conversation and asked him how to get this done. He said, "Just do it."

So I invited Greg down to The Broadmoor to select a hole. We had a few suggestions and then Greg discovered the 16th.

The 16th hole at The Broadmoor is a par 3 that runs along an access road. I told Greg that if he could get his marshals to the championship site, we could figure out a way for them to park near the 16th. They could marshal from the tee through the green, and have the added advantage of a nearby snack bar and rest room. We were able to make that happen and for the first time individuals with disabilities marshaled a hole at a national championship.

That same evening in Denver, Greg talked to me about scooters, which are single-rider carts, at the Women's Open. In the past, individuals with disabilities had been limited to watching from one site set up for their wheelchairs. They were never able to move around on the course.

We agreed to offer 20 single-rider carts for individuals who couldn't walk. For instance, Nancy Lopez's dad was once again able to follow her, hole by hole, on the scooter. These single-riders were first at the Women's Open in 1995, and now are offered at every USGA national championship.

The Women's Open and all of the amateur championships are always going to be an *artistic* success. The reason is because the USGA knows how to run a great-looking championship, set up the test, and define the best player of the week. That they do very well.

But it always seemed to me that one of the keys to conducting a great championship is to get people to come out to watch. That's what is so much fun about the amateur championships, because there are not a lot of ropes out on the golf course to keep spectators away from the action. I think, for example, that when three-to-four thousand people watched the final match of the 2001 Women's Amateur at Flint Hills National Golf Club in Andover, Kansas, it was great that they could walk with the players right out in the fairways. It's pleasant walking and, unlike watching a championship on television, you really feel as if you're part of the game.

My whole premise for the Women's Open was that we needed to get people to come, and try to have a sell-out. In fact, I once attended the Final Four of women's college basketball, in Charlotte, North Carolina, just because I wanted to see a women's sporting event that was sold out. Whether it's an event for men, women, or donkeys, any sell-out has a certain frenzy and excitement. If it's sold out, it's sold out.

In 1990, I had a USGA brainstorming session with Karen Moraghan, Kendra Graham, Betse Hamilton, and a few others on ways to attract more spectators to the Women's Open. One of the things we came up with was a program called "Kids Get a Front-Row Seat," in which we would admit children to the Women's Open, free of charge, if accompanied by an adult, and provide special seats in the bleachers for them.

In 1991, Ann Beard and I (she was chairman of the WC at the time) tried to arrange for children to get in free at the Women's Open at Colonial in Fort Worth. We couldn't do it because the club had already sold some tickets, and several members of the local committee thought free admission for juniors was prejudicial against seniors. We did manage to start the U.S. Women's Open Junior Golf Club at Colonial. A tent was set up where children were given a chit for a hot dog and soft drink, along with a cap. Five hundred youngsters came that first year. It was a start.

This program continued at Oakmont, Crooked Stick, Indianwood, The Broadmoor, and Pine Needles when these clubs hosted the Women's Open.

In 1995, we let more than 1,200 kids in free at The Broadmoor but "Kids Get a Front-Row Seat" officially started at the 1997 Women's Open at Pumpkin Ridge near Portland, attracting more than 2,400 youngsters. In 1998 at the Women's Open at Blackwolf Run Golf Club in Kohler,

Wisconsin, a record 6,600 youngsters participated. Several innovations to the program were included: kids went around our putting course, Polaroid shots of each junior were taken in the tent, and they were given a short tour around the golf course with an explanation about how to watch a golf championship. USGA memberships were given to each young spectator, and a scavenger hunt using golf terminology was conducted.

In 2000, at the Merit Club outside of Chicago, the Fellows at the USGA Foundation came up with another theme for the junior program at the Women's Open and other selected championships. The new name, "Catch the Spirit," is a message to juniors that we are including them in the game. "Kids Get a Front-Row Seat" became part of this initiative.

The USGA conducts "Catch the Spirit" days at a few amateur championships by offering a golf clinic and lunch. In fact, in 2001 in Tulsa, Oklahoma, on Monday of U.S. Open week, a Catch the Spirit Day for 300 children was conducted at a course near the Southern Hills Country Club championship site. The day started with the Dennis Walters Golf Show, a drive-chip-and-putt contest for kids by the Golf Channel, lunch provided by Outback restaurants, and then a guided tour of a practice round of the U.S. Open at Southern Hills. Dave Bryan, Director of Golf at Southern Hills, spoke to the children about sportsmanship and the spirit of the game.

It's a great program because, first of all, they see the best of a class of player, whether it's at the Girls' Junior, the Women's Amateur Public Links, or the Women's Open. It's a quick read because youngsters' heads are like sponges. They see how to behave, how to make shots, and how to use their imagination. They're not focused on the practice tee and just making swings.

I know that after I attend any USGA championship, even if I don't hit balls during the week, I'm a better player when I come home. With that visual asset of watching great players, I play pretty well for a while, until I get back into my old, bad swing habits.

Youngsters can take advantage of that visual experience. I've seen it here in Colorado where little children easily pick up skiing. They do it because they have no fear. They just point those skis and go, because they've seen other people do it.

We're all like that, as youngsters. My golf swing today, for example, is exactly like Dave Trufelli's swing, because I mimicked him.

We had a lot of fun selling the 1995 Women's Open. The most important part was talking Mimi Griffin into being the Championship Director.

She put a staff together of Lisa Luigs, Margie Cole, and Kate Cunningham. This was a dynamite team that coordinated every activity involved with the Women's Open.

Right off the bat we sold 45 skyboxes, a record number. About a year and a half before the championship, we were rolling right along when our ticket chairman quit. Until that time, my responsibility had been the golf course and all that goes with it, but now, with no ticket chairman, I got involved in all phases of ticket sales. Those of us on the local championship committee had to take up the slack.

Our ticket sales started to take off. By the time the first round began, we could see that we were going to do well. On three of the four days of competition, we had great weather. And since Colorado people like to be outdoors, we began to see big galleries. The people of Colorado Springs, the people of the surrounding area we call "the Front Range," and the entire state supported the championship.

I carried a little notebook around in which I wrote things I had to do. When the championship started, I still had quite a long to-do list. I said, "Well, we're not ready yet."

Then I thought: *What you really need to do is just get out of the way and let things go. Some of this stuff you are just not going to get done because the Women's Open is a work in progress, it just keeps going.*

To celebrate the 50th anniversary of the Women's Open, we invited all of the past champions. Early in the week, past champions who weren't playing in the Women's Open appeared with Patty Berg in one of the greatest golf clinics I've ever seen.

In the early days of the LPGA tour, Patty conducted clinics with various players to help attract spectators with an event called "The Swing Parade." One of the USGA people had suggested we resurrect the Swing Parade for the 50th anniversary. When we did, it was a big hit, attracting about 3,000 spectators, young and old. To see Patty out there as the emcee, with Louise Suggs, Betsy Rawls, Catherine Lacoste, Sandra Spuzich, and all of the others hitting balls, was quite a special scene.

We had a great 50th birthday party for the champions. Nearly all of them were there, from Patty, who won the first Women's Open in 1946, to Patty Sheehan, the defending champion. Pat Bradley was there, Betsy King, Liselotte Newman, JoAnne Carner, and many more. Barbara McIntire sat at a dinner table with Kathy Cornelius, who had beaten her in that Women's Open play-off so many years before.

With so many champions gathered in one place, it was a terrific night. Each champion had the microphone for a time and, at the end of the evening, Patty Berg stood up to speak. Even then, Patty was a bit frail and when she stood the room was totally silent out of respect for what she has meant to the players and the game.

Patty is, I think, everyone's hero and one of God's great people. What she has given to golf, and particularly to the women's side of the game, gave it a great boost. The thing I like most about Patty is her positive attitude.

Patty gave a very gracious speech and ended it with her traditional closing, "God love you. God bless you. And God bless America."

She received a long, loud, standing ovation and, even now, thinking about it gives me goose bumps.

The championship itself *nearly* went off without a hitch.

On Thursday, just before the start of the first round, I got a call on my two-way radio to go to the second green. A sprinkler head had stuck during overnight watering and the section where the hole was located was saturated. It's a smallish green, so we didn't have many hole locations anyway, but neither did we think we could sop up all the water.

Barbara McIntire, who was chairman of the USGA Women's Committee that year, was on the first tee helping start the players. So here we were, at zero hour, and the hole cutter from the grounds crew was cutting a new hole on the second green. In fact, we were putting the hole in a location where I'd never, in all my years there, seen the hole cut. That made me pretty nervous, too.

We then got a call from Barbara saying there was no flagstick at the first green. I jumped into my cart, tore down to the first green, and saw the flagstick standing sentry, so we were okay.

We managed to get through the first round without further mishap, but a thunderstorm forced suspension of play rather late in the second round. The players marked their balls, and the course was evacuated for the rest of the day. We were told that all of the players had completed at least 14 holes.

The following morning, the second round had to be completed before the players began the third round. We left the flagsticks in place on those last four holes for players who hadn't completed the second round, and began cutting new hole locations on holes designated for the third round from hole one through hole 14.

I got another radio call to go to the 14th green. Evidently, we'd had bad information on how far the last group of three players had advanced in the second round before evacuating the course.

One of my players from the 1988 U.S. Curtis Cup team, Caroline Keggi, had marked her ball on the 14th green when play had been suspended the previous night. She had marked it about eight feet from the hole, which was located in the right-center portion of the green. We now had had a new hole cut in the back-left portion of the very large green. Caroline's ball was now some 60 feet from the new hole.

I radioed for the hole cutter and told him, "You don't need a hole liner," which is the plastic liner that many people call "the cup." I said, "You can just cut the hole and she can putt without a liner in it."

Then I asked Caroline if she wanted the liner. She wanted that liner. She had a right to ask for one if she wanted to, but she didn't *have* to have it.

"Captain," she said. "I want to hear that ball hit the bottom of the cup when I hole this putt."

Now, I had to get a liner. Our communication was bogging down, she was standing there waiting for an opportunity to putt to the old hole location, and now the first group of the third round had made the turn. They were coming!

It was unbelievable how quickly all of this was happening. The hole cutter arrived, but he didn't bring a hole liner. Luckily, The Broadmoor has 36 holes. I sent him to the other course to get a liner, but we were running out of time. That first group was on the 12th green. Finally, he came back and installed the liner. We made it, just a few minutes before the first players arrived.

After all of this folderol, Caroline missed the putt.

We had a lot of excitement in that final round. Meg Mallon was playing in the last group as the leader after three rounds. It became a battle between Meg and Annika Sorenstam, a new player from Sweden. They seesawed back and forth in regard to the lead. Annika was playing in the group just in front of Meg. Meg hit into a water hazard on the 4th hole and made a triple-bogey and that's when the battle intensified.

Annika held up under the pressure and came into the final hole with a one-stroke lead.

Meg was behind her in the final pairing and Barbara McIntire, as Women's Committee Chairman, was officiating. Meg had a chance at the par-5 17th to pick up a stroke but didn't get her ball up and down from 20 yards out for a birdie.

As the players and officials walked down the 18th fairway, we lowered the ropes to allow people to walk in with the players. Spectators were everywhere, crowding each other in the fairway and walking down the rough. Rows and rows of people were gathered around the 18th green. As we crossed the bridge to the 18th green, I heard a hissing noise and looked up to see The Broadmoor's hot air balloon rising nearby. I almost had a stroke and called Kendra Graham, the USGA staff point person for the Women's Open, on the radio. She got things under control and the balloon mechanism was turned off. Then I looked back down the fairway to see a band of horses and riders coming down the fairway from the tee to participate in the prize-giving ceremony. I just hoped they wouldn't make any noises while the players were putting. Never a dull moment.

Seeing all of those people made Barbara teary as she walked down the final hole. I had joined the group on 15 and was walking in as an observer. I got pretty emotional myself. I was proud of our effort. Colorado Springs had come through. We had the most spectators the Women's Open had ever had with nearly 95,000 people. The championship was set in a new direction and the bar had been raised by the work of so many good people, which is exactly the idea. That's the legacy we wanted to pass on for future championships, to make the Women's Open better and better.

Meg had a final chance to tie, but her 15-foot birdie putt curled just right of the hole and Annika won her first Women's Open by one stroke.

The 1995 Women's Open is one that I'll never forget. That year, my Christmas card was a panoramic photograph of the final hole surrounded by thousands of people who were there to watch women play golf.

I can't wait to see the Women's Open become a sell-out. I'd love to walk up to the gate some day and have someone tell me, "Sorry, there aren't any more tickets."

Chapter 25

[Becoming Vice President]

During 1995, I became even more heavily involved in the USGA as vice president.

I was chairman of the Championship Committee, chairman of the Members Committee, chairman of International Team Selection, and served on the Finance Committee, Communication Committee, and the Management Committee.

The USGA is unique in that committees decide its policies. While the USGA president has the influence to promote his or her personal agenda, and the executive director is the staff person charged with implementing policy, the Executive Committee governs the USGA with input from sub-committees.

The members of the XC always serve on a number of these committees, which demands research, study, and a great deal of time away from our own occupations.

I served on nearly every USGA committee while a member of the Executive Committee. Two assignments were particularly difficult. I began serving on the Implements & Ball Committee in 1987 and it was tough because of my lack of knowledge. I had to work really hard to get up to speed and to understand the issues and the discipline. I was Chairman of the Handicap Committee, which virtually runs the handicapping system used throughout the United States, and that was also very tough. Again, it was my lack of knowledge.

I was one of those golfers who had always walked into the ladies locker room and handed my scorecard to Helen, the locker room attendant at The Broadmoor Golf Club. She is a beautiful person, and she always posted my score for me.

Incredibly, when I became chairman of the Handicap Committee in 1988, I had no clue about how to post my own score, so the first thing I did was talk to Helen.

"Helen," I said, "you've got to walk me through these steps. I don't even know how to post a score."

I had no interest in it, none, but I had to quickly acquire an interest and learn how this committee did its basic work. I then attended a course-rating seminar to get up to speed. I knew I couldn't participate in changing policy until I knew where the working concepts came from.

One of the key innovations of the Handicap Committee at that time was to change the rule about the number of people it took to form a club, because you had to be a member of a golf club in order to get a USGA handicap. You needn't belong to a club that owned real estate, but you had to be part of a group, or club, of golfers in order to have peer review. That was part of the rules.

When I became chairman, the USGA had previously specified that it took 50 people to form a club. I lobbied the committee to have that number changed to 10. As far as I was concerned it could be four people, because I never thought of building a handicap system to keep out the cheaters. Our game is based on honesty, fair play, and a sense of integrity. You leave that up to the golfer. The only person who gets hurt in a cheating matter is the cheater. But that wasn't the way the world saw it. Other people wanted us to specify having more people in a club, to supposedly guard against cheating. I would have been for four members. Between four and 50, I supported 10, which was my idea of a good compromise.

The Handicap Committee was concerned about the lack of knowledge among golfers. We had implemented ESC, Equitable Stroke Control, in an effort to make the USGA handicapping system more fair. ESC is a concept that a limit be imposed on the score a player could take on each hole. The limit was determined by their present handicap index. The purpose of this concept was to keep players from running up their score on one hole to deliberately and unfairly inflate their scores and their resulting handicap index. Hopefully, ESC also helped pick up the pace of a round of golf.

While ESC achieved both purposes, it was a difficult concept for golfers to understand, so we decided to put out an instruction book on handicapping and ESC, which the USGA would distribute.

I thought the best way to approach this book was to make it as simple as possible, almost in a comic book format. So with Dean Knuth, the USGA's Director of Handicapping and GHIN® (Golf Handicap Information Network), and Rhonda Glenn, we published "Uncle Snoopy Wants You to Use Your Handicap." Charles Schulz, creator of the wonderful "Peanuts" cartoon strip, came to our rescue by providing the artwork. The book is still a valuable guide for golfers and, as of this year, the USGA has distributed more than three million copies.

When I was chairman of the Members Committee I thoroughly enjoyed working with Chris Law, the staff member in charge. I attended a lot of meetings and, because this kind of program is fairly complicated, we had a lot of outside experts helping us.

The USGA Members Program was founded in 1975 to create a communications link between the USGA and individual golfers. It's an exchange, with the USGA communicating its goals and the individual members communicating their ideas and support.

About 600,000 members had been signed up and our goal was to enlist one million. We never reached that goal under my watch. I pushed hard to get a whopping computer for the program, with a database to give us more information about our members. I believed that we needed that computer and database badly, but it never came to fruition while I was chairman, or even while I was president. We didn't get it until after I left.

An interesting side effect of my USGA presidency is that we lost a number of USGA members who wrote to Golf House saying they were dropping out because the USGA had a woman at the helm. David Fay replied to those letters and took a "good riddance" stance on those resignations, I'm happy to say.

These complex issues that I was assigned make me recall something I learned from the great player, Mickey Wright. Mickey once told me of an instructional film she made with several male professionals. The men's segments were filmed first and they covered driving, chipping, and putting. When Mickey arrived for the filming, there was but one shot left to cover. "Of course," Mickey said, "it was the buried lie in the bunker."

She had to hit a number of those shots perfectly, I might add.

"They always give the buried lie in the bunker to the woman," she chuckled.

Being chairman of the Amateur Status & Conduct Committee from 1992 through 1994 was a little easier. I learned a tremendous amount from John Glover of the R&A, who had worked with P.J. Boatwright and Frank Hannigan for a lot of years. When Tony Zirpoli was assigned to amateur status from the USGA staff, I just loved working with him because he was so dedicated and had such great understanding of the issues, along with a keen sense of humor.

The USGA has perhaps the best golf museum in the world and certainly the finest golf library, but it's a small, unknown museum in New Jersey. While I was on the Museum Committee, only about 20,000 people a year visited the museum, and that's if you counted the deer on the grounds of Golf House. Even in 1990, when a number of guests attended the Curtis Cup match at Somerset Hills Country Club, which is down the road from Golf House, only 22,000 people visited the museum.

For a while, we were spending a million dollars a year running the museum and special exhibits and it was pretty hard to justify the expense with that kind of turnout.

While it wasn't my idea, I certainly favored the proposal of taking our show on the road with traveling exhibits. The traveling exhibits are extremely labor-intensive, but in 2001 the USGA mounted its 100th traveling museum exhibit, tastefully staged by Andy Mutch, who was director of the museum. The museum has since managed to reach many thousands of people with these displays.

I also believed that the USGA needed a video on the museum. We needed the video to have something of informational value to take out to people because they sure weren't coming to Golf House, and we ended up doing that.

The museum is a special place. It now occupies nearly all of the space once used for offices in a wonderful old mansion on the grounds of Golf House. Architecturally, the museum is lovely with its sweeping staircase, fine chandeliers and a number of graceful rooms. One of the rooms we're most proud of is the Bob Jones Room, which is just off the foyer. The room is devoted to Jones's career and the walls are lined with books that attest to his magnificent life. His medals, displayed in a modest glass case, are perhaps the single most inspiring sight at Golf House.

The room's fireplace and comfortable furnishings make it as cozy and comfortable as a fine home library. Not long after I was named to the XC, I found myself sitting in the Bob Jones Room with Mickey Wright.

Since our semifinal match in the 1952 U.S. Girls' Junior Championship, Mickey had become the greatest woman player in the history of the game. Ben Hogan and Byron Nelson each said she had the greatest golf swing they'd ever seen.

While on the Museum Committee, I'd been campaigning to add portraits of the great women in the game to our collection. Along with our golf artifacts and collections, the museum housed a number of wonderful portraits, but only three were of women: Glenna Collett Vare (six-time U.S. Women's Amateur champion), Margaret Curtis, and Babe Zaharias. In 1987 we commissioned a portrait of Patty Berg, a Curtis Cup player who won the U.S. Women's Amateur and U.S. Women's Open, along with 14 other major championships.

The museum's curator and librarian at that time was Janet Seagle, an old friend of mine, a fine player, and one of the most knowledgeable people in golf. Janet helped ramrod the oil portrait of Patty Berg. It was truly a wonderful painting and I believe captured Patty's indomitable and jolly spirit. Only one thing was wrong—the portrait showed Patty in a beige skirt and I knew that she nearly always wore blue or gray. I had the portrait sent back to the artist with orders to change the skirt color. If you look at the portrait closely today, you can see that the skirt was repainted.

My next goal was to have a portrait painted of Mickey Wright. We lined up a few friends to privately finance the project and the portrait was painted. I wanted to stage the unveiling at the museum, but the tricky part was getting Mickey to participate.

After all of her years on the road, Mickey no longer enjoyed traveling and refused to fly unless it was the only way to get to her destination. She's also somewhat shy, so all of the honors and awards she has been given have been more of a distraction for her than anything else.

We talked on the phone several times and I convinced her that we would simply hold an intimate afternoon reception with her friends.

"It's going to be very simple," I told her. "If you want us to just serve milk and cookies, that's what we'll do."

Frankly, I was a little surprised when she agreed to come.

We put together a guest list that I thought would please her. Helen Sigel Wilson, a Curtis Cup player and captain; some of Mickey's friends from the Far Hills area; Dot Porter, the 1949 U.S. Women's Amateur champion, who Mickey had said was one of her favorite playing companions; and Mickey's close friends Peggy Wilson, Betsy Rawls, and Kathy Whitworth, along with a few USGA officials she knew and liked.

Mickey drove to New Jersey from Florida and on a beautiful autumn afternoon, we had our little gathering in the Golf House library. The USGA sent a car to New York to pick up Herbert Warren Wind, our great American golf writer who had covered so much of Mickey's career. And it's one of the few times I can recall when Mr. Dey, P.J., Frank, and David Fay were all together in the same room.

The unveiling was a very simple ceremony for perhaps 40 people. P.J., David, and Frank spoke, Mr. Dey said a few words, and Kathy and Betsy related their memories of this historic player. I introduced Mickey by recalling that she was one of our first customers at A Short Story, but because we were such a small business at that time we couldn't just give her the shorts that she ordered, we had to charge her for them, at cost.

Mickey is one of the most gracious people I know, and she responded with touching remarks about her fondness for the USGA. We capped off the day with a small candlelit dinner for 10 in a private room of a nearby restaurant. Mickey sat at the head of the table with Kathy on her right and Betsy on her left. I remember that Kathy and Betsy were talking about Mickey as if she wasn't there, recalling the many great shots she had hit in her career.

"The only thing she *wasn't* great at were putts of four feet or less," Kathy said.

"That's right," said Betsy, "that's the only thing she wasn't great at."

"Well, she wasn't *that* bad!" Mickey said.

It was a fine evening with a lot of stories and laughter.

In 1993 the Nominating Committee asked me to take on the job of vice president of the USGA. It crossed my mind that I could now at least see the light at the end of the tunnel. I knew I would either go out after my years as vice president, or eventually be asked to be president.

I now knew my exit strategy, let's put it that way. In my mind, I didn't go beyond being vice president.

I was absolutely, totally involved with the USGA at that time: I'd been chairman of Amateur Status, I'd done Handicapping and the Golf Handicap Information Network, or GHIN®. GHIN® was good for me because it was very entrepreneurial in spirit, which it needed to be. We needed to define who our customers were and take as good care of them as we possibly could, so I enjoyed that quite a lot.

I had been up to the kazoo in USGA merchandising because I was really a committee of one, in that I was the only XC member who had been in the clothing business. With the staff, I'd been heavily involved in starting new projects, so my commitment to the USGA was definitely getting more intense when I became vice president.

The USGA was changing. The association had always been perceived as a stuffy organization, Eastern-bent, private-club, and male oriented. I believe my presence as a woman on the XC changed that perception a little bit.

The USGA is an organization of golfers, but also an organization of clubs and courses. By the 1990s, more of our member courses were public than private. This was a good thing since the USGA has become very interested in reaching out to more golfers.

My USGA friends reacted with a lot more excitement toward my position as vice president than I did because they thought I was getting closer to the presidency. I don't recall anything specific that was said, but they were clearly anticipating my eventual move into the top post. The press was on top of it from day one, speculating that I would head the organization in a couple of years.

I didn't have time to think about it. I was on the XC because I wanted to serve the USGA and really didn't mind in what capacity. The presidency wasn't anything I was seeking. If I were asked to do it, I'd do it, and I'd do it to the best of my ability, but I wasn't out there pushing for the job.

Our businesses were doing well up until the time I became vice president. Then we began to struggle because there was more competition and the philosophy at The Broadmoor Hotel had changed. In terms of local customers, we were dealing with a different set of circumstances.

Majority ownership of the hotel had been sold. The hotel was being renovated, which was exciting, but at the same time, torn-up parking lots and buildings hurt us. The services offered at The Broadmoor also changed and, for one reason or another, not as many local residents used the hotel. At least 50% of our business had been local customers, so we were hurting.

In 1994 I decided to try my hand at being a retail consultant. The Homestead Resort in Hot Springs, Virginia, talked to us about opening some shops there, but we couldn't justify opening just one shop in a remote place like Hot Springs. We'd have to do several shops and if we did, it would be such a big commitment that somebody would need to move to be there all the time, because we'd have that kind of stake in it.

I said to Gary Rosenberg, president of the Homestead Resort, "The hotel staff would be the best people in the world to run these retail shops and I'd be very happy to help with the buying and the training of the employees as a consultant."

I began consulting in Hot Springs early in 1995. It's a grand resort but definitely a destination spot and getting there was sometimes an all-day adventure.

I was taking on an awful lot as I advanced into the vice president's seat. Later, in 1995, we opened two new shops for the Homestead and I began to oversee the buying and operations. I say "we" because some of my Colorado Springs associates pitched in, too.

The two new Homestead enterprises were their kitchen shop, "Southern Taste," and a men's clothing shop, "Wm. S. Flynn."

We did it all, including the concept, the buying, the way the stores looked, all supplies, and coordination with the architect.

I went directly to the Homestead from Shinnecock, where the U.S. Open had just been played and where I had been chairman of the Championship Committee. When Southern Taste opened in June 1995, I didn't go to the U.S. Senior Open at Congressional because construction on this store had been delayed. Our part had been ready earlier, but the space wasn't ready.

There were plenty of XC members at the Senior Open, but I was disappointed not to be there. When we finally opened the store, it was just before the 1995 U.S. Women's Open, of which I was a co-vice chairman, at The Broadmoor Golf Club. I had been in Hot Springs for two critical weeks before the championship.

In September, we opened the Wm. S. Flynn store, named for the architect of the wonderful Cascades Course at the Homestead, which in my view is the finest mountain course in the world.

A friend came in to help, along with Gloria Lindsay of the Homestead staff, or we never would have been able to open. Just tagging the merchandise was a big job. This was new for the Homestead, so nothing was tagged in their receiving department.

This was my first role as a consultant, and hands-on has never been a problem with me. I think that by the time I got my role figured out, I just wanted to spend more time with USGA work.

When we opened Wm. S. Flynn we didn't even have a manager for the store. It's such a remote spot that it's difficult to find new employees, so I flew in Bob Boylan one of our staff members from Colorado Springs, to manage the shop for the first couple of weeks because we didn't have anybody to run it. I was interviewing people as quickly as I could.

At this point in life, 1994 and 1995, I was vice president of the USGA, chairman of the Championship Committee, and co-vice chairman of the 1995 U.S. Women's Open at The Broadmoor. I was also consulting retail director for the Homestead. In Colorado Springs, we were still in the deli business, and we had five shops at The Broadmoor Hotel. There was plenty to hold my interest.

Meanwhile, the chairmanship of the Championship Committee was the one lead role that I believed I was most equipped for, because of my history of playing in 32 USGA championships. It's also one of the most fun roles in the USGA because that person had always worked closely with P.J., who had been in his role for more than 30 years. P.J. probably did a lot of things that weren't in his job description.

P.J. had passed away by the time I became chairman. Instead, I worked with David Eger. David and I had our moments. It wasn't anything concrete, but there was resentment there and I think that David struggled with the fact that he had to report to a woman.

David had come from the PGA Tour and wasn't accustomed to working with so many people in operating a championship. I believed that championships were something I knew about because of my experience with the WC, as a player, and riding shotgun with P.J. I wanted to be involved but my relationship with David was just a push-me, pull-you, up one side and down the other. There was some speculation in the press about whether David and I got along. We worked together, after a fashion, in 1994 and 1995, and he resigned from the USGA in July of 1995 to rejoin the PGA Tour.

I will say this on David's behalf and on my behalf. We've worked through our problems and I now consider him to be a good friend of mine. But we had a rough go for a while.

Tom Meeks, a longtime member of the USGA Championship staff, took over the lead staff role at the U.S. Open and U. S. Amateur. Tom and I got along fine.

In 1997 the Homestead hired a full-time retail director. I was consulting director and they wanted to keep me on for a little while, but it really didn't work out with this other new person.

I think she was threatened by me, although I was clear about my role and didn't want to intrude in her role. It was an uncomfortable situation. I told Gary Rosenberg that I thought the only way he was going to know if she was any good or not was for me to just get out of it. The Retail Director was hired in January 1997 and I left in April.

While I didn't work for Gary at the time, I absolutely love the place and there isn't anything I wouldn't do to help. I'm always thinking about new ideas for them and, of course, I'll pass those on. In 1998, in early summer, Gary called and said the retail director had left and he wanted me to evaluate the situation.

I flew in and did an in-depth evaluation, which was some of my best work. I also proposed what I thought they should do, going forward, and offered my services for a couple of years.

I began working for them again in September of 1998. Late in 2000, I told them I really needed to back off and spend more time with the USGA Foundation. As they began to look for someone else, I stayed until August of 2001. In the interim, from when I left and came back, they had opened five stores in the hotel corridor, which was part of the master plan that we'd worked on.

My analysis said the Homestead shops had way too much inventory and there were a lot of disciplines that needed to be put in place. It was out of balance. We opened two new stores and I worked hard on staff and merchandising, bringing in some of our people from Colorado Springs to do visual merchandising.

It was interesting to identify the various managers and their strengths and give them a chance to run with those.

Bill Campbell used to say to me that I work in "fits and starts." When Bill was USGA president, he wouldn't hear from me for a while, then get volumes of correspondence. He meant that as a compliment, but he picked up on my style of operation. I get bored if I'm focusing on just one thing.

I've always been a multitask person. In fact, I think I would have been a better player if I hadn't been multi-task oriented because I would have focused more on the task at hand—playing one hole at a time.

Chapter 26

[Madame President]

Everyone in the insular little world of golf, it seemed, was speculating about whether I'd ever be asked to be president of the United States Golf Association.

While I was vice president, Bill Campbell was chairman of the USGA Nominating Committee. Whenever Bill and I were seen together, Barbara McIntire or my pals on the Women's Committee would ask if Bill had asked me about "the, you know, the PRESIDENCY!"

I had lunch with Bill at the 1995 United States Open at Shinnecock. We were just talking, one on one, about a member of the Executive Committee.

Ann Beard, a good friend and former chairman of the Women's Committee, and her husband, Lee Beard, were in the dining room having lunch. Ann was certain that Bill was asking me to be president. She just couldn't stand it until we left the table and the minute she saw me alone, she ran up to me and asked, "Did he ask you? Did he ask you? Did he ask you?"

Reporters were very big on it and they'd ask Frank Hannigan if I were qualified for the office. I remember that Frank once said, "She's forgotten more about playing the game than most of them know." It wasn't true and he shouldn't have said it, but Frank always popped off like that.

The press was speculating, big-time. I had to tell the reporters who asked, "I don't even know how it works and I don't even know who decides. I've gotten a big kick out of what I've done."

Tim Rosaforte, who then worked for the *Palm Beach Post*, began asking me about it when I was first nominated to the XC in 1987. I told him he needed to call somebody else because I wasn't even in the club yet!

When I became vice president, a past president told me that I might one day be president "if things work out." It has to be a mutual thing. You've got to want to do it, and they've got to want you.

I was on the XC because I wanted to serve the USGA and didn't mind in what capacity. The presidency wasn't anything I was seeking. If I were asked to do it, I'd do it and do the best I could. But I wasn't out there working for the job.

In 1995, former United States President George Bush and Barbara Bush went to St. Andrews to watch the British Open and spend a few days in Scotland.

I was staying at Walden House, the R&A house adjacent to the 18th fairway of the Old Course. The Bushes and Reg and Diana Murphy were also guests there. The Bushs was on the top floor, I was on the floor below, and Reg and Diana were the floor below me. One night at dinner, I said, "This is the first time I ever slept between two presidents."

George and Barbara dined with us every night. On one occasion he said, "I hear you're going to be president of the USGA."

"Well, I don't know that," I said.

"Trust me," he said. "It's a done deal."

With all due respect, he'd been president of the United States but he didn't have a vote in *this* election.

I think I can say that George Bush and I are friends. I like him a lot.

In 1998 he came to the Women's Open at Blackwolf Run Golf Club in Kohler, Wisconsin, for the 18-hole playoff between amateur Jenny Chuasiriporn and professional Se Ri Pak and watched with his friend Herb Kohler. President Bush was in town to participate in the opening of Whistling Straits, a marvelous test of golf along Lake Michigan that was created by Pete Dye and Herb.

Then, in 2000, President Bush and Barbara Bush visited Bert and Sandy Getz at the Merit Club in Libertyville, Illinois, the site of the Women's Open. He said he wanted to see me. I was then told on the radio that he was on a conference call. Bert Getz, the Merit Club's founder, was with Bush and said, "When he comes back, I'll find somebody with a radio, call you, and say, 'The eagle has landed.'"

We couldn't hook up that day, but I spent some time with Barbara Bush. She's absolutely terrific, and I'm disappointed that she didn't run for president between George and George W.

At that time, I hardly ever had a conversation in which someone didn't ask me about my future role with the USGA.

Finally, in November of 1995 I was at Golf House for the fall meetings. During a break on Saturday morning, Bill Campbell asked to talk to me. We sat down in the lobby at Golf House.

By then, I figured he was either going to ask me to become president or send me out to pasture.

"I'm sure this isn't a surprise to you," Bill said, "but I want to ask you to become president of the USGA in January."

I said simply, "I accept."

There were no fireworks. I didn't do any fist pumping. And I didn't get teary. I was just quietly pleased.

Bill said he knew I could do the job, he was willing to help in any way, and was glad I agreed to be nominated.

The suspense was over. I telephoned my brothers, who were extremely excited for me, then I told Barbara McIntire. She was thrilled for me, but also extremely pleased because of what it meant to all women in the game.

Barbara had been speculating that this was going to happen, so we didn't have to discuss whether she thought I could do it and still handle our businesses. Frankly, you're no busier as president than when you chair other committees. For sure, your exit strategy is in place when you become president. You know where you are going next.

Neither was my health a concern. As far as I was concerned, since I'd had the bypass operation, I was cured. In those days, whenever I was faced with a medical questionnaire that asked if I had heart disease, I always checked "No."

Barbara's work in the businesses was invaluable. During this period and the two years following, she ran them almost totally alone, except for the restaurant. She also watched over The Men's Shop and looked after my house when I was traveling. In 1995, and again in 1996, the first year I was president, she had a full plate with her own duties as chairman of the Women's Committee. That's a lot.

Barbara is like a sister to me, and the Bell family considers her to be one of their own. Few people in this life are fortunate enough to have someone like Barbara to head the list of their devoted friends.

Barbara had sold her house next door and, with Tish Preuss, moved into my house two weeks before the 1995 Women's Open.

When I became president, Barbara, our CPA Dolly Wong, and all of

the people who worked with me kicked in to help. I thanked them pro-
fusely because I wasn't around much and they had to shoulder a lot of
responsibilities.

In November, with my nomination official, I began preparing myself
for office. I spent a lot of time talking to then current USGA President Reg
Murphy about long-range goals. Reg was a very good visionary and had
certain projects in the works that I needed to know more about.

I talked to a number of the past presidents, getting sound advice, and
spent a great deal of time with David Fay. I wanted to be sure that I was
ready to assume this new role.

David first came to work for the USGA in 1978. When we had the 1983
Annual Meeting in Colorado Springs I called him "Knives and Forks"
because he was in charge of planning the food and scheduling our dinners
and meetings.

David and I became fast friends as we worked together to rally the
Colorado troops and get a good turnout for the Annual Meeting. Out here
in the hinterlands some 500 people came, which was then a record.

When David went through a battle with cancer, beginning in 1984, I
called him or wrote to him whenever possible. Fighting lymphoma, David
went to the edge, and almost over the edge, nearly losing his life four
times.

At the time, I'd ordered some white pique knit shirts embossed with
the Bell's Deli logo, which is two crossed bells. I sent one to David. Later, I
sent a shirt to Frank Hannigan when he had heart bypass surgery in 1985.
It was kind of a crazy thing to do, but I just wanted to send them something
to show my support.

For a while, it seemed that the *only* way you could get a Bell's Deli shirt
was to have a serious operation.

David was determined to whip cancer, and he whipped it, but that's the
kind of guy he is. He has a lot of courage and places a great value on life.

After Frank left the post of senior executive director, David was named
interim executive director and ran Golf House. The XC hired a search firm,
which searched the country to find a new executive director.

The XC decided that David was the right person for the job. I've always
said that we spent a large amount of money finding David Fay, who was
right under our noses.

The great thing about David is that he's extremely bright, yet well bal-
anced. He has a wife and two daughters, a nice life, and he's very interested

in things other than golf, so he keeps his job in perspective and doesn't let it eat him up.

He became executive director when he was in his early 40s, and will serve the USGA well until he retires. It's nice to have that kind of continuity. David Fay is one of the best things that has happened to the USGA, and someone of whom I'm very proud. Many saw his relative youth as a handicap. I saw it as an advantage because he could provide years of continuity for the association.

After being nominated as USGA president, I knew that I once again needed more education. I also had to figure out how I was going to communicate and whom I was going to appoint to various committees, which is part of the president's job. I flew back to Colorado Springs and began working on it right away.

We needed people with experience, knowledge, and interest in certain subjects to head committees. Consulting Reg and David, I completed the assignments by the first of December.

The president's relationship with the executive director is a key to a good administration. I told David that I considered our relationship to be a partnership, that I'd been in a business partnership for a number of years, and that I understood how partnerships worked quite well.

I also told him that that I wanted to communicate with him electronically. Computers and e-mailing, in 1995, were still unknown to both of us. We didn't use personal computers throughout Golf House at that time, but it was clearly the way of the future.

I'd bought a computer after my bypass operation and tried to work on it while recuperating. But I had real problems with my memory right after the surgery because of the anesthetic, so at that time the computer didn't work out. Now, I wanted to get back into it and begin to communicate electronically with David and the USGA. Also, I wanted to see more electronic communication throughout the USGA and with state and regional golf associations.

When I mentioned this to David, he could have said, "You've got to be kidding. I don't know anything about computers."

Instead, he said, "Fine."

It would be a formidable task to get all of the staff and committees on line, so I called Dean Knuth, Director of GHIN® and Handicapping, who was a computer nerd. Dean ordered laptops for David and me and we began to learn what to do. In the beginning, one of us would send a message, then telephone the other to see if it had been received. Believe me, we had our moments of frustration and, looking back, plenty of humor. One day David told me he was going back to the typewriter and fax machine and this was after we'd both been working at the computer for a few months.

"Fine," I said, "but I'm going to continue writing to you on my laptop."

Today, everyone at Golf House and most of our volunteers communicate via the Internet.

Reg Murphy's last meeting as president of the USGA was a meeting of the USGA Foundation.

Reg said to me, "You chair the meeting, because there are some things I want to say and I don't want to say them from the chair."

I was pretty nervous when I took over the meeting. I was not yet president and not really sure that I was ready to host important meetings.

At the meeting, Reg pushed. "Look," he said. "You've got all of this television revenue, these funds will be coming in. If that's going to continue to happen, going down the road, we've got an obligation to get these funds back into the game."

The USGA was undergoing prosperity. As Reg said, the prospect of landing our new television contract was attracting high bids. The contract, which would eventually align us with NBC for five years, would bring a lot of money into the association. We also had more than 600,000 USGA members and their dues added more prosperity.

Reg's remarks in that meeting charted our course: Here's where we need to go, but how are we going to get there?

After Reg was nominated as USGA president in late 1993, I had attended a testimonial dinner for him in Baltimore. It was a night of sincere tributes from his friends, along with a video that outlined his career and used the song "One Moment in Time" as a soundtrack.

Two years later, Barbara McIntire, Ellie McColl, and Paula Petrie hosted a surprise dinner party for me at the Cheyenne Mountain Country Club in Colorado Springs after I had been nominated as USGA president.

I love parties and we've had a couple of memorable ones. One year Paula Petrie hosted a surprise birthday party for me. Without my knowledge, everyone was told to come dressed as "Judy Bell." We had a roomful of people wearing eyeglasses, hats, khaki slacks, and tennis shoes.

At a Halloween party at the home of Billy Syms and his wife, the great amateur and three-time Curtis Cup player Nancy Roth Syms, everyone came in costume. Billy showed up in a dark brown curly wig, tennis shoes, white-rimmed eyeglasses, and a brightly colored Lilly shift over his wide girth.

I came dressed as part of a six-pack of Budweiser beer. At one point during the evening, Billy and I traded costumes. One of our mutual friends slapped me on the backside and said, "Billy, you even walk like Judy."

Another funny party was at Halloween when I told everyone on the invitation list to come dressed as a rabbit. I was in the hospital having knee surgery when I came up with the idea, so I had little better to do than spend hours on the telephone, calling costume rental stores from Colorado Springs to Salt Lake City. We corralled every available rabbit costume. Nearly 100 people dressed in costume and it was hilarious to see them arrive, then to look out over the room and see nothing but rabbits.

The party at Cheyenne Mountain Country Club was a lovely and meaningful night. I thought I was meeting a couple of people for dinner, but when we walked into the club, a host of friends, including Marty Parkes and Karen Moraghan from Golf House, and my great-nephew Chris Bell had gathered in the living room of the club.

After drinks, we moved into the dining room. Barbara, Ellie, and Paula, who gave the party, have great taste. Round tables for eight were formally set and decorated in the USGA colors of red, white, and blue. The flower arrangements at each table included small American and USGA flags.

A number of friends made nice remarks, but I nearly came undone when my great-nephew Chris raised his glass in a toast. I'm very close to Chris, who is Carl and Gwen's grandson. He lived with me for several years while he went to school and worked in The Men's Shop at The Broadmoor. At the time, he was about 21 years old but his words that night belied his youth and he spoke very movingly of our relationship and his pride in what was happening to "Aunt Judy."

Barbara had commissioned a video tribute of lots of old photographs fading in and out to the song "Somewhere Over the Rainbow," sung with wonderful power by the Mormon Tabernacle Choir.

I've always identified with the character of Dorothy in *The Wizard of Oz*. It's not just the Kansas connection; it's because the story is about the amazing adventure of life. We all follow a yellow brick road and sometimes face adversity and scary events, but I'm such an optimist that I always believe we'll find the other side of the rainbow. "Somewhere Over the Rainbow" is truly a favorite song of mine and, when you closely listen to the lyrics, there's almost a religious message.

My friends know of my fondness for the song, the story, and for Dorothy, but I had another surprise when, just before becoming president, I received a pair of ruby slippers from my friends Karen and Tim Moraghan, both of whom work for the USGA.

At the end of January, it was off to Orlando and the Disney Resort for the USGA annual meeting and my election as president.

From Colorado Springs, Tish and Ellie attended. Barbara, who was chairman of the Women's Committee, and Joanie Birkland, the vice-chairman, were of course there. Dolly Wong, on her honeymoon with her husband Dave Kast, was there, which was a lovely surprise. Steve Bartolin, president of The Broadmoor, flew in for the occasion. I was so very fortunate that friends from all over the country attended, which I'm sure beefed up the attendance.

Thirteen members of the Bell family came down for the show. As I recounted earlier, the night of the election was one of the most moving experiences of my life but a lot of fun, too. After the ceremony and dinner, I was up most of the night, talking with old friends and reading the telegrams and greetings I'd received in honor of that day.

I was extremely touched by all of the letters, particularly one from Tom Kite:

Dear Judy,

Let me add my name to the long list of those who are so proud for you this day. It is a wonderful honor for you being named the President of the USGA. Those of us in the golf industry who have watched you for so long cannot think of anyone more qualified for the job. There will be many challenges and obstacles to your goals over the next few years. But, as you have always been able to do with your golf game, there is little that you cannot handle. Somehow it seems that having you at the top of the USGA is as secure as watching Ben Crenshaw over a ten-foot putt, you know the result is going to be very good most of the time. I look forward to seeing you soon so I can personally congratulate you. Have a wonderful evening.

Sincerely, Tom

During a dinner of the Women's Committee the night before my induction, Maureen Garrett had read a poem from an anonymous source. I didn't hear it as I was at the Links Club dinner, but in Maureen's wonderful rolling voice and British accent, it must have been a smash. The poem was called, "It Couldn't Be Done."

> Somebody said that it couldn't be done
> But she with a chuckle replied,
> That maybe it couldn't, but she would be one
> Who wouldn't say so 'til she tried.
> So she buckled right in with the trace of a grin
> On her face; if she worried she hid it.
> She started to sing as she tackled the thing
> That couldn't be done, and she did it.
>
> Somebody scoffed 'Oh you'll never do that,
> At least no one ever has done it,'
> And she took off her coat and she took off her hat,
> And the first thing we knew she'd begun it.
> With a lift of her chin and a bit of a grin,
> Without any doubting or quiddit,
> She started to sing as she tackled the thing
> That couldn't be done, and she did it.

Following a press conference the next morning, it was time to take a deep breath and have some fun before the hard work began. With the rest of the Bells and a few friends, I spent a couple of days touring the attractions at Walt Disney World, losing myself for a time in the fantasy.

I then went to South Florida to attend a party given by my dear friend Katherine Graham at her club at Jonathan's Landing, then headed home and rolled up my sleeves for the serious work ahead.

As Reg had emphasized, as a nonprofit organization and the governing body of golf in America, the USGA is obligated to put the funds it receives back into the game for the benefit of golfers. Not only do we have that charge, it's what we, as volunteers who care deeply about the game, really *want* to do and we want to do it well.

With the increased revenue from television rights, a large amount of which is made up of the rights to the telecast of the United States Open, we were now fortunate to have more funds and we could do more to help the game. But where and how would we spend the money most effectively?

We sent questionnaires to the presidents and executive directors of all state and regional golf associations. If they were making wish lists, we asked, what would they like to see the USGA do? Their answers gave us a grassroots volunteer and staff perspective about future projects to help golf. We gathered input and data from all over the country and from volunteers who serve on USGA committees.

In April, at the 1996 Masters Tournament in Augusta, I chaired one of the most effective meetings of my term when the executive committee had a brainstorming session.

David Fay was there, but it was strictly an executive committee long-range planning meeting. The session was to give XC members the information we'd gathered about potential projects and to get their feedback and direction.

We had the meeting in a small dining room in a house the USGA had rented in Augusta. We were just packed in there and the tiny room seemed jammed. People were talking excitedly, carrying on, and interrupting each other with their ideas. But this was a brainstorming session and I loved it. It was absolutely super because people were enthusiastic about what they were talking about.

I wasn't trying to get from point A to point B, or seeking to walk away from the meeting with a solid plan. All I was trying to do was get everyone involved in an exchange and see what came out of it.

We were just whipping along when suddenly Roy Ritchie, an XC member who was one of the lawyers in the room, passed a note to me That basically said, "You've lost complete control and you need to call the question."

I just smiled at Roy, winked, and mouthed the words, "Thank you."

We kept going and going. Everyone was talking at once and people were shouting out their ideas. One idea was popping off the other. Someone would say something, and someone else would expand on it. It sounded like a Bell family dinner, so I was very much at home. It was getting started. It was a good exchange.

People shouted and carried on even more, throwing anything out on the table. I wanted to have everyone in the meeting be so comfortable that if they said something asinine, something off the wall, it was okay because nobody was going to get on their case.

If one of the XC members said, "We ought to build golf courses all over the country," or some idiotic thing like that, nobody was going to give them a hard time because this was an idea session. If we walked out of there with 50 ideas, that was okay with me. That didn't mean we were going to do them all, this was just part of the process.

In a few minutes, I got a note from Peter James, another lawyer and member of the XC. Peter's note basically said, "I would think it would be good if you did this, this, and this to get better control of the meeting."

I smiled at Peter, gave him a wink, and mouthed the word "Thanks."

Then I just went back and let everybody go the way they wanted to go.

A couple of years later, after my presidency was over, I had lunch with Peter when he was attending a meeting at The Broadmoor. We're great pals, and he told me that when I was elected, a few past presidents showed some concern that I had never run a big corporate meeting. They believed that I might need a bit of help from the lawyers on meeting protocol, Roberts Rules of Order, and process so that we'd be able to get things done.

I believe that they probably, in an informal way, spoke to every lawyer on the XC about giving me "guidance."

But as Peter said, "We learned pretty quickly about you, because you would just smile, and go on and do it the way you wanted to do it."

In the XC's brainstorming session, we honed in on a few things that we'd like to start doing, one of which was assistance to state and regional golf associations. Another was getting the USGA on the information network. Another was expanding the USGA Foundation through a strong grants program.

In August 1996, in Portland, we had a special meeting of the XC to reconfirm these programs. We voted to give a million dollars to state and regional golf associations to get them equipment that they desperately needed, such as computers and two-way radios.

The Portland meeting was also to consider a USGA fellowship program that would be tied to the grants initiative. Another plan on the table was to set up a foundation office in Colorado Springs in order to receive guidance and support from the El Pomar Foundation, which is based in that city.

Bill Hybl, a former Colorado state representative and president of the United States Olympic Committee, was chairman and chief executive officer of El Pomar. Bill offered the USGA space in a building with other nonprofit organizations.

In the spring of 1996, I became a trustee of El Pomar Foundation, the first woman director in 40 years. Becoming more familiar with El Pomar's fellowship program at each trustee meeting, I thought that what I was seeing would work beautifully for the USGA Foundation.

The Foundation began immediately after the 1965 U.S. Open when Gary Player, the champion, donated a portion of his purse to the USGA to benefit junior golf. Now, 31 years later, through careful investments as well as new monies from television, we had a sizeable amount of funds to distribute.

The XC, meanwhile, responded to the state and regional golf associations. Their people had responded to our questionnaires and we listened, I think, very well, which is what you must do. If you're going to ask people about something, you've got to listen to the answers and work back through them.

We decided to help with some of their association projects in-kind. One example was expanding the P.J. Boatwright Jr. Internship program by making it not quite as restrictive. The program assigns interns to go out in the field to help state and regional golf associations. Now, a person could be an intern for a longer period of time and renew for another year.

We voted to begin seminars at Golf House, bringing the Boatwright Interns in for an orientation period. If they were going to be USGA-assigned people, we wanted them to be able to have a pretty good working knowledge of the USGA. That seminar program later expanded to other personnel and to volunteers of state and regional associations, which was wonderful.

Since Reg had passed a charge to me when I became president, because we needed to figure out ways to put dollars back into the game, I knew we would have to expand our own services.

Expanding our grants initiative was key. At that time the effort was very small and because of that, not as well organized as many larger grant programs. I wrestled with several questions: How much should we dedicate to these grant programs? Who would research the grant applications and determine the value of the many programs that were crying out for financing?

When I became an El Pomar trustee, the timing of my new education was right, considering the issues faced by the USGA.

El Pomar takes new trustees through an expansive education process. If you're going to be a trustee you have to really understand what trustees do, so I learned about what El Pomar does in terms of its grant-making and fellowship program. There was a lot of material to review: videos, annual reports, and brochures on their programs. It was quite an involved learning experience.

At the same time, it was very valuable because if we were going to increase the size of our USGA grant giving, we needed to be sure we had our ducks in a row and that we were running our program in a sound fiduciary manner.

I sat in on El Pomar meetings for several months before proposing the fellowship concept to anyone. First, I asked David Fay to come with me to visit with the senior staff of El Pomar. After these meetings, we were both sold on the idea of a Fellowship program and an office in Colorado Springs.

It made no sense to me to reinvent the wheel every time we wanted to start a new project, so I brought two El Pomar fellows and their director to explain their grants initiative and fellowship program to the 1996 XC meeting in Portland. When they spoke, the XC members began to understand exactly what I'd been talking about and how the El Pomar fellows worked on grant requests.

I believed it would be necessary, I said, to start our own fellows program because everyone on the staff at Golf House clearly had plenty to do. There was no way we could actually pull staff members out of Golf House to administer grants. If we were going to expand our grant making, we were going to have to set up another way to conduct it.

David and I later sat down and talked to the El Pomar people about their grants program, learning every phase of how it operates.

That's how the USGA Fellowship program came to Colorado Springs. El Pomar was the role model. Their foundation held our hands through the learning curve and provided office space and, because of El Pomar, we are much further along the road to being the foundation that we want to be.

Not that other foundations couldn't have helped us, but El Pomar, with a new fellowship program, was just perfect for us. It was also a good fit because, most importantly, El Pomar operates with an entrepreneurial spirit and is not a passive foundation. Consequently, that's what I thought we should be, so it was a great role model.

In that August 1996 meeting, the Executive Committee approved funding and expansion of the grants initiative and the start of the USGA Fellowship program.

Finally, in October 1997, the expanded grants initiative called "For the Good of the Game" was approved to the tune of $50 million over the next

10-year period. We would help fund programs that opened the game to new groups of players—concentrating on providing affordable and accessible golf for economically or physically challenged people. Each program that applied for a grant had to have a strong local champion who could drive the program to success.

This was an extremely large amount of money, but we were blessed with having the funds to get these things done and it was at the right time.

Now, as then, the USGA Grants Committee is made up of volunteers from the XC and from outside the XC. Three times each year, the committee meets to review all grant applications and to make recommendations to the XC about the amount of dollars to give and how these funds will be used.

The USGA Fellows collect all the data about requests through site visits and telephone calls, then present each application at the grants meeting. This is extremely valuable to the Grants Committee and an excellent opportunity, in terms of leadership and service, for the fellows.

Other programs began to expand. In the communications area, we began promoting our own amateur championships. In 1996, I had seen real results when two of our staff members worked hard to promote the U.S. Women's Amateur in Lincoln, Nebraska. With no budget, they were able to generate a lot of free promotion on local radio and television stations. For the semifinal matches and the final, that promotion resulted in slightly more than 1,000 spectators each day. I began thinking about how we could promote all of our amateur championships because they're the USGA's great showcases of how golf should be played. Not only would promoting them expose more people to fine shot making, it would showcase the true spirit and sportsmanship of golf as demonstrated by the finest players.

Besides, I thought, if we don't promote our own amateur championships, who *will* promote them?

I was very keen on this idea and pleased when the XC voted to fund this new program. By prompting our communications department to advertise, we were soon seeing several thousand people in the galleries of previously sparsely attended championships, such as the Junior Amateur and the Women's Amateur.

We tried a lot of different things, including advertising in local newspapers, billboards, and radio and television spots. The promotions familiarized people with the amateur championships and with the USGA as the governing body of golf and caretaker of the game, a governing body that is there to serve them.

Like any new project, it worked well for certain championships and not so well for others. We had some good results, but the XC has since backed off of this advertising project a bit by cutting the funding, which is disappointing to me.

We began hosting media relations meetings at Golf House with representatives from the clubs that host our amateur championships. The gatherings improved our already fine relationships with those clubs and their members.

The one thing that I'd always hoped we could get done was to earmark monies from the merchandising and licensing programs for junior golf, so that people could understand that purchasing our products is very beneficial to the game. We had a vote on that at an XC meeting but nothing happened until the 2001 U.S. Open when a new hangtag for the clothing sold by the USGA was authorized, explaining where the merchandise revenues were going.

Chapter 27

[Presidents and Champions]

The USGA president makes small and large decisions on the direction of the association and, in order to get honest input, every USGA president has a kitchen cabinet.

There is, for instance, a management committee made up of the USGA's officers. Some presidents use the Management Committee as a sounding board, and some don't.

When I was chairman of the WC, I certainly consulted a kitchen cabinet of Kay Jackson and Martha Martin, both longtime WC members, as well as other WC members—Katherine Graham, Betty Richart, Ann Beard, and Joanie Birkland—who would go on to become chairman.

After I was elected president, I continued to use these women as sounding boards. I also consulted past-presidents Will Nicholson, Bill Campbell, Jim Hand and, Reg Murphy.

I used what I considered to be a working cabinet of XC members which included Trey Holland, a urologist; Reed Mackenzie, a lawyer; Jerry Stahl, who is in the lumber business; Tom Chisholm, who has an automotive parts business; David Boyd, an insurance executive; Peter James, another lawyer; and Carol Semple Thompson. They were the seven people I talked to most.

The beauty of the USGA presidency is that each president brings a different style and set of skills to the table. Some presidents use their Management Committee more; some use the Executive Committee more. Some presidents like to build a constituency, some like to act more as benevolent dictators, if you will. It's all a question of style.

Each USGA President has an agenda. Bill Campbell, who was a tremendous player, having won three USGA championships and having played on eight Walker Cup teams, was the most hands-on of the presidents I worked with. Bill brought the playing side of the game to the table and was also a successful businessman, which is extremely valuable. He was a great supporter of the women's championships. So was Bill Williams, a brilliant lawyer who made a strong contribution in organizing the Rules of Golf.

Will Nicholson was fascinated with the Rules of Golf, was a great student of the game, and strongly believed in golf's traditions. As a businessman, Will had no problem in knowing what it was he wanted to protect and keep going.

Jim Hand was fascinated with the playing of the game and with the championships. He did a great deal in organizing the conduct of the U.S. Open, and got involved in course setup and course preparation. Before becoming president, Jim spent four years as chairman of the Championship Committee, which is an extended term. He was such a sound thinker and an absolutely outstanding president.

Stuart Bloch was deeply involved as chairman of the Implements & Ball Committee. He was so strong on the technical side of golf. He also pushed for better communications.

Grant Spaeth could probably work the street better than anybody I knew. He was very, very good with reaching out to public course players and with state and regional golf associations. He was a student of the Rules of Golf, a good player, and knew the traditions of the game.

As vice president, I worked very closely with Reg Murphy. Reg was quite remarkable. As a journalist and publisher, he had top-grade communication skills. He oversaw the USGA Centennial, the USGA's big 100th birthday celebration in 1995. Reg promoted the women's side of the game, gave the Women's Committee more responsibility, and was a keen observer at our women's championships.

I remember when Reg and his wife Diana attended the 1994 U.S. Women's Open at Indianwood Country Club in Lake Orion, Michigan. A few of us, including Diana, who is a public relations expert, were having an informal discussion about promoting the Women's Open. Several people kept comparing the Women's Open to the U.S. Open, which is a slightly unfair comparison.

In a very pointed way, Diana said, "But *this is* 'The Open,' isn't it?"

That's the kind of spirit that moved the Women's Open to the next level.

Every USGA president is so *dedicated* to the USGA's mission of preserving and protecting the best interests of the game, but each president had a different style.

My style was pure Judy. It was exhausting. I had anticipated that working in my role as president would take up about 50% of my time but it wound up taking 75%.

I wanted to build a constituency and at the same time make sure that everybody had a time to speak and to say what they wanted to say. I never just went with the crowd, but always liked to hear the whole story. That's my style, so I tried to communicate in every way I could.

Perhaps because I was the first female to hold the office, I was asked to give a number of speeches, a lot more than most presidents. I also had the women's side of the game to think of, because that's where I came from. I wouldn't just attend the U.S. Open, I'd go to the Women's Open, too. I wouldn't go just to the U.S. Amateur, I'd go the Women's Amateur. I wasn't the first president to do that. Reg Murphy was very involved in the women's championships and Bud Semple attended every USGA championship during his term of office.

Time management has always been a challenge for me and now, with all of my other responsibilities, I had a tiger by the tail.

The USGA's financial growth was strong on my watch and my two years as president seemed pretty upbeat. We were blessed in not having any real controversies at that time. We did have one difficulty in the Implements & Ball category about markings on the clubface, but we were able to flush that out.

Our 13 national championships grew in stature and more people entered than ever before. That was just timing and the natural evolution of our championships, which seem to attract more entries each year.

Spectators were another matter. We worked hard to get more people to attend our three open championships and our ten amateur championships and we had some very good results.

We also had what was at that time the largest crowd in Women's Open history at the 1997 United States Women's Open at Pumpkin Ridge Golf Club in North Plains, Oregon. More than 109,000 spectators came to watch, largely because Nancy Lopez was in contention throughout the week.

Nancy is the sweetheart of golf fans everywhere. She had won a host of tournaments, but had never won the Women's Open, although she had finished second three times.

I had helped to set up the course for the championship and thought we had established a good test for the field. When Nancy fired her third straight round in the 60s, she was seven under par and earned a spot in Sunday's final pairing, just three strokes behind the leader Alison Nicholas, a fine young English player.

Never have I seen so much excitement at a Women's Open. It was a beautiful, sunny day on Sunday. When it was time for the final pairing to tee off, Nancy was escorted through a crowd of several hundred people stretching from the women's locker room to the first tee. Thousands more lined the first fairway, 15 deep. When Nancy was introduced, there was a huge roar from the spectators and many of them shouted, "Nancy! Nancy!" The atmosphere was electrifying.

As the round began, both players were firing iron shots at the flagsticks, exchanging birdies on the second hole. Then, on the fourth, a par 5, Alison holed a 56-yard wedge shot for an eagle just after Nancy hit her third shot stiff to the hole. Alison went to 13 under par, a plateau that had never before been reached in the Women's Open.

The crowd was jovial, pulling for Nancy but also responding to Alison's fine shots. The media was another story. At least 50 photographers came to shoot what might be a historic Lopez win and their jostling for better vantage points caused unwanted confusion.

Through 13 holes, Alison and Nancy played brilliantly and Alison kept her three-stroke lead. At the 14th, a longish par 4, she made her first mistake, hitting an iron through the green into a very bad area of rough, dirt, twigs, and dry leaves. Alison made a double-bogey. Nancy made par and was now within one stroke of the lead with four holes to go.

The 15th hole was a medium-length par 3 and I had tucked the flagstick in the right portion near the entrance to the green, about eight paces from some heavy grass that made up the collar. It was the easiest hole location I had used all week on the 15th. In fact, Grant Spaeth needled me about using such an easy location in the final round. Nancy went for the flagstick but brushed her iron shot slightly to the right and her ball nestled in the rough. She faced a very difficult chip and could not stop the ball near the hole, making a four. Alison parred to take a two-stroke lead with three holes to play.

As Nancy walked to the 16th tee, I heard her mutter, "Stupid bogey," under her breath.

Not a single spectator had dropped out. In fact, we picked up hundreds more who wanted to see this showdown firsthand, and they streamed down the rough along the 16th fairway. When Nancy made a 15-foot birdie putt to again pull within one stroke, there were shouts from the spectators.

We heard another thunderous roar from the vicinity of the 18th green, and I knew the scores had been posted on the monster scoreboard.

A few skyboxes stood in back of the 17th green and one of them may have saved the Women's Open championship for Alison. Her approach shot bounded over the green and would have rolled much further down the hill had it not been stopped by the skybox. She was able to get a drop and chipped back toward the hole.

Nancy, meanwhile, was bunkered. Both players bogeyed.

A single stroke separated Nancy and Alison as they hit their approach shots to the par-5 18th. Alison hit safely on with her third shot, some 15 feet to the right of the hole. Nancy faced a third shot from about 20 yards short of the green but misjudged her chip, and it skipped 18 feet past the hole. We were down to the putts.

I cannot stress enough how loud the cheers for Nancy became. If Arnie had once again been in contention on the last hole of the U.S. Open, the commotion around the final green could not have been more intense. Several past champions, including Betsy King, Annika Sorenstam, and Laura Davies, squatted near the green to see the finish, which was something I'd never seen before.

To get to the meat in the coconut, Nancy missed her birdie putt. Alison safely two-putted for a par and the Women's Open championship, thrust her arms into the air, then went to Nancy and hugged her. Both players were in tears.

Once again, I marveled at the drama of women's golf. I was so proud of both of those players. Going head-to-head in an intense battle for a trophy that meant so much to each of them, they had shown the greatest sportsmanship and grace.

A few minutes later, Nancy was in the media tent for her press conference. She had telephoned her father, Domingo Lopez, and she repeated what he had said.

"You know, Nancy, maybe you are not supposed to win this tournament," he told her.

With all my heart, I hoped he was wrong.

~

In 1997 the Executive Committee voted to give one million dollars for each of the next three years to the First Tee. The First Tee is an initiative started by the World Golf Foundation to build short courses and learning centers in order to introduce youngsters to golf.

The USGA's contribution was considered very carefully. Three million dollars was a lot of money, but we looked at the First Tee's checks and balances, their intent, and their mission, and decided we would support this initiative.

A kickoff ceremony for the First Tee was scheduled in New York City's Central Park in November. Former President George Bush, who was Honorary Chairman, Tim Finchem, Commissioner of the PGA Tour, and Tiger's father, Earl Woods, were all scheduled to speak. I was to speak on behalf of the USGA.

I flew to New York, then took a cab to our hotel. That night, I had dinner with President Bush, Tim Finchem, and Earl Woods in a hotel suite. Earl did most of the talking and nearly all of it was about how he had raised Tiger. After dinner, President Bush asked if I wanted to ride over to The Tavern on the Green the next morning. I accepted and his Secret Service agents told me where to be and at what time. I showed up on time at the side entrance where an entourage of Secret Service agents was waiting.

President Bush came down the elevator and once we were in the limo, he pointed to a sort of odd-looking man on the street.

"See that guy?" Bush said. "He's always trying to hustle me for an autograph, then he sells them."

"Well, this morning," Bush chuckled, "I *stiffed* the guy!"

In my speech at the ceremony, I made a point of mentioning that the USGA had been funding junior programs for more than six years.

In 1993, our $90,000 grant helped jump-start the "Hook a Kid on Golf" initiative. We'd given the Metropolitan Golf Association $100,000 for its "Golfworks" program, which helped children get jobs at metropolitan-area golf courses and clubs. In 1996 we helped fund the start-up of a joint program with the Girl Scouts of America and the Ladies Professional Golf Association, which would hopefully result in thousands of girls playing golf.

I wanted to make sure that people knew the USGA Foundation had committed to supporting programs in a big way for those who are economically or physically challenged.

While I was president, I also spent a bit of time with United States President Bill Clinton. We met at the 1997 United States Open at Congressional Country Club in Bethesda, Maryland.

President Clinton had indicated early in the year that he wanted to attend. We began talking to the president's staff prior to the championship, then had meetings the weekend before and during the championship. It was heavy-duty stuff.

The president was going to attend Sunday's final round. Virtually overnight, the USGA staff built a tent on the 16th hole from which Clinton could watch the action. On Sunday, his Secret Service agents had their game faces on and carried machine guns hidden in golf bags.

We didn't know if President Clinton was going to participate in the trophy presentation or not. His Secret Service people did *not* want him to do it because the presentation was to be on the 18th green, a small island green, and they felt they couldn't assure the president's safety. But he always made up his own mind about where he would appear, so we weren't sure.

I was standing in the tent with Dick Ebersold, president of NBC Sports, when the president arrived with his daughter, Chelsea, a friend of Chelsea's, and a Secret Service retinue. I tried not to stand close to Clinton because I was sick with a terrible throat and bronchial infection.

When the president wanted to go to the NBC booth at the 18th hole, we all left the tent and I got in a golf cart with Dick.

The head of Clinton's Secret Service detail approached me and said, "Since you're president of the USGA, I think I'd better tell you that we've had two bomb threats."

"Do you know what time the bombs are supposed to go off?" I asked.

He said, "Sixteen-thirty," which is 4:30 P.M. in military time. By the time I figured that out, it was 4:25 P.M.

Everything flashed through my mind. In 1977 there had been a death threat against Hubert Green when he won the U.S. Open at Southern Hills Country Club, in Tulsa, Oklahoma. We hadn't stopped play then, and we were fortunate that nothing had happened. Now, I wondered, should I stop play? Should I get everybody off the golf course?

I had two radios and a cell phone, so I had three different communications pieces and could have reached everybody. I asked the Secret Service agent what their plans were.

"We're going to stay the course, unless the president decides differently," he said. "We're talking to him now."

That was the best guess of the Secret Service agents. They knew more about the situation than any of us. They must have believed it was a crank call or they wouldn't have said they were going to stay the course.

I said, "I guess we will, too."

I took Dick back to the TV compound and drove to the far corner of the property, as far as I could to get away from where the president was. I'm no fool! Frankly, I was afraid but I also wanted to think about the situation. By that time, "1630" had passed. I called Mike Butz, the USGA's assistant executive director, and told him of the situation.

Mike had been monitoring the television broadcast of the championship and said, "We have another problem. President Clinton has said on the air that no one has invited him to present the cup! Perhaps you should go to the broadcast booth and invite him to do it."

"I'm not going to do it," I said. "David Fay is in that booth. I will be happy to call David, or you can call David, and tell him we need to extend the invitation to the president and to explain to him that we didn't invite him earlier because his Secret Service escort didn't want him out there on that island green."

That's what happened. David invited President Clinton, but the Secret Service talked to him and persuaded him not to go. No one told me of the final decision.

The championship ended and Ernie Els won. I went to the scoring tent and waited for Ernie to sign his scorecard then we began walking to the 18th green for the trophy presentation.

Ernie is a big, hunk of a guy, so I got on the inside of him, so that he walked between me and where Clinton might still come over the bridge. If somebody were going to fire at the president, I wanted to have Ernie between me and the target!

I remember that I kept my eye on that bridge to see if Clinton was coming over while I introduced the champion. Ernie gave a speech, then I gave him the trophy. It was probably the quickest concluding ceremony that we've had in a long time. Believe me, this was one time when I was extraordinarily brief and to the point!

From Congressional Country Club, I went to the United States Women's Amateur Public Links Championship in Center Square, Pennsylvania.

The Women's Amateur Public Links was our first crack at promoting amateur championship attendance and the results were pretty amazing. Here we were in rural Pennsylvania, conducting a championship that traditionally attracts little attention, and our grassroots promotional effort brought a lot of people out to watch. Based on the number of cars in the parking lot and the number of people we saw out on the golf course, we had some 800 spectators each of the last two days of competition.

At the time, we had no formal pairings sheets, just typed sheets that we posted for the players, so I helped photocopy the pairings and passed them out to spectators, telling them how glad we were that they had come.

I visited with people in the gallery, asking them how they heard about the championship and discovered that a lot of people found out about it in stores, where we had placed posters and complimentary tickets. It was terrifically rewarding. We'd had an idea and the first time out of the box it was working.

When I returned to Colorado Springs, I picked up my messages on my answering machine.

One of the first messages was from my brother, Carl.

"Oh, honey," Carl said. "We just saw you on television with President Clinton. Gwen and I are just so proud of you. Dad would have been so proud to see you standing next to the president of the United States."

The very next message was from my brother, Fred.

"Judy," Fred said, "we were just watching the broadcast. What in the hell were you doing in a tent with that guy? I'm certainly glad that Dad wasn't here to see it. He must have rolled over in his grave!"

Like so many Kansans, Fred is a staunch Republican while Carl is obviously a bit more on the liberal side.

Chapter 28

[No Women Allowed]

When I became president, there was quite a lot of speculation about whether Augusta National Golf Club and the Royal & Ancient Golf Club of St. Andrews would invite me to join their all-male clubs. There was speculation in the press, speculation among my acquaintances, and speculation among my friends.

I was never invited.

Augusta National doesn't have any rule that specifies that the club must be all men. It just is. Frankly, if I'd been invited to join, I don't know if I could have done it. I don't know when I'd have had the time to really use an Augusta membership properly, as you should and would want to. I did not feel badly *at all* that I wasn't invited.

The R&A was a bit more tricky because all previous USGA presidents had been invited to be members.

Over the years, I'd also served on some of the R&A's committees. When I was chairman of our Amateur Status Committee, for example, I also served on the R&A's Amateur Status Committee. But I never, ever thought much about being a member of the R&A because it is an all-male club, period. It flat is. That's just the way it has been for 400 years.

I am a member of another club in St. Andrews, Scotland, the St. Rules Club, and I'm also an honorary member of the Troon Ladies Golf Club on the other coast of Scotland, near Prestwick, and I'm very honored to be a member of both.

I believe that some R&A members felt badly that I wasn't invited, but it never hindered me. I would have had a very different attitude if it had hindered my work on behalf of the USGA with the people of the R&A, such as the chairman of the General Committee, the captain, the chairman of the Championship Committee, the Amateur Status chairman, the I&B chairman, all of those people who make up their General Committee. I would have felt very awkward if it had negatively affected that relationship, but it didn't. Not one iota. Not once at any time.

One of my very dear friends, Maureen Garrett, a past Curtis Cup player and captain who received the USGA's Bob Jones Award in 1983, was extremely upset when the R&A broke tradition by not inviting me, as USGA president, to be a member.

Maureen is one of the most gracious people I've ever known, and one of the best at smoothing over difficult situations, so her venom about this particular subject surprised me. I was taken aback because Maureen is English and as the sort of grande dame of British golf has lifelong ties with the R&A, of which her son is a member.

"I was very upset that the R&A was hidebound and didn't acknowledge you because you are a woman," Maureen said. "I thought it was dreadful, not inviting you because you are a woman when they should be honoring the USGA presidency.

"Men get jealous, I think," she said. "They've got to be pretty big to accept the fact that a woman is better than they are. Thank God you were given the chance to prove yourself as president, and you proved yourself."

I have great personal relationships with a lot of people who live in the British Isles. When I'm in Scotland, I've been invited to the R&A and made to feel very comfortable. They've been most gracious.

In April 1997, I was in St. Andrews for an R&A meeting held every four years for all of the world's governing bodies of golf.

I walked and played golf with three women delegates. It was my last walk around the Old Course. I hadn't been playing much golf, certainly hadn't walked, and it was tough to make it on my bad knees.

I swore, "If I have to walk on these *stubs*, I will."

I'm happy to say that I made it around the Old Course and had a marvelous day.

David Fay and I met Richard Cole Hamilton, chairman of the R&A's General Committee, in the office of my friend Michael Bonallack, secretary of the R&A. Women aren't normally permitted in the R&A dining room, so I was amused because I wondered what we were going to do about lunch.

When we went to the dining room, by chance it was absolutely packed. Neither Richard nor Michael had thought about making a reservation, so we had no table. It had nothing to do with my being a female.

We went to the Town Hall where the meeting was going to begin. On the way, Richard, being a Scot, bought some candy bars—two for the price of one—and that became our lunch.

When the captain is in St. Andrews, he is in residence in the Captain's Suite at the Walden House. That night, Harvey and Nadya Douglas had a dinner party in the suite for me, Helen Webb, Ian Webb, who was vice chairman of the R&A's General Committee, Richard, David, and Michael and Angela Bonallack.

As we sat for drinks, we had that spectacular view of the R&A clubhouse, across the 18th hole, across the 1st hole of the Old Course, across those golden, sunny links to the sea. It is one of most special views regarding golf that I have ever seen. I love it.

Richard is a very funny man and tells great stories. He was telling a story, when he suddenly stopped. "Oh, I have to do a little presentation," he said. "I have to do a little speech."

He had been pulling my leg and I'd been pulling his, when he said, "And it's about you, Judy."

"Oh, Richard," I said, "would you get serious. Be quiet and sit down."

Then he said the nicest, nicest things about the cooperation we'd had, and the relationship he'd had with me, and how the R&A and the General Committee felt about me, then he gave me a very special gift from the General Committee, a sapphire and diamond brooch.

It was another of those rare times when I was literally speechless. I stood up and fumbo-jumbo'd around and told them how much I appreciated it. In this wonderful setting with good friends, with that historic view through the towering old-fashioned windows, it was a fabulous evening.

They gave me that wonderful token of appreciation, of which there are only two in the world. I was given the first one. Angela Bonallack, a dear friend of mine, received the same pin when her husband Michael retired as secretary of the R&A.

I think their gesture and their gift came from their hearts and I accepted it from my heart.

This was a two-day meeting that gave me the perfect opportunity to meet golfers and golf administrators from around the world.

That same year, we began working on the USGA's "Spirit of the Game" initiative about etiquette and the Rules of Golf and how to educate golfers at large about these two subjects. The idea really came from Arnold Palmer.

In 1997 I was in Florida and visited Dow and Linda Finsterwald at their winter home at Bay Hill. It was right after Arnold's surgery for prostate cancer. Arnold and the Finsterwalds have been close friends for many years, and we visited Arnold so that I could give him my best wishes and those of the association.

That night Arnold went into great detail about the fact that, as the game grew and expanded to nontraditional players, some of the courtesies of the game, the etiquette you use around the golf course, were missing.

Arnold was worried because he felt strongly about proper dress and behavior on the golf course. His concerns struck a chord with me.

Arnold had been the honorary chairman of the USGA Members Program since it began in 1975 and contributed a great deal to the program as well as to the game.

I thought he was right and made a lot of sense, so we started working on the "Spirit of the Game" program through our Communications Department. We decided to produce a video. The one thing I didn't want to have us mention was "etiquette" because the word is a turnoff to children and a lot of other people, as if by saying "etiquette" we were invoking all of the piety of Miss Manners or Amy Vanderbilt.

The idea was to produce a video about courtesies on the golf course and Karen Moraghan, a consultant to the USGA, took the ball and ran with it. She developed an excellent video. It's still available and we have thus far distributed some 400,000 copies.

Right at the core, the USGA has a responsibility and a commitment to teach people *about* the game. We're the historians. We have the finest golf library in the world today and it's up to us to teach people about golf's history. In my mind, it's also up to us to teach people about the spirit of the game, which is as important as seeing three knuckles on your left hand with the "V" pointing between your right shoulder and your chin.

It's so important because if you don't have that fabric around the game of golf when you play, you're playing something, but it isn't golf.

Golf's code of conduct has been really important in my life. From the time I first set foot on a golf course, I was taught about this code. I was taught where I needed to be, where I needed to stand, who attended the flagstick, who raked the bunker, whose turn it was to play. All of those things were taught to me by my parents, particularly my mother.

Mother believed that people should be considerate of other people. That's why I love the game, because of the friendly spirit in which it is and should be played. Whether it's playing for fun or in serious competition, this conduct is woven through this game. It has to be there.

We also expect a certain code of behavior from spectators. At my first U.S. Open as USGA president, the 1996 Open at Oakland Hills Country Club, in Bloomfield Hills, Michigan, we had a problem with some of the spectators. Early in the week, I had our security people escort four spectators off the course because they were out of line. They were loud, obnoxious, and had obviously had too much to drink.

The USGA constantly has to review all of its policies, and alcohol is certainly one of them. At the Open, we need to not only look at the issue of what time alcohol service starts and stops, but also at whether alcohol sales need to be barred completely.

Another policy that needs constant review is what prices we allow the host clubs of national championships to charge spectators and contestants for food and beverages. I regret to say that I've been to host clubs where the price of the food was so high that the contestants couldn't eat there. There were, in fact, two clubs where we went off site to have lunch every day because the prices were too high.

When you invite guests to your club you should want things to be reasonable and affordable. Spectators and contestants are also guests of the club, and the USGA needs to constantly be aware of that.

When I was on the WC, I remember suggesting to certain clubs that they have a contestant's menu with reasonable prices. Some host club memberships just don't think of it because they sign for their food. A lot of clubs require members to spend a minimum amount of money at the club each month, so they might as well spend $10 on a hot dog because it makes their minimums go quicker.

On the other hand, one of the finest examples of hospitality was the way Southern Hills Country Club in Tulsa, Oklahoma, treated contestants in the inaugural U.S. Women's Mid-Amateur Championship in 1987. The club offered contestants a complimentary buffet breakfast each morning. It was a great idea and I give the credit to Dena Nowotny, a Southern Hills member who was on the WC and the first chairman of the Women's Mid-Amateur Championship Committee.

Chapter 29

[My Exit]

It was January 24, 1998, Tucson, Arizona. For the last time, I stood at the podium of the USGA's Annual Meeting as president. My term had ended and Buzz Taylor would become the new president.

My journey as USGA president had been smooth.

The USGA is like a great clock, each gear meshing with the next, reliably ticking off the years. No single person really makes a difference without the meshing of all of the gears—the volunteers and staff.

Honesty, diplomacy, discretion, humility, and loyalty to the game matter most in the association's leadership. Every two years that leadership is passed to other individuals and for the next two years, they're given an opportunity to help look after the game.

I loved the work, loved the people and, above all, I loved the game. While I was president I'd traveled to dozens of American cities and to England, Scotland, and the Philippines on USGA business. I knew the routine well: the scurry to the airport, a seat in coach class, a pile of papers on my lap, a flight spent scribbling away on our shop accounts, inventories, and letters on behalf of the USGA. Land at an airport, get the rental car, try to find the hotel, meet hundreds of new people, attend meetings or make a speech.

The trips became a somewhat harried routine but the work was a challenge I loved.

Some people say that I brought a certain toughness to the presidency, and a willingness to do the small things as well as the large, to pass out pairing sheets as well as meet with the R&A. I asked a great deal of the staff, but never asked them to do something that I wasn't willing to do myself. I tried to be a cheerleader for the staff and volunteers and tried to keep things upbeat. I preferred to *think* about the game, rather than react emotionally. And because I never cared about who got the credit, I think we were able to do a lot of good.

As president, I loved being very close to the national championships. Watching the best players in the world compete against each other was a special thrill.

Another great part was making friends and meeting people from around the world through the USGA's relationship with the Royal & Ancient Golf Club of St. Andrews, the World Amateur Golf Council, and other allied associations.

Any USGA president must have a good relationship with the R&A because we have so many common interests, such as writing the Rules of Golf. I had enjoyed very positive experiences with the R&A's general chairman, Richard Cole Hamilton, Michael Bonallack, a good friend who was secretary of the R&A at that time, and Ian Webb, the R&A vice chairman who had been chairman of the R&A's Amateur Status and Conduct Committee when I held the same position on the USGA side. Over the years, I had the good fortune to make many friends in the United Kingdom through both men's and women's golf.

Oddly enough, my only really unpleasant experience as president had been with an R&A member.

Whenever I went to the British Open I had dinner with the R&A members and committee people. One night, I sat at a table with former USGA president Will Nicholson, his wife Shirley, and several members of the R&A. An R&A member sitting next to me asked, "Now, what do you do with the USGA?"

I said, "I'm on the Executive Committee."

He was sort of full of himself and 10 minutes later asked if I knew Will Nicholson. Of course, Will was sitting right there at our table, but he knew that Will had a lot to do with the Masters, and proceeded to also tell me, "You know, Will Nicholson has been president of the USGA."

Another 10 minutes passed and he again asked me, "Now, what do you do with the USGA?"

I was getting bored with the conversation and said, "I am president of the USGA. I have the exact same job that Will Nicholson had, and he's a great friend of mine."

The fellow almost fell off his chair, but he was condescending to me as a woman, I thought, and he had pushed my buttons a little too much.

While president, I got a big kick out of working with USGA staff members, who are very dedicated to looking after this game. I looked forward to each visit to Golf House and, during my second year, tried to be there for a couple of days each month. David Fay and I could have done our business almost anywhere, but I would have missed the interaction with the staff.

Now, I was ready to fade into the background. As I gave my last speech as president I looked out at the audience with sheer appreciation.

The friends who had come to the 1996 Annual Meeting to usher me into office were now there to ring me out. Members of the XC and WC sat in the front of the room. My brother Carl, his wife Gwen, and my nephew Chris Bell were there. Paula Petrie, Ellie McColl, and Tish Preuss had come from Colorado Springs. Dean Knuth, the USGA's former director of handicapping, had flown in from San Diego. Barbara McIntire, Joanie Birkland, and Dena Nowotny smiled up at me in support. The USGA staff, the USGA Fellows, and most of the USGA committees were represented.

People seemed relaxed. These were my friends.

In two years I had given some 80 speeches. I'd answered some tricky questions; Rules of Golf questions, equipment issues, concerns about Equitable Stroke Control. I no longer had as much fear of the microphone as I'd once had.

I looked out at my pals in the audience. Nearly every one of them had helped me in ways large and small. Barbara had run the business. Former WC chairmen had given me advice. The XC members had given me advice and support. I was extremely grateful to them all.

The previous day had been hectic. I had chaired my last XC meeting, and it was a good one, but my composure drained away when we met with the USGA staff.

We gathered in a fairly large room that afternoon. After everyone filed in, the members of the XC and staff sat in folding chairs, completely lining the room's perimeter. I had to smile. I'd heard that the word around Golf House was that staff members came to work each day, then just waited for the phone to ring so that Judy Bell could give them something else to do.

I was surprised that so many staff people had bothered to come. David Fay, Mike Butz, Maggie Giesenhagen, Tom Meeks, Tony Zirpoli, Marty Parkes, Tim and Karen Moraghan, the regional managers, the communications and championship departments, the handicapping department, the USGA Fellows, and many more.

Members of the Women's Committee sat at a long conference table and I stood at the end of the table with Joanie Birkland, the chairman.

I opened the meeting with a few comments of welcome, then looked around the room at all of the familiar faces.

"I'd like to thank the staff," I said in a quavering voice, then broke down in tears. I tried to hold back, but I knew I would miss all of these relationships going forward. I couldn't get through it, and bowed my head as I welled up. What got me was seeing all of the staff members in that room and my memories of working so closely with so many of them over the years. All those people. All that work. All those years.

They began applauding. I couldn't stop sniffling and, one by one, each person in the room stood up until everyone was standing and applauding. A few were as emotional as I was.

When they finally sat down, I couldn't continue for a few moments and Joanie, who was also a little choked up, stepped in. "On behalf of the Women's Committee," Joanie said shakily, "I'd like to thank the executive committee for giving Judy to us as president. It meant a great deal to us all."

It was a very poignant moment in my life.

Things got back to normal that night when we had the annual Links Club Dinner, which is attended by the executive committee, past presidents, past XC members, and the winner of the Bob Jones Award. Nancy Lopez had been named recipient of the award, which pleased me no end.

There's a tone of levity to the Links Club Dinner—a lot of ribbing and laughter—so I felt very upbeat. During the program I confessed to Nancy that it was my fault she had lost the 1997 Women's Open because of where I had located the hole on the 15th green on Sunday.

Nancy laughed, and said, "Judy, I'm relieved. Now I can quit blaming myself for brushing that shot to the right."

At the end of the dinner, Buzz Taylor, the incoming president, gave me a few pointed gifts that related to facets of my style with which all XC members were familiar. Buzz gave me a poster-sized telephone credit card with unlimited minutes, which referred to my penchant for long-winded telephone conversations. He presented an old-fashioned windup alarm clock that had "Judy Bell Time" printed on it in reference to my *occasional* late entry into meetings. And as a final spoof, Buzz gave me a one-quart mason jar full of scotch.

Buzz had done his homework. He had talked to Dow Finsterwald who told him about a diet I had tried with Dow's wife Linda and another friend Eunice Moore. Our rule was that we were allowed one drink a night and no more. One night, just for fun, when Linda and Eunice came to my house for dinner I served them their single drink of choice in a quart mason jar.

The Links Club dinner was upbeat and fun.

A few months before, as the end of my term had drawn nearer, I worked a lot of hours trying to finish the USGA projects I was involved in. The USGA Fellowship Program was just one year old, so I was helping with the process of getting it going. I worked on the process of the grants initiative and also made sure that our USGA assistance to state and regional golf associations was meeting their needs. I'd worked right up to the end at a sure-footed pace.

Now, I would give my final speech and I was ready to hand over the reins to Buzz, who had become a good friend. It was his time to take over and promote the causes that he believed would keep the USGA on course.

A few minutes before I was scheduled to begin, Trey Holland, the USGA's vice president, was to give his Rules Committee report.

I don't have a closer friend than Trey. What really bonded us at first was that he has a very different sense of humor and so do I. When Reg Murphy was president, Trey and I usually sat together at XC meetings. Trey would whisper something inane to me, I'd have trouble stifling my laughter, and finally Reg had to separate us. We must have seemed like a couple of schoolchildren.

Trey and I had since worked on a lot of projects together. Trey is a brilliant guy, very cerebral, and is probably one of the most knowledgeable people on the Rules of Golf today. I've always told him, however, that underneath he's just an Indiana Hoosier. He can't help it.

Trey is a brilliant doctor and has a very, very caring side to him, although you're lucky if you see it once. I adore Trey and his wife Cheryl. I'm crazy about them and wouldn't trade anything for their friendship.

At that time, neither Trey nor I could foresee the critical role he would one day play in my life.

When he was introduced at this, my final annual meeting as president, Trey stood up and didn't say a word about the Rules of Golf. He had always been right on point in his previous reports but this time he told a very funny joke about pigs, said that was his report, then became choked up.

"Judy," he said, "it's been a great ride."

From my perspective, Trey was right.

In my speech, I wanted to do well and finish on a high note. I had a moment of panic when I thought I would just look at the first page of my speech while another person addressed the meeting.

I couldn't find my speech. It wasn't with my papers. It wasn't any place. I didn't know what to do. A couple of people in the audience had helped me write it, so I thought, *I'll just invite them up and we'll give the speech jointly!*

Finally, I looked to my left and Trey had a sick smile on his face. He'd taken my speech and was hiding it from me.

After he handed it over, I stood at the podium to speak.

"It has been a pure joy to be so closely involved with the United States Golf Association," I said. "I know of no other sport where those who play the game give countless volunteer hours back to the game."

I spoke of some of the goals we'd reached during the last two years and the thrill of watching golfers, from a disabled child to the players in the Walker Cup match. Then I issued some challenges.

"Do all you can about the pace of play," I told the audience. "It is what most threatens enjoyment of the game.

"Try to figure out how more golfers can get handicaps within the system. Sometimes I think we throw up obstacles along the way, so take a look at getting rid of Equitable Stroke Control once and for all. Why not turn in the score you shoot?

"Deal as quickly as possible with the issue of fancy equipment and the ball going too far. I know that *my* ball isn't going too far, but I can't say that for the best players in the world. Good golf and low scoring must be based on skill.

"Be vigilant about the spirit of the game. It's clearly our charge to educate golfers, young and old. Otherwise, they are playing *something*, but it isn't golf."

I ended and my friends stood up and applauded. Maybe they stood because, while I wasn't perfect, they knew that I had given my all. I stuck it out, and I did not fail.

That night we had the Bob Jones Dinner and I participated in the introduction of Nancy Lopez.

It was a pleasure to recall Nancy's triumphs and grace. I spoke of her victory in the New Mexico Women's Amateur Championship in 1969 when she was 12 years old, then addressed a more serious issue.

"It's tragic that even at that late date, discrimination was still commonplace in our country," I said. "Nancy experienced those rites of exclusion, but she survived them and was tempered by them. It's a mark of her great character that she has never chosen to discuss them. She simply kept her eyes on the prize and, with the help of a devoted mother and her father, Domingo Lopez—who simply told her to smile in the face of adversity—Nancy began her march to one of the greatest careers in the history of the game."

I said that Nancy was that rare person who will be remembered with the very highest regard as long as the game is played.

"For what you have given to this game that we all love, in recognition of the example that you have set, for your integrity, strength of character, and your grace, it is my greatest honor and pleasure to present you, Nancy, with the 1998 Bob Jones Award."

Domingo Lopez sat at a table near the podium. In her speech, Nancy thanked him for all he had done for her over the years. When she said with great emotion, "You've been a great father," I doubt there was a dry eye in the room.

The evening ended. My term was finished.

As I lay in bed that night, I thought: *Now, it's over. You did the best you could do at the time. Don't look back and wish you had done it any other way.*

I slept like a baby.

The next day was Sunday. We had an informal retreat for the USGA Fellows. Various staff members coached them on communications. We had lunch by the hotel pool then played golf. The Super Bowl was televised that night, and Denver was playing Green Bay, so we didn't miss that. Marty Parkes, director of communications, is a devoted Packer fan and wore his cheese head, but it didn't do any good and I was thrilled when Denver won.

There were still committee meetings to attend, so a number of people stayed over. On Monday night I had my last dinner of the annual meeting with Barbara McIntire, Tish Preuss, and Rhonda Glenn. It was a relaxing evening, very low key. We had drinks on the patio of a wonderful Mexican restaurant, talked golf, and reminisced a bit about the past two years. It was a fine, clear desert night and the tiny white lights on the trees around the patio sparkled and shone.

It was time to get on with my life.

Chapter 30

[A Short Story Ends]

That winter, Barbara McIntire was named captain of the 1998 United States Curtis Cup team. She was delighted and quite surprised, because she had been captain in 1976 when she led the U.S. team, which included Beth Daniel and Nancy Lopez, to a victory.

I was very pleased for her. I felt that the WC's somewhat surprising selection had come about because Barbara was a proven winner. The Curtis Cup Match had become so competitive and we had won only one of our last four encounters with Great Britain and Ireland. We needed another victory.

In July, before we left for the match at the Minikahda Club in Minneapolis, we felt the first stirrings of trouble with our businesses. In the summer of 1988, Oklahoma Publishing Company, of Oklahoma City, had bought 65% of the stock in The Broadmoor Hotel. In 1990 the company acquired another 15% to secure 80% interest. Its president, Edward L. Gaylord, was also involved in Gaylord Entertainment Company, a publicly held company that, among other properties, also owned the Grand Ole Opry in Nashville, Tennessee, and the Opryland Hotel. Thayer Tutt and Karl Eitel had always encouraged a friendly environment that hotel shop owners had enjoyed, but the new owners were interested in having their own retail division.

The hotel had always had a family feeling, with the same guests returning year after year and a solid group of members at the golf club, but things change. Now the clubhouse of The Broadmoor Golf Club had been torn down and a new structure was being erected, along with the reworking of the parking and the grounds. While these actions were progressive, it was very disruptive to business until the work was completed. A modern interior replaced the homey old clubhouse and the new owners had added a state-of-the-art spa in an attempt to attract more business. Changes were in the air that, in the long run, would grace this wonderful landmark, but the start posed some struggles for us and for our customers.

In addition, we felt the pressure when the new management kept raising the rent for shop spaces. It had been a constant worry that our sales couldn't keep up with the rising cost of doing business. Then, in May 1998, The Broadmoor management told us they wanted more space for hotel-owned shops. They wanted A Short Story.

It was a closed subject, no negotiation. We had officially been put on notice.

We would have to close this original shop after the first of the year and we believed it foretold the closure of our other shops. They had already taken over our tennis and golf shop operations.

We kept working, but we knew the end was near.

Meanwhile, the Curtis Cup Match was a bright gleam on the horizon. Barbara was working hard to assemble and captain a great team. I was looking forward to the Minikahda encounter, simply because all Curtis Cup players love to go to the match.

Not only is the Curtis Cup a spirited contest, it's a huge reunion of past players from both sides. If you were a past player and could travel, you wouldn't miss it for the world.

The reunion of old friends is the best part of each Curtis Cup and there are wonderful activities for past players. A golf match called "The Supporters Saucer" pits past American players and current WC members against their counterparts from GB&I and the Ladies Golf Union. The Curtis Cup dinner at the end of the match is always entertaining and warm, with many toasts and reminiscences from both sides.

One of my favorite evenings is the dinner for past players and captains, a tradition started by Maureen Garrett and Jeanne Bisgood in 1972. Whether you are president of the Ladies Golf Union, captain of the R&A, president of the USGA, or the wife of the president of the host club, you cannot attend this dinner unless you are a past Curtis Cup player or captain.

It's a doozy of a night. Because no officials can attend, players and captains can say anything they want—no matter how critical—and what they say will never leave the room. At one dinner, the players talked about how they felt on the first tee of the Curtis Cup Match. They talked about how they felt about their partner in alternate shot. And let's just say that officials have been discussed *in detail.* It's a riot, and no past player would miss it.

Barbara takes great pride in being an American and she used nationalistic fervor to light a fire under her 1998 team. In the van used to transport the team, she played a tape of patriotic songs over and over. At the hotel, she invited past players and Captains to a team meeting to give inspiring pep talks, and she gave her players inspirational sayings to hang on the walls of their rooms.

It worked and we were all elated, especially Barbara, when the United States of America won the match, ten to eight. The night of the celebration dinner, Barbara, Joanie Birkland, and I flew with Judy Eller Street in her plane to Philadelphia for the 50th anniversary of the U.S. Girls' Junior Championship at Merion Golf Club.

After the Players Dinner, Barbara and I returned to Colorado Springs to prepare for the closing of A Short Story. We'd seen it coming. Still, it was an emotional wrench, but probably more so for Barbara. A Short Story was our mother ship. I had been extremely busy with my volunteer work for the USGA and my retail consulting business, but Barbara had been running our shops on a daily basis. It was tough for her, but not as tough for me, as I probably like change better than she does.

We'd had a good run at The Broadmoor for 36 years, from 1962 through 1998. We still had the other stores; The Second Story, the Men's Shop at The Broadmoor, the Little Kitchen, and Pappagallo, and I guess I thought we'd have those four stores for quite a while longer. We closed A Short Story in February 1999.

In the spring, the hotel management told us that they wanted our other spaces as well, and that we needed to be out by the end of February 2000.

We prepared to go out of business. We hired a firm from California that specialized in running going-out-of-business sales. We worked on the newspaper and radio ads, and sent some 5,000 letters to our longtime customers. We were going to start the sale in November and wanted to invite our customers in first. They were the reason we had lasted so long. We said in our letter that we regretted that we would no longer be in business to serve our customers and that we were looking forward to seeing them along the way. We wanted to let them know that we appreciated their loyalty and all the purchases they'd made over the years, so we wanted them to have a head start in purchasing sale merchandise.

It was a time of emotional valleys, but there were peaks, too.

Late in the year, the USGA announced that Barbara was to receive the Bob Jones Award, the USGA's highest award, which is presented for distinguished sportsmanship. The award was presented at the 2000 Annual Meeting in San Francisco. It was a great tribute to my business partner, and a little scary, too.

Trey Holland, who was now USGA president, and Carol Semple Thompson, who had played on both of Barbara's Curtis Cup teams and was chairman of the Bob Jones Award Committee, escorted Barbara to the stage. A photographer snapped away as Trey and Carol presented the award to her. The photographer told them to back up, which they did, but the stage was so narrow that Barbara fell off the back and Carol, trying to hold Barbara up, also landed behind the stage.

After everyone was righted, Barbara, who is extremely poised in the most difficult situations, began her speech. It went off without a hitch until the very end. She had copied a poem on the last page, and the page was missing. Without skipping a beat, Barbara recited the poem from memory.

Once again, Barbara had finished like a champion.

The next day we returned to The Broadmoor to finish running the sale, which went on until the end of February. Then we closed the stores for good.

The reaction of our community amazed and touched me. Three television stations had covered the beginning of our sale. Now, they came back to cover the end. The gist of their stories was that this long-time business had been an asset to Colorado Springs for 36 years, but changing resort business trends had put us out of business.

Reporters from the newspaper and the three television stations wanted to interview Barbara and me. We held up fine until one occasion, when Barbara said she couldn't do an interview because she was so emotional that she couldn't talk about it any more. I had to do the interview alone.

The TV stations ran the stories in their midday news programs and again at night. One night they led their nightly news with the story.

On the night when we closed the stores for good, we met in the Little Kitchen and shared champagne with our 12 remaining employees, then took everyone to dinner at Bell's Deli.

I was resigned to the fact that we were out of business. We'd been trying to get it done for three months. It was a hard push at the end, a lot of work, and it was finally over. I felt a sense of relief.

By then, our employees had found other things to do and those who didn't want to work any more simply retired.

The next morning, we had no shops to go to, but after being on my feet for more than three months, I felt pretty good.

Now we had to decide what to do to make a living. I had the Bell Retail Group, a consulting business, and worked with the Homestead Resort in Hot Springs, Virginia, and Birdwood Golf Course, a public facility in Charlottesville owned by the University of Virginia. We still had a lot to do to get the businesses sorted out, and at the time we were doing fulfillment for USGA volunteer uniforms and art prints. So, we had some activity going.

I wasn't that concerned about the future. I figured that we would do something in the way of merchandising and just needed time to figure out what that would be.

Barbara felt uprooted, but I tried to be positive and look at this as an opportunity. We talked a lot, sorting it all out and discussing whether we wanted to open another store. We had kept our display antiques from the shops, just in case. We considered opening a store and looked at different locations in town, which took up some time, but the economics of it didn't look favorable. At one of two locations we seriously considered, we'd have had to buy the property. We couldn't justify paying the asking price because, with that mortgage, we would have set up the business to fail.

The other opportunity was quite attractive and appealing, but we just weren't ready to once again make a commitment to run a day-to-day retail business.

In August 2000, the USGA followed tradition by naming a past president as captain of the United States of America World Amateur Team. The only difference was that, while it was a men's team, I was that past president. So, I became the only person in the world to have captained both a men's and women's World Amateur Team, again making the record book in an unusual way.

The 2000 U.S. Amateur Championship was played at Baltusrol Golf Club, in Summit, New Jersey, just before the World Amateur Team Championship at Sporting Club Berlin in Bad Saarow, Germany.

USGA President Trey Holland asked me to go over a week early to support the U.S.A. team in the Women's World Amateur Team Championship and to stand in for him at the opening ceremony.

When I arrived in Germany I was a captain without a team. In fact, I didn't even know who would be on the team because after a lot of discussion, the decision had been made that final selection would depend on performance in the U.S. Amateur. I had lobbied hard for this decision because I wanted to be sure that our U.S. Amateur Champion, if he was an American, would be a member of our team.

It was an intriguing process. During the Amateur Championship, Bryce Molder, David Eger, and Ben Curtis were named to the team. The selection committee then made an unprecedented move. The committee asked John Harris, who was on the cusp as far as being selected for the team, to make the trip to Germany with the possibility of actually playing for our side once the outcome of the Amateur Championship was determined.

John was a past Amateur champion and remained one of our best amateurs. He would, of course, make the team if he won the Amateur or went to the semifinal round and he could even make it if a foreign player won the U.S. title. John, however, failed to qualify for match play.

Luke Donald, of Scotland, went to the semifinals and looked as though he could win the whole thing. David Eger also advanced to the semifinals and Bryce Molder went to the quarterfinals and both were on the team.

John Harris and Ben Curtis arrived in Germany on Friday, six days before the competition started. David and Bryce arrived around noon the next Monday. We now had four U.S.A. players in Germany but we still didn't know who the fourth member of the team would be. When Luke Donald got beat in the semifinals, two Americans, James Driscoll and Jeff Quinney, advanced to the final. John Harris's chances of being named to the team diminished severely.

But John is such a fine player and has a wonderful competitive spirit. He played four practice rounds with Ben that gave Ben a lot of confidence about learning the courses.

David and Bryce, who arrived Monday morning, three days before the championship started, got three practice rounds under their belts so our team was slowly coming together. Whoever won the U.S. Amateur would be invited to play on the team. Who knew if either player would be free to go to Germany? Jeff and James were all square after 36 holes and went to sudden death. They couldn't finish because of darkness that night and had to continue the next morning (Monday). Jeff won on the 39th hole. He accepted a spot on our team, flew to Germany Monday night, and arrived at the resort in time to play the last five holes with the other members of the team. Jeff had to be pretty tired but he was keyed up about winning the U.S. Amateur and was raring to go in Germany. With this helter-skelter schedule, the USGA had to deal with passports, travel arrangements, and uniforms, all at the last minute. In fact, we brought in a tailor to fit the uniforms in Germany.

David Eger and I had talked before going to Germany. We had had our differences in the past, but now we were on the same side, together, without any conflicts.

I could tell that we had both put the past behind us. He knew what it took to win and what it took to be a team player, and he was determined to show a lot of leadership with his teammates. He accomplished that.

We had one team meeting before the competition began at which David, John Harris, and I talked about the losing teams we'd played on. We talked about the fact that we weren't the favorites and we needed to go out and just play the golf course. Bryce Molder knew what we were talking about because he played on the U.S.A. Walker Cup team that lost at Nairn.

The Faldo course at Sporting Club was an excellent test of links golf. The Palmer course there was more of a parkland course, well treed. We played the Palmer course, the easier course to score on, the first day, so our strategy was to come out of the chute with three scores under par. Then when we played the Faldo course we would try to hold our own to par.

Our supporters were strong, but few; Joanie Birkland, Barbara McIntire, Trey and Cheryl Holland, David Eger's parents, and Wendy Uzelak, a USGA regional affairs manager.

In the format of this championship, the best three out of four scores count each day toward the team's total.

We opened the first round on the Palmer course with David shooting 67, Bryce firing a 69, and Ben and Jeff both shooting 71. We were at 207, nine under, tied with Canada for the lead. South Africa was four back.

The second day, on the Faldo course, we took a one-stroke lead over Germany when Bryce led off with a 71 and Jeff Quinney shot 72. David and Ben both shot 73, for 423. It was a strong team effort at level par for the day.

We'd had sunny weather the first two days but lightning struck on Saturday, literally and figuratively. We separated ourselves from the pack with 205 on the Palmer course, despite a 45-minute lightning delay. Bryce shot an amazing 65. David followed with 69, and Jeff's score of 71 counted. We moved into a seven-stroke lead over Germany. GB&I was third at 11 under par, one shot ahead of Australia. We never knew how we stood with the other teams until the end of the day. We just knew how we stood with the golf course.

The final day was rainy, windy, and cold with temperatures in the 50s and we were playing the more difficult Faldo Course. "Be patient," I said to my players. They played their own games and let the results speak for them.

Bryce was brilliant with a 68, the best round in the championship considering the conditions. Ben Curtis shot a two-under-par 70, and David Eger shot 75 to bring the bacon home. We won by 16 strokes, with GB&I second. Australia finished third.

The USA had won its 11th victory in 22 tries at the World Amateur Team Championship, better known around the globe as the Eisenhower Trophy.

The awards ceremony was held in the pouring rain. Luckily for us, we were still wearing our rain suits. We lowered our American flag as a band played "The Star-Spangled Banner" for the winning team. Even in the rain, it never sounded better. I gave our acceptance speech in German. Before leaving for the championship I had checked out my speech with Anna Bonnelycke, a German friend in Colorado Springs, just in case.

After we received the Eisenhower trophy, we attended a reception where the German Golf Federation gave me a life-sized Gund bear. I brought it home on the plane.

This was a special group of guys and I was proud of their performance and proud to be their captain. I never had more fun.

Chapter 31

[Beginning Again]

The year 2001 was the most hectic and frightening year of my life.

It started out pretty well, however, because in December 2000, I had taken a new job. I began working as Consulting Director of the USGA Foundation. I wanted to see the Foundation build and get started on the right foot and I was interested in working with the USGA Fellowship and on the grants initiative.

I had a lot of confidence in the USGA Fellows. The greatest thing about my role was to help them to grow in their decision-making and in leadership skills. Steve Czarnecki and David Shapiro were from the first class of USGA Fellows and now worked in the USGA office as managers of the Fellowship and Grants programs. The three of us were a management team. I had so much confidence in David and Steve and to watch them grow in these positions gave me tremendous enjoyment. In my book they were top-notch.

The culture in the office was very collaborative and collegial, with 12 to 14 Fellows working at any one time, plus Steve, David, our administrative assistant, Wilma Jordan, our technical assistant, Mark Boger, and me.

We shared a common goal—to run this part of the USGA Foundation with an entrepreneurial spirit as a grant-making agency and to take proactive steps with new projects. The USGA Grants Committee—made up of volunteers from the XC and from outside the association—meets three times a year to review all grant applications. The committee makes recommendations to the XC about the applicants in terms of dollars and how the funds would be used. The Fellows collect all the data about the grant request through site visits and phone calls, then present each application at the grants meetings. This process worked just as we had planned. It was extremely valuable to the committee and an excellent opportunity for the Fellows in terms of leadership and service.

I was glad to have the new position. After we closed the shops at The Broadmoor, I needed to do some meaningful work or I'd feel useless and bored.

Barbara, too, seemed at loose ends, so we finally decided to look around for certain niches where there was a need for our services. There seemed to be a need for a strong retailing presence in the merchandise end of special events, namely golf championships such as the United States Women's Open and the United States Senior Open.

This was right up our alley, so we pursued those two venues for 2001, when the Women's Open would be at Pine Needles Lodge and Golf Club in Southern Pines, North Carolina, and the Senior Open would be at Salem Country Club in Peabody, Massachusetts. Although both championships were being played in the same year, we bid on them, thinking that we'd probably get only one. Much to our surprise, we won both contracts.

But retailing, especially golf retailing, was something we surely knew how to do. We developed buying plans, worked with the fixture vendors, set up the merchandise tents, received all the goods, made certain that everything was in inventory, and supervised the volunteers who worked in the merchandise tent.

From the first week in March through the end of the Women's Open, in June, Tish and Barbara lived in Southern Pines. From mid-March until the end of the Senior Open, in July, we had a staff person, Helen Kirkland, in Massachusetts. I came in periodically to work at both sites. After the Women's Open, we all went to Massachusetts to work the Senior Open.

It was a tremendous amount of work but a lot of fun because, by this time, we'd all recovered from the closing of the shops and this was an exciting new enterprise. I particularly enjoyed working with Kelly Miller and Peggy Kirk Bell at their course, Pine Needles. Kelly is Peggy's son-in-law and the Bells run Pine Needles as a family enterprise. It's a special place.

The week of the Women's Open, Pine Needles was nearly overrun with spectators, caddies, players, media, and the 2,500 people needed to work the championship. We set up the merchandise tent as we would a large, luxurious shop, buying North Carolina country antiques to display soft goods.

We filled the tent with live plants to soften the displays and added Peggy's beautifully restored Model T Ford as a centerpiece. The merchandise center looked great and business was brisk.

For the first time since I've been attending the Women's Open as either a contestant or rules official, I didn't see much golf. We were too busy taking care of customers. At the end of the championship, however, I was gratified when more merchandise had been sold than at any other club in the history of the Women's Open.

Our operation for the Senior Open also went very well. The goal for corporate sales was set at a half-million and we did more than $600,000. Our merchandise tent sales were second only to the 2000 Senior Open in Des Moines, Iowa, in terms of the amount of sales and profitability. The plan was to do around $2 million and we did $2.4 million. Salem members had been so nervous about the merchandise and believed they had a chance to have a lot of leftovers, so they were looking for some sort of guarantee or someone who could help out in this situation. I was sure that, if managed correctly, there wouldn't be that much left over and agreed to buy back whatever remained on Sunday night, providing we could have a two-day sale immediately after the championship concluded.

We ended up running a sale on the property for two days after the championship and then rented a kiosk at a nearby shopping center for another week where we were able to move a strong amount of goods. Buying the leftover merchandise probably wasn't my most brilliant decision but I didn't think we could get hurt and I was willing to take the chance. After all was said and done, some of my partners and I expressed that it was possibly the most stupid thing I'd ever done. We ended up with some $35,000 in leftover merchandise. It's still in storage.

I then returned to Colorado Springs where I lived in a large house on El Encanto that my parents had bought in 1967. After they died, the house became mine. I had lived in it for more than 30 years.

During those three decades the house was the setting for hundreds of parties and a number of USGA meetings. It was a fun house with flowing spaces, four bedrooms and baths, and I had entertained many, many houseguests over the years.

But the house seemed so large for my present life. Besides, the upkeep was expensive so I'd been thinking about selling it for quite awhile. I'd first put the house on the market in 1995. Then Barbara sold her house next door and it seemed foolish to sell both at the same time. Where would we live? My house was the larger of the two, so when Barbara sold hers, she and Tish moved into my house and Barbara bought a half interest.

After Dad died in 1980 and the house became mine, I had thought about selling. I just couldn't find a house that I liked as well, so instead decided to do some additional renovation. I added a sunroom on the front, enclosed the porch on the back, gutted the bedrooms and bathrooms and remodeled to give every bedroom its own bath. I reworked the living room, put in new heating and air-conditioning, and added new thermopane windows.

Renovation is extremely expensive. Putting in new heating and air-conditioning is a little like buying expensive underwear—you spend all this money on something you can't see.

Whenever I saved some money I used it to put Mexican tile on the floors, just because I loved Mexican tile. I eventually did the floor of every room except the bedrooms. But by 2001 I had bad knees and walking on the tile was killing me.

I'd invested even more in the landscape. On the front portion of the lot, I'd had a number of specimen trees and bushes planted to screen the house from the street. They'd now become so large that maintenance was constant and quite costly.

In fact, the alterations I'd made were the very reasons that made me sell the house. I recognized that. I'd also lived there for 34 years. That was probably long enough to be in one place. Selling it was fine with me. It was time.

Meanwhile, Barbara, Tish, and I had rediscovered Southern Pines when we stayed there for the Women's Open. It's a place we all liked to visit and we had very fond memories of the town. Barbara worked at the Mid Pines Club right out of college and had won six North & South Women's Amateur Championships at nearby Pinehurst. Tish had won the 1991 USGA Senior Women's Amateur at Pine Needles. I'd always loved the place because of my fondness for the wonderful golf courses I'd competed on. I also loved the climate. The proximity to our friend Peggy Kirk Bell made Southern Pines even more special. So, the three of us bought a cottage in Southern Pines in July 2001. We now had two homes, in Colorado and in North Carolina.

Our new cottage was about three blocks from Peggy's home, which overlooked the 18th hole of her golf course. Peggy is one of my heroes. She's such a good person and I like the way she has lived her life. She always stands for what's right, she's proud to be an American, she's extremely honest, and has high integrity. I look up to her.

We decided to try living in Southern Pines for a few months. We wanted to see how much we used the cottage. If we spent enough time there and found it to be worthwhile, fine, I could even see retiring there. If it didn't work, we'd sell it.

Southern Pines was to be a seasonal adventure but Colorado Springs was home. Selling the house on El Encanto was still in the back of my mind and I got serious about it when we found a large townhouse that we liked at the beginning of the year.

The transactions took place. My house was sold and we closed on the townhouse all in August of 2001. I didn't have one pang of remorse about selling the house in which I'd lived for so many years. It seemed a time for new beginnings. After the new owners moved in, I dropped by one day to pick up some paperwork. I'm glad that I did. They had arranged all of their furniture so very differently that it didn't seem like my old house anymore. I was ready to move on.

In August, Barbara, Tish, and I moved into the new townhouse and, true to form, immediately began making renovation plans.

I wasn't feeling well, however, and I didn't know why.

Chapter 32

[My Greatest Challenge]

"Judy, they removed a liquid cyst from your abdomen and there were signs of a malignancy."

Barbara McIntire had just said the word I dreaded and didn't want to hear. Malignancy. I had just opened my eyes after two hours of surgery. I was groggy from anesthesia, but that word registered.

I wasn't frightened because Barbara, Tish, Carl, Gwen, Fred, and Sally were in the room and I felt I had a lot of support.

My strongest emotion was relief. I finally knew what was wrong with me. Now we could do something about it. It was September 27th, 2001.

Four days earlier I had celebrated my 65th birthday. The previous week, Barbara had hustled me downtown to sign me up for Social Security and Medicare. It was a prospect I didn't enjoy, but the ordeal of filling out forms and admitting I was old enough for those benefits became fun when my competitive nature kicked in.

"I don't care how much my Social Security check will be," I told the clerk, "as long as it's one dollar more than Barbara's."

It was. Thirty-eight dollars more.

Joanie Birkland drove down from Denver for my birthday. As part of the celebration Joanie, Barbara, Tish, and I were going to do what we liked best—play golf. I didn't feel well enough to play that day, so I stayed at home while they went to the course.

I'd been feeling lousy for a couple of months. In the last 10 days I'd begun to feel even worse. I felt terribly bloated and couldn't seem to catch my breath.

In mid-August, the 101st United States Women's Amateur Championship had been conducted at Flint Hills National Golf Club, just outside of Wichita, in Andover, Kansas. It had been a great opportunity to spend time with my family and I'd entertained a lot, cooking dinner for the Women's Committee a couple of nights at the golf course lodge where we stayed.

The championship was hugely successful. As a result of community loyalty and the advertising efforts, some 3,000 spectators came out to watch the final. The crowd was everything I'd dreamed of for the Women's Amateur. It meant even more because Carl, Gwen, Allen, his wife Kim Bell, and their sons Jeffrey, Richard, and Scott were spectators. Jeffrey and Richard worked during the championship, alternating carrying the status board in two matches, including the 36-hole final.

But I had not felt well, the bloating and breathlessness had begun, so I never left the lodge to watch any of the golf until the final day, which was highly unusual for me.

After the championship I returned to Colorado Springs and went to see my doctor. He suspected that something was once again wrong with my heart. The worst part was my confusion. My heart checkups had been good and my current symptoms were unlike any I'd experienced before my heart bypass. I didn't know what I was dealing with so I had this helpless feeling because I had no idea what to do.

All of the usual pictures were taken at the office of my cardiologist, Dr. Buzz Sellers.

His technician seemed pleased with what he saw. "Judy," he said, "you almost have the heart of a world-class athlete."

"I find that hard to believe," I said. "I can't even bend over to tie my shoes. And you're going to have to help me get off this gurney."

The day after my birthday, I had a CAT scan and X-rays. The radiologist saw a liquid mass in my abdomen and called Jack Speer, my primary care doctor, who told me to immediately check into Penrose Hospital. Terrence O'Rourke, a surgeon, came to see me and ordered more tests. I would have exploratory surgery on September 27th.

On September 26th, I knew I was in for a fitful and frightening time, so I called a couple of friends and talked well into the night. I was pretty matter-of-fact about my illness. After all, I had nothing new to tell them. Mostly, I just wanted the distraction of everyday chitchat. Just tell me your news. Let's have a conversation.

Meanwhile, the 2001 USGA Women's State Team Championship was underway in Wayzata, Minnesota. I had hoped to go because the championship cup was the "Judy Bell Trophy," just as the trophy for the USGA Men's State Team Championship is named for Jim Hand, past USGA president and a good friend of mine. Now, of course, I was in the hospital.

I'd shared the news about my health with a few close friends. When they heard of my predicament, several members of the Women's Committee were in Wayzata, including the chairman, Cora Jane Blanchard, Betsy Clifford, and Pat Clarke. They stood outdoors in a circle and held hands while a prayer was said in my behalf.

Pat then said, "I have to go back on rules duty, but I will be praying. And I can't think of a better place to pray than on a golf course."

Their little meeting had been an emotional one and when I heard about it, I was extremely touched.

Christi Dickinson of the Women's Committee was in charge of the championship. She faced so many responsibilities that my friends chose to wait until the championship ended to tell her of my condition.

Christi was, however, very intuitive. On the morning of the 27th, she saw several WC members whispering in a corner of the USGA office. Christi suddenly appeared nervous and shaky. Oddly, she asked, "Is something wrong with Judy?"

"No. No. Judy's fine," she was assured.

Despite her misgivings, Christi carried on. At the presentation she told of the trophy's origins: Evie Moreland was the mother of past Curtis Cup player and captain, Judy Oliver. Both were great friends of mine. Evie owned a beautiful silver bowl, embossed with scenes from American history; Washington crossing the Delaware, farmers at the plow, settlers in covered wagons, soldiers raising the flag at Iwo Jima. Evie offered this lovely bowl to the USGA Women's Committee as the Judy Bell Trophy. Thank heavens the WC accepted Evie's generous offer, as I can't think of any trophy that better represents America.

I underwent my surgery the morning after the championship ended. My brothers, my sisters-in-law, Tish, and Barbara came into my room in intensive care after I woke up.

I said, "Well, what's going on?"

I looked at the faces of Carl and Fred. They seemed grave, and had trouble looking me in the eye. Barbara broke the news, then said, "The malignancy is in your peritoneum."

"What's the peritoneum?" I said.

I began asking questions when Jack Speer came into the room. The peritoneum is the lining of the abdominal cavity. The malignancy was mostly liquid. Some of it had been removed through surgery, but it was also microscopic and there could be a million malignant cells in an area the size of a dime.

Jack, a former oncologist, said he'd never seen a case of my particular kind of cancer. That shocked me and, for the first and only time, I became emotional. I wasn't crying because I had cancer. I cried because there seemed to be nothing I could do about it. I had some weird form of the disease and, at that time, no one seemed to know what it was. What was it? What was the treatment? What could I do to fight it?

I began to work things through in my mind. An oncologist, Dr. Paul Anderson, joined our team. He had seen this type of cancer before, he said, and eight of his patients were presently being treated for it.

I saw several doctors that day and asked each of them just one question: "Is this treatable?" Their answers were consistently affirmative.

I settled down. I began thinking in a really positive way. I knew I needed to immediately sort out my priorities. Getting well was my first one.

A couple of minutes after I was diagnosed, I telephoned Trey Holland. Besides being one of the best friends I've ever had, Trey is a respected urologist in Indianapolis, Indiana.

When I gave him the news, Trey became very quiet and listened to everything I said.

"We'll go to work on it," he said.

"Will you be a part of my decision-making team?" I asked.

"Yes," Trey said.

He immediately became involved. Trey was always there for me and we talked on the telephone every day. I'd tell him what I was worried about, or what I had been told, and he would talk me through it. He checked with the doctors in his office and other doctors. He talked to my doctors, my primary care physician, Jack Speer, my oncologist, Dr. Anderson, and my surgeon, Terrence O'Rourke.

My case was discussed with doctors at the Mayo Clinic in Rochester, Minnesota, where Will Nicholson had given me a contact. The case was also presented to doctors at the M.D. Anderson Cancer Center, in Houston, and the National Cancer Institute, in Washington, D.C. I wanted a group effort to define the treatment protocol for my type of cancer.

After we got responses from the three treatment centers, much to my surprise they were united in their opinions and we had received a consensus. I would undergo a program of 36 chemotherapy treatments, three treatments every month, with one week off each month.

I now had a plan and I wasn't alone. I had an entire group of experts to help me, which was heartening. I didn't want to think about what was ahead, so I began to approach my disease with the same philosophy I've used throughout my life. How do I solve the immediate problem? I didn't want to know if I had six years to live, or two years, or four years. I just held on to the thought that it was treatable and set out to do everything in my power to get ahead of it.

As I write this, it is April and I've been undergoing chemotherapy since the end of October. I'm almost halfway there.

For my treatments I go to the Rocky Mountain Cancer Center in Colorado Springs. As I sit in a lounge chair with the chemicals flowing through my groshong, the plastic portal to my system, I'm either on the telephone or working on my laptop. Rocky Mountain Cancer Center is a great place and has some private treatment rooms. I finally decided to start using one when I saw that all my yakking on the telephone was disturbing other patients in the main treatment room.

Trey pointed out that my disease hadn't changed my work ethic or my passion for golf. "One day," he told a friend, "I was talking to Judy on the telephone. We were discussing a future site for the Women's Open. She had some concerns about the site. She was passionate about it and began talking louder and louder. She was literally *yelling* into the phone while she was undergoing chemotherapy!"

Old habits die hard. Much of the work on this book, in fact, was done while these lifesaving chemicals were being pumped into my body.

I've been pretty lucky with chemotherapy in that I've not had some of the side effects that affect a lot of people, such as nausea. I have had joint and bone pain from the chemical Taxol. Most people who take Taxol experience some pain but mine is aggravated because I have both osteoarthritis and psoriatic arthritis. It's very hard for me to get up and down. Rising from a chair is a major undertaking. I also have a little trouble walking. I've lost most of my hair, which at first bothered me a lot. It's only hair. It's the least of my worries. My hair will grow back.

After a couple of months of treatment I received some very encouraging news. A particular blood test, CA-125, is commonly known as a "tumor marker." If your CA-125 count is between zero and 35, you're in the normal range. At the time of my surgery, my count was about 256, which indicated a very intense presence of malignant cells. My CA-125 test in December showed a reading of 42. In January, the reading dropped to 18 and I was ecstatic. In February it was 14. In March it was 13. In April it was 10. As long as the readings stay in that range, we're on the right road.

My friends say my energy is high. Outside of my bone and joint pain, I feel okay but I don't think my energy level is astounding. I've always had a lot of energy. That's pretty much me.

My balance is affected by the chemotherapy so I'm working on that with a physical therapist, Jackie Thomas. She has me stand on one foot, close my eyes, then stand on the other foot. I keep trying to walk in a straight line. It's fairly difficult, so I find it's easier to get around using a cane. That's okay; it works.

I can't wait until the chemotherapy ends and my bone and joint pain go away. One of the things I really miss is playing golf. One of golf's great benefits is that you can't think of anything else *but* the game when you're practicing or playing. When you're hitting balls, your mind is in limbo. You have a sense of well-being because you're in rhythm and in balance. Besides, it's fun. I remember all of those feelings so distinctly. I can't wait to chase the butterfly again.

Chapter 33

[Up the Mountain]

On September 28th David Fay sent an e-mail to the entire USGA staff.

RE: Judy Bell

Bad News. Judy has cancer.
She had a cyst partially removed from her abdomen yesterday in Colorado Springs. The hope was that the cyst was benign. It was not.

I've spoken with Trey who will speak to the type of cancer, treatment protocol, et al, in a report either this weekend or early next week. I'm afraid I can't provide you with more information at this time. But since news—especially bad news—travels fast, I wanted to tell you all what I presently know—which isn't much.

Miracles do happen. Let's pray for one.

This has been one lousy month...

David

P.S. I spoke with Barbara McIntire a few mintues ago. She recommends no phone calls at this time (but with Judy, we all know that will certinly change soon!) but cards are encouraged.

Within a week of my surgery, news of my diagnosis appeared in *Golf Illustrated, Golf World,* and on the front of the sports page of *USA Today.* David and Trey had confirmed my condition whenever reporters called them.

Barbara, Tish and Helen Kirkland took turns spending the night in my hospital room. Despite David's request that people not call, my bedside telephone and cell phone rang constantly. I *wanted* to talk, but "my keepers" were vigilant and waylaid my calls. Occasionally, when they were out of the room, I managed to make a call or two.

I was amazed and touched by the outpouring of affection from friends. Every day for months, I got telephone calls and several dozen cards and letters from my family, USGA people, media people, golfers, and old friends from around the world. Their support cheered and strengthened me. A lot of people told me they are praying for me and, believe me, I can feel the strength of those prayers. It's helping me through this battle.

One of the most touching letters came from Frank Hannigan. Frank can be a crotchety guy but his letter was affectionate and dear. He just wrote to me about his travels and his news of the day, but he had an affectionate tone and his letter meant a lot.

In referring to our time together in golf and in the USGA, Frank wrote, "Judy, you and I have seen the best of it."

In November, the City of Wichita honored my brother Carl. The city commission paid him special tribute for his work on behalf of Wichita as mayor and as a member of the city commission. In the ceremony it was announced that the convention hall at the Wichita Civic Center had been named "The Carl Allen Bell Jr. Convention Hall."

Because of my treatments, I couldn't attend. Carl later sent a tape of the ceremony to me and I watched it with friends. I'm so proud of Carl, just as I am of my other brothers.

After undergoing chemotherapy for nearly two months I didn't feel great, but I didn't feel too badly either. I still worked nearly every day. My chemotherapy took half a day on Tuesdays and I'd go to the clinic accompanied by Barbara, Tish, or assorted other friends.

Over Thanksgiving, I did additional work on this book. While I underwent my Tuesday chemotherapy, I lay back in a lounge chair, speaking into a tape recorder while Rhonda sat nearby asking me about my life.

"I feel like I'm at the psychiatrist!" I laughed.

Tuesday's weren't too difficult but Wednesdays, the day after my treatment, could be rough. I pressed on, working in the office full-time for three days a week, half a day on Tuesday, at least half a day on Wednesday and Thursday, and some weekends.

In November, I went to St. Augustine, Florida, to be inducted into the World Golf Hall of Fame. Trey, as USGA president and my good friend, would introduce me during the ceremony.

While I'd talked to Trey every day, I hadn't seen him since learning I had cancer. We met at the hotel. He hugged me. I kissed him on the cheek. I was glad to see him and our reunion was as emotional as it *can* be for a couple of cold fish.

The night before the induction, I had a dinner party for about 40 friends who had come to the ceremonies. My brothers and sisters-in-law were there, as well as Allen Bell, my nephew, and my niece, Carolyn Bell.

Despite my illness, I looked pretty healthy but I'd lost some weight and a small amount of hair. I also had to use a cane because of gouty arthritis. I asked Allen to help me get through the ceremonies by letting me hold his arm when I mounted the stairs to the stage.

Just before the ceremony began, I spotted a friend of mine in the audience. The year before, John Glenn had been terribly ill with lymphoma and his prognosis had not been good. The previous winter, I'd flown to Florida to spend some time with him while he was in the hospital. Now he was in remission and, for the first time in a long while, had made a trip to watch my induction.

I hadn't seen John since he'd recovered. Now he sat in his wheelchair with my other friends, wearing a blazer and bow tie I'd sent to him for the occasion.

I wanted to let him know how pleased I was that he was in the audience. Allen helped me to find the right row and I went straight to John and kissed him.

"I just wanted to make sure the tie was right," I said, and made my way back to my chair.

When Trey introduced me, I stood backstage and avoided listening. I didn't want to become emotional—I had to keep myself pulled together for my speech—but I heard the first part of the introduction, which was classic Holland work. The bottom line was that when I'd shot 67 in the Women's Open so many years before, I had only played well for nine holes.

When my name was called, I walked to my mark, leaned on my cane, and, with a big smile, waved at the audience. Many people seemed emotional and their response touched me enormously.

I got through my speech just fine, thanking all of the people who had written and telephoned to encourage me. "It has been," I said, "like a big, warm hug."

While I've been lucky to be honored a few times, I don't feel emotional at these public occasions. I plant my feet solidly on the floor, and try to do my part by giving a good talk and remembering to say thank you. Otherwise, I just enjoy the festivities.

After the induction, I had to do television interviews. This was my first public appearance since my diagnosis.

"What did they ask you about?" Fred asked.

"My health, of course," I muttered. I appreciated the support and concern although I was frankly a little bored with talking about it.

But I must. My treatment protocol is set. There's no reason to alter it because I'm responding well. Trey still keeps up with my stats and I call him frequently. Friends and family members stay in close touch and give me lots of love.

Except for my treatments, life seems to have changed little. Barbara, Tish, and I went to Florida for Christmas, then to Southern Pines to celebrate the New Year and to honor Peggy Kirk Bell on her 80th birthday.

In February, the 2002 USGA Annual Meeting was held at The Broadmoor Hotel. I loved seeing my old friends from the USGA. An added treat was that Maureen Garrett flew in from England and stayed at our house.

In late February, Barbara, Tish, and I went to Hutchinson, Kansas, to work on the merchandising operation of the 2002 Women's Open. We then drove 45 miles to Wichita to spend a couple of days with my family. It reinforces me a lot to once again be at the Bell family dinner table.

From Wichita I flew to Philadelphia to attend meetings in my role as a director of IKON, an office solutions corporation.

My first priority today is my health. I continue on in a role as a consultant at the Foundation. My business opportunities are interesting and Barbara and I are looking at a new venture in North Carolina. In Colorado Springs, Barbara, Tish and I recently bought the townhouse next door, which we're tackling as a remodeling project with resale in mind. It's something that we've always wanted to do and, if it works, we might do it again. That door is open.

Learning new things remains one of life's greatest pleasures. Sometimes

I learn from an extremely surprising source. A few years ago, in fact, I learned a lot about courage, fortitude, and the ongoing search for adventure even when we're older and more infirm. I learned it from our dogs.

On that evening, our yellow Labrador Retrievers, "Bear" and "Glenna," escaped again from the house on El Encanto. On the gate leading to my backyard I'd hung a wooden sign that was shaped like a tombstone that said, "Here lies the son of a bitch who left the gate open." At night, mountain lions sometimes came down from the mountains and woe to any dog in their path.

There were so many times that I heard Tish or Barbara shout the terrifying words, "Bear's out!"

To Bear and Glenna, however, it was a game. If they found the gate or a door open, they'd take a leisurely walk while we frantically drove around the neighborhood calling their names. Fortunately, we always found them and brought them home.

On this particular day, it was bright and sunny so I opened the front door for fresh air just before dinner. I never thought our dogs would want to leave home. I couldn't really blame them for taking off again, but they were now very old and slow-moving.

Tish and I had just finished eating when the telephone rang. Our friends Frankie and Bill Tutt called to say they'd been driving up Cheyenne Mountain Boulevard when they thought they saw two mountain lions walking up the middle of the road. They stopped and discovered to their amazement that these animals were Glenna and Bear. Frankie and Bill promptly coaxed them into their car, took them to their house, and called us.

I couldn't believe that our dogs weren't still in the house and went from room to room calling their names. Sure enough, no Glenna, no Bear.

After we brought them home, the dogs walked into the house rather sheepishly. But they seemed frisky, too, and had big grins and sparkly eyes. They had enjoyed such a good time on their two-mile, up-the-mountain hike.

They were 14 years old, which in dog terms is like being over 90. So here they were—Bear and Glenna—trudging slowly up the mountain together, breathing hard, but once again in search of new places, new friends, a fresh adventure, a new challenge.

It's one of my favorite memories and the spirit behind it always makes me smile. Glenna and Bear are gone now, but we have two new black Labs, another brother and sister named "Captain" and "Rosie." Believe me, we've had a riotous time trying to train them while moving into the townhouse and doing some remodeling.

I am very, very blessed. My life has been interesting and I've been able to do so many different things. I was lucky to be born into my family. I believe in God. I have a great heritage. I had the opportunity for a good education. Playing sports, golf in particular, was a very important part of my life. I couldn't ask for anything better.

And as my friend Bill Campbell once said, "It isn't the destination that matters, but the journey."

So far, it has been a great trip.

[Acknowledgments]

I would like to thank the following people, without whose help this book could not have been written. They provided support, ideas, history, details, transportation, research, and office space. So to Carl, Gwen, Fred, Sally, Allen, and Ruth Bell, and to Barbara McIntire, Tish Preuss, Barbara Romack, John Glenn, Kathy Williams, Paula Petrie, Robert Champlin, Trey Holland, David Fay, Marty Parkes, Rand Jerris, Aunt Ellen, Betty Richart and my co-author, Rhonda Glenn, I offer my most sincere thanks.

— *Judy Bell*

[Judy Bell's Awards & Honors]

1976 Colorado Golf Hall of Fame
1981 Person of the Year, Colorado Golf Hall of Fame
1986 Hall of Fame, National Golf Coaches Association
1986 Honorary Lifetime Membership, Prairie Dunes Country Club
1990 Kansas Golf Hall of Fame
1991 Spirit Award, Summit of Women's Golf
1995 Isaac B. Grainger Award, United States Golf Association
1996 Colorado Sports Hall of Fame
1996 PGA of America Honorary Member Award
1996 Second Century Distinguished Alumnus, Wichita State University
1997 Patty Berg Award, Ladies Professional Golf Association
1997 LPGA Commissioners Award, Ladies Professional Golf Association
1997 Arnold Palmer Lifetime Service Award, Golf Association of
      Philadelphia
1998 Inducted as Member of Captain's Club, Memorial Tournament
1998 Distinguished Service Award, Metropolitan Golf Writers Association
1998 Distinguished Service Award, International Association of Golf
      Administrators
1998 Donald Ross Award, American Society of Golf Course Architects
1998 Woman of Distinction, Women's Western Golf Association
1998 Mercedes Benz Legends of Women's Golf
1998 Lifetime Achievement Award, Colorado Golf Hall of Fame
1998 Cochina Award, Arizona Golf Association
1999 Graffis Award, National Golf Foundation
1999 Order of the Rose, Delta Gamma Sorority
2000 Walk of Fame, Wichita State University
2001 First Lady of Golf, Professional Golfers Association of America
2001 Legacy Award, Wichita Urban League
2001 Kansas Sports Hall of Fame
2001 Colorado Sports Hall of Fame

2001 World Golf Hall of Fame
2002 William Richardson Award, Golf Writers Association of America

Team Competitions

Member, 1960 United States Curtis Cup Team
Member, 1962 United States Curtis Cup Team
Captain, 1986 United States Curtis Cup Team
Captain, 1988 United States Curtis Cup Team
Captain, 1988 United States Women's World Amateur Team
Captain, 2000 United States Men's World Amateur Team

Positions in Golf

1961-1964	USGA U.S. Girls' Junior Championship Committee
1967-1997	Chairman, Broadmoor Ladies Invitation
1968-1984	United States Golf Association Women's Committee
1981-1984	Chairman, United States Golf Association Women's Committee
1981-1984	World Amateur Golf Council Women's Committee
1968-2001	Rules Official, United States Women's Open
1987-1997	United States Golf Association Executive Committee
1987-1997	Rules Official, United States Open
1988-1997	Rules Official, Masters tournament
1988-1992	Chairman, United States Golf Association Handicap Committee
1988-1992	Chairman, United States Golf Association Golf Handicap and Information Network Committee
1991-1992	United States Golf Association Treasurer
1992-1993	United States Golf Association Secretary
1992-1993	Chairman, United States Golf Association Amateur Status Committee
1994-1995	Chairman, United States Golf Association Championship Committee
1994-1995	United States Golf Association Vice President
1995	Vice Chairman, United States Women's Open
1996-1997	United States Golf Association President
1964-present	Board of Directors, Women's Western Golf Association
1999-present	Consulting Director, United States Golf Association Foundation Fellowship & Grants Programs